To my parents, in loving memory

THE AMBER COAST

A Latvian Family's Journey

By

Ilse Zandstra

ISBN: 978-0-99529-100-3 (PB)

Prologue

Dressed in the navy blue uniform of the girls' school I had attended in Göteborg, Sweden, and with my blonde hair coaxed into two skinny braids, I squirm on a bench outside Principal Henderson's office. Beside me sits Father, a worried look on his face, and to his right, my older brother, Peter, who is examining his cap as if he half-expects to find some treasure inside. Father glances at his wristwatch, turns his steel-grey eyes on me, and I stop wiggling. We are waiting to be admitted into Van Horne Elementary School. It is February 1951, and we have just arrived in Montreal. I am seven years old and my brother is eight.

Unfamiliar sounds float in the overheated air, and I strain to catch even one of the English phrases Father made us repeat as we walked to the school: "Good morning," "My name is Ilze," or "How do you do?" I wish my stomach would stop turning somersaults, and that beneath the thick woollen dress I am wearing, my skin would stop begging to be scratched. Peter too, is wearing his Swedish school uniform—a dark blue jacket; knickers that button below the knee; long, thick wool socks; and a cap with a visor. He sits perfectly still and straight-backed, but I see his eyes follow the children as they pass. It doesn't take long to realize that he is the only boy wearing knickers and knee socks.

Father hisses at me again, and then stares at the closed door of the principal's office, willing it to open. He fingers his homburg, still wet from the melted snow. On his knees rests the battered leather briefcase that accompanies him everywhere, except on evening walks. I know that Father is also worried, but his worry is different from mine. Just yesterday, he and Peter had been turned away from the boys' school around the corner from our apartment building. "Mama," he said, when he returned with Peter in tow, "they won't take our Peter, all because we're not Catholic." Mother tried not to show her concern as Father continued. "Seems there are two, and who knows, maybe more, different kinds of schools. When I said we were Lutheran, the principal shook his head and handed me back Peter's report card."

"Oh, dear. What now?"

"I'll try the Protestant school tomorrow."

Father dislikes setbacks at the best of times, and there haven't been any of those for a long time. He is anxious to have us back in school, for we have already missed one precious month of learning during our move. As the son of a mother and father who were both schoolteachers, Father believes that nothing is as important as education. "Education," I've heard him repeat so often that it must be true, "is an immigrant's only road to a decent future." I want desperately to start school in Canada and walk that road.

Father shifts on the bench to reach the handkerchief in his coat pocket. He shakes out the clean white cloth, and I see his initials, JAZ, neatly embroidered in one corner. For a brief moment, before he crumples it up to wipe his forehead, it is like a flag of surrender. Two mornings in a row, the annoying mix-up about schools is causing him to be late for his new job at Canadian Vickers. I know he secretly wishes Mother were able to help him take care of these schooling matters so that he could concentrate on his real job, but like us, Mother knows only a few words of English. Father speaks better than any of us, but often his pronouncements meet with quizzical glances, and every time he says his name, he is asked to spell it. His English consists of phrases plucked from a battered language text and words tweezed from the dictionary. German, Russian, Latvian, and Swedish—he is fluent in them all, but now despairs of having to learn a fifth language at his age. Father is forty-four.

Just when I think I cannot sit still another minute, there is movement behind the glass door. A tall, slightly stooped man with glasses opens the door and motions us into his office. Father and the man shake hands, and then Father places a heavy hand on each of our shoulders as he says our names. Peter bows, and I offer a limp half-curtsy. The interview does not last long, as both Father and the principal are eager to get back to work. After reminding us to be good children and listen to the teacher, Father hurries away. Peter takes my hand, and I hold on tight. Soon however, an older boy arrives to take away Peter, his cap in hand, while I await my fate, nervous and alone.

When I reach my classroom, my teacher, Mrs. Bindman, does not look pleased to see me, but does her best to paste a cardboard smile on her face. Her grade one classroom is full, every desk already occupied. I stand, knees trembling, at the front of the class like some curious object on display and listen as the teacher mispronounces my name. "Class, say hello to Elsa." Then she steers me by the shoulder to an empty desk in the last row, beside an open doorway through which coats and a jumble of boots on the floor are visible. My only hope now is that there might be another Latvian girl in my class.

Mrs. Bindman returns to the front of the class, sighs audibly, and squares her bony shoulders. Then, in a tone that I guess is meant to assure the class that she would continue to do her best in a difficult situation, she begins the lesson. I sit up straight and fold my hands on top of my desk the way I have been taught to do in my Swedish school. I try to pay attention, but the sounds coming from her lips convey no more to me than the crackle and sputter of the nearby radiator. I can feel myself getting sleepy.

Even today, decades later, I remember the strangeness of my first day of school in Canada as clearly as if it had happened yesterday. Schools were overcrowded. Teachers were overworked, with separate morning and afternoon sessions. No special considerations were given to non-English speaking students, many of whom had arrived from war-torn Europe. It was sink or swim, and I decided to swim. In a few short months I had some new friends, mostly immigrant girls like myself, and together we mastered English and, much to the horror of our parents, discovered comic books and chewing gum. I adapted quickly to my new country.

That first winter had been one of the coldest winters on record. Even the shipping lanes in the St. Lawrence had frozen solid, and we had been forced to journey inland from Halifax by train. Then, in our Montreal apartment, the space heater struggled to keep us warm. Each morning as my brothers and I prepared for school, Father scratched at the frost on the window to check the outdoor temperature, shaking his head in disbelief. The voice in his bedside radio had already told him how cold it was, but Father was an engineer and believed in double-checking his figures. "Bundle up well," he admonished, and disappeared out the door.

The train ride from Halifax to the Eastern Townships where we had first stayed, had come as a welcome relief from our ocean voyage across a wild North Atlantic which had tossed the *Gripsholm* about as if it were nothing more than a piece of balsam from one of Peter's model ships. As our Canadian National Railway train chugged across a dazzlingly white landscape, Peter and I would run up and down the length of the car and make unnecessary visits to the bathroom to throw scraps of paper into the toilet and watch them disappear onto the rushing track below. Mother tried in vain to get us to stay in our seats, but it was all too easy to ignore her silent entreaties. Mother was suffering from laryngitis, and she had her hands full with our two-year-old brother, Roland. A fellow passenger kindly offered her some penicillin chewing gum to relieve her aching throat, which she diligently sucked on and chewed, but even so, she wasn't able to speak above a whisper. We made matters worse by tickling Roland just to hear him squeal each time we ran past him. After changing trains in Quebec City, we finally tumbled out, tired and disheveled, onto the platform in Plessisville, a sleepy town southeast of Montreal.

Today, as the *Baltic Star* sails toward Latvia, the homeland I left so long ago, I am thinking back to our arrival in Canada. That sea voyage took place in 1951, across a stormy North Atlantic in mid-winter. Today's voyage in the summer of 1990 is smooth, the day warm and sunny, and the mood cheerful, despite some underlying anxieties. Barely two months earlier, the Supreme Soviet of the Latvian SSR voted to restore independence to Latvia. It is independence in name only; the battle for real freedom must still be fought and won.

I am with my father, my brother Roland, and other relatives, as well as over three hundred fellow passengers, most of them Latvian. While we are in Latvia, our Swedish ship, the Baltic Star, will serve as our floating hotel, and each time we disembark or get back on board, we will have to show our passports to the Soviet border guards. Some of the older Latvians are dreading having to face Soviet officials; their wartime memories are still raw. I, on the other hand, am worried that the Latvian I speak is that of a child rather than an adult. Growing up, my brothers and I spoke Latvian at home and English elsewhere. To my parents' dismay, I even changed the spelling of my name, Ilze, a popular name in Latvia at the time of my birth, to what I thought was a more Canadian-sounding Ilse. Peteris became Peter, and Rolands was changed to Roland. For a while, my older brother even used his middle name, Roman, instead of our last name, Zalite. Too many zeds, we countered, if anyone asked why. On this trip, I am Ilze again, although the spelling on my passport reflects the unofficial name change I made as a child.

The modification in the spelling of a name was nothing compared to the profound changes that took place in our lives as a result of World War II. What was a large, close-knit extended family, living in a small, independent country, became part of the Latvian diaspora, its members spread across the globe, a few even reaching far-away Australia. Some relatives chose to remain in Latvia and take their chances, and an unfortunate few, like Mother's brother, Janis, and Father's nephew Varaidots and his family, were illegally deported by the Soviets to Siberia. The one thing that was true for all of us was that not one of our lives would remain the same.

What am I going back to, I ask myself. The Latvia of my parents and ancestors, celebrated in a thousand *dainas,* has not existed for many decades. For me, it was a song on my mother's lips, a longing in her heart, a country spelled *Latvija* on my birth certificate. When we fled that Latvia just ahead of the Soviet tanks that overran it, we lost everything. I had been a baby and had no memories of my own to resurrect, but I wonder if my father will be able to unearth anything of his former life. He had abandoned most of his physical possessions, including the contents of his apartment in Riga and a locked car at the dockside in Liepāja, but the intangibles—language, culture, and love of country—have stayed with him.

Many Latvians have lived their lives in exile dreaming of the day their country would be free and they could return. Not Father. He does not believe in holding on to false hopes and impossible dreams, and until May 4, he did not believe for one second that the Soviets would ever loosen their grip on Latvia. But time and history were proving him wrong; the Berlin wall had fallen, and the Iron Curtain was showing signs of cracking. We were on our way to Latvia to see for ourselves and to meet our relatives. A special highlight of our visit would be the Song Festival.

Growing up in Montreal, much of what I knew of Latvia came from folk songs and picture books sent to us by our Latvian relatives. Mother's repertoire of folk songs was vast, and the songs she sang to us varied with her mood. When she felt content, her songs were light and cheerful, but often they were sad, particularly on days when a letter from home had arrived to remind her of all that we had lost. Then, she would sing of motherless children and of brothers lost forever on some distant battleground. On those days, all I could do was cover my ears and bury my face in her soft bosom. Father did not sing as often, and when he did, they were very different songs. If he let his guard down, he might sing a German hymn that he had learned as a child from his mother. He possessed a fine baritone voice, and at Latvian get-togethers, he would join in to sing about bravery or love of the fatherland; other times, after a glass or two of *šnaps* he would sometimes belt out a song in Russian. He sang about the River Daugava, the Danube, or the mighty Volga, but never about the St. Lawrence. Early in my life in Canada, I discovered that, unlike us, Canadians did not sing very much, even about their mighty river.

The books our Latvian relatives sent us usually contained blurry photographs of narrow streets and old-fashioned streetcars or of statues and churches, all on greyish paper. Looking through them, I wondered if my homeland was continually enveloped in a thick fog. The reproductions of paintings by important Latvian artists were so poor that I thought the artists had carelessly smudged their canvases before the paint was dry. When, after studying a recently arrived book, I had mentioned this idea to Father, he told me not to blame the artist. "It's about all we can expect in a book put out by the Soviets," he said. For Father, this was explanation enough. The word *Soviet* said it all—bad, shoddy, suspect, and much worse. Over the years, I had been taught that nothing good or beautiful or honest could ever come from communist hands. I did not bother to read the accompanying text that was printed in both the Latvian (Roman) and Russian (Cyrillic) alphabets; the first required more time and effort that I was willing to expend, and the second, with its letters facing every which way, was impossible for me to decipher. Many Latvians, including Father, thought it almost traitorous to even own such books. More than once, after examining the place and date of publication, Father had pronounced with authority, "Ha! Khrushchev is laughing now. The rubles spent on this book will buy him another screw for one of his missiles pointed our way."

Even as Father railed against the evils of communism and worked to defeat it, he, along with most other Latvians, had been taken by surprise when the USSR began to unravel. President Gorbachev's *perestroika* and *glasnost* had allowed his people a glimpse of life beyond the iron curtain and over the wall, and it was enough to make them like and want what they saw. The sudden agitation for freedom by the swallowed-up Republics was beginning to give the Soviet bear indigestion. The fall of the Berlin Wall in 1989 meant that the time was right for the Baltic countries to finally reclaim their independence.

In early 1990, I had received a surprising telephone call from my eighty-three-year-old Father. "Would you like to go to Latvia?" he asked. I almost dropped the phone. "I just read in *Laiks* (the Latvian newspaper) that the Latvian Church here in America is organizing a special sailing from Stockholm to Riga," he said, speaking to me in Latvian, as always. "I've already sent off my cheque but thought you might be interested, too."

"When?" I asked as I glanced at my calendar. In the last few years, I had begun to feel a growing desire to see Latvia for myself, not just through the eyes of my parents or through the lens of someone else's camera. I welcomed the opportunity to bring into sharper focus the blurred photographs and distorted childhood images that I carried in my head.

July 1990 Flags Flying the Baltic Star docks in Riga.

(left)1927 Grandfather Peteris Zalite surrounded by his six children. Father is wearing his sailor's garb. (right) August 1936 Wedding of my parents, Erna and Janis Zalite in the Dom Cathedral in Riga.

1941 Father and Mother with their new Opel.

LATVIA

One

Six months later, at the end of June, my father and I and four hundred other souls are on our way to Latvia. I have flown to Stockholm from the Philippines where I am now living; others have arrived from cities all over North America and as far away as Australia. This is not only a historic voyage; for me it is also a family reunion. My father and my brother Roland, and his wife, Janice, one of only two non-Latvians on the manifest, are here. My older brother, Peter, who is a Canadian diplomat serving in Germany, will meet us when we dock in Riga, along with his three teenage daughters, Alex, Kristi and Tammy. My mother's sister, Elza Rabacs, and her daughter Mara are on board, as is another of my cousins from New York, Walter Zalite, with his wife, Irma. Amid the excitement, I feel the absence of my mother more than ever, sad that she did not live long enough to see this day. My childhood friend Anitra Halliday (nee Beikmanis) is my cabin mate. Our parents were friends, and we both had summer cabins on Ile Perrot, west of Montreal. She, being an only child of working parents and my mother's godchild, spent many hours at our house. I like to think that we were as close as sisters, alternately playing and bickering, then making up again and sharing secrets.

The mood is upbeat and heady, but beneath the surface gaiety flows an undercurrent of apprehension, and for some of the travelers, fear, especially among the older, returning Latvians. The crumbling Soviet Union is still determined to hold on to Latvia and its Latvians, and it is hard to forget past abuses. Who knows which of our names appear in KGB dossiers? I refuse to be afraid; I am Canadian and my non-Latvian married name is my amulet. Still, at times I wonder if I might be somehow detained or harmed.

We board the *Baltic Star*, and all our fears are momentarily quashed. The words *Happy Ship* are scrawled in bold black letters across its white hull, and soon it is riding out of the harbour like a knight off to the Northern Crusades. For its previous exploits, the *Baltic Star* has also been nicknamed the *Freedom Ship*. Five years ago, in the summer of 1985, the *Baltic Star* took part in a peaceful, patriotic demonstration against the Soviet Union's illegal World War II annexation of the three Baltic countries. The ship steamed defiantly up and down the amber coast, as close as it dared to the shores of Estonia, Latvia, and Lithuania, testing Soviet determination and strength. The *Baltic Star* was soon forced to retreat into international waters. Four years later, in 1989, in a spectacular display of solidarity, one million Estonians, Latvians, and Lithuanians, young and old, forged a human chain that stretched from Tallinn in the north, through Riga, to Vilnius in the south, to protest the signing of the Molotov-Ribbentrop Pact fifty years earlier. A secret clause in the pact between the USSR and Third Reich had cost the Baltic countries their independence and turned them into unwilling Soviet republics.

"Have you checked out the ship's gift shop?" asks Roland when we meet in the bar for happy hour.

"Not yet," I answer. "Should I?" My suitcase is already crammed with gifts.

"They're selling bananas! Mostly booze and bananas."

"Enough for a thousand banana daiquiris," Janice laughs, taking a sip of her mineral water.

"Now I get it. Earlier I overheard someone referring to our ship as the *Banana Boat*, but I didn't get it." I settle into a leather chair and place my camera on the low, glass table. Apart from a distant hum and a faint vibration, there is no sensation of movement.

"*Come, Mister Tallyman, tally me* banana...." sings Janice, as she taps her fingers in time to the beat. In a Latvian world, one thing she can relate to is the familiar Belafonte song.

Father has just joined us. "You joke, but I bet many young Latvians have never tasted a banana."

I can't imagine someone not knowing the sweet taste and smooth feel of a banana in their mouth. Back home, supermarket bins overflow with the golden fruit, and it was the first solid food I fed my babies. But suddenly, an unexpected memory floats unbidden to the surface.

Bananas were once special to me too, consumed only as a rare treat. On my birthday, when I could have any fruit I wanted, I asked for bananas. Winter bananas from the tropics were once an exotic and expensive luxury.

The evening passes quickly as friends and family exchange news while fighting off jetlag-induced drowsiness. At this northern latitude it is still light at eleven when I say goodnight and head for my narrow bunk. The following morning at breakfast, Father helps us with the names of relatives we are likely to meet and their relationship to us; he has been corresponding with them, and they know we are coming. I have met only cousin Janis Freimanis, a scientist, who visited us in Canada several years ago.

"Janis Freimanis is my sister Marija's son," Father explains, patiently at first, "the only one of my siblings who stayed behind. Janis and his wife, Arija, have two children, Janis and Ligita. Ligita is married with two small boys...."

Father continues as I write the names in a small notebook. I leave off the diacritics, hoping Father won't inspect my jottings. Most of the names are unfamiliar and sound as if they have leapt off the pages of a Latvian name day calendar—Alvils, Inguna, Egils. Will they understand my rudimentary Latvian? Will my accent bring forth a scowl or a smile? The fifty-year gulf that spans two generations suddenly seems impossibly wide.

"It's possible it was a political statement," suggests Father when I ask about the origin of the names. "The more Latvian, the better."

For most of the morning there is nothing to see but an expanse of smooth water, high clouds stretched into long, thin ribbons, and a sun that shines at us from an unlikely northern angle. The gift shop is slowly emptying of bananas except for their telltale odor; on the shelves sit only a few remaining bottles of spirits. Someone has brought out a guitar, and the sound of singing wafts from the dining room.

After lunch, Father joins me on the foredeck. He is formally dressed in a white shirt, jacket, and tie, with heavy, old-fashioned Zeiss binoculars dangling from his neck. His cane is crooked over one arm, and it swings to and fro as he walks to the railing. More at home on board a ship than on land, Father has no need for his cane now; he and the ship move as one. He has learned to read the ship's smallest movement with his feet and is able to anticipate its every sway. With his feet planted wide and the binoculars pressed to his thick glasses, Father strains to make out a distant shore, hoping to get a first glimpse of the land he left so many years ago. I want to ask him if they are the same binoculars that were responsible for my parents' chance first meeting.

***

"What do you see through them?" a young, raven-haired Erna had inquired oh-so-sweetly and innocently of the young man at the rail. He was dressed in a white sailor uniform, with a cap on his head. Behind her, her sister Elza was attempting to suppress the giggle that somehow managed to escape her lips. The two sisters were touring a navy ship docked in Andrejosta, Riga's main harbour. The sailor had smiled, then removed the leather strap from around his neck and gallantly offered Erna the binoculars. She pressed the glasses to her forget-me-not blue eyes and exclaimed, laughing, "Oh dear, I don't see a thing." Janis smiled indulgently and reached forward to show Erna how to adjust the focus. One year later, in August 1936, Erna and Janis, my parents, were married.

***

Father repositions his feet to steady himself against the mounting swells, as the ship groans and tilts a few degrees. All his life, Father had worked in shipyards, designing, refitting, and repairing ships and overseeing their construction. Like a test pilot, but without the accompanying glamour, Father had supervised many a ship's maiden voyage, breaking in the engines and confirming the ship's stability and seaworthiness. He lowers the binoculars, raises a hand to shield his eyes from the sun's glare, and squints into the distance. I can almost feel him willing the land to meet his searching eyes. Again, he lifts the glasses to his eyes and peers intently southward. Suddenly, a small involuntary cry escapes from Father's lips. He is not one to let his feelings show, but I suspect he has sighted land. Soon, he hands me the binoculars. "Ilze, look out there—about two o'clock. Kolkas rags!"

"Kolkas rags," I murmur, and lean against the railing as I search the misty horizon where sea and sky meet. I'm not sure what I am trying to find.

"We're getting close," Father explains. "Kolkas rags marked the entrance to the protected waters of the Gulf of Riga."

I glance at Father and wonder if he really has spotted land. I see only sky and water. Father knows these waters well. In his youth, he recklessly ventured past Kolkas rags on the *Tobago*, the small wooden sailboat he owned with his brother, Juris. Later, during his obligatory year of military service, and on his way to and from Sweden with his young bride, he would also have passed this way.

Father is waiting for my reaction and tries to hide his annoyance that I do not see what he sees. I lift the binoculars to my eyes once again, steady myself, and suddenly, there it is: a spot of land bobbing up and down like a ship on the horizon. "I see it!" I cry, grateful that we can share this special moment.

I cannot help but feel regret that this strategic piece of Latvian coast that guards the entrance to the gulf was unable to hold back foreign invaders; the Vikings and Celts, Teutonic Knights, Danes and Swedes, and the Third Reich all passed this way. At least Kolkas rags could not be blamed for allowing the Soviets to overrun our small country. The Russian bear invaded Latvia from the east, fording streams and splashing across the shallow lakes and peaty bogs of the heartland to its capital.

As I hand back the binoculars, I turn and see that the deck has filled with passengers, all pointing and staring in the direction where land has been sighted. "Look, the amber coast," I hear someone behind me exclaim. A few of the passengers are crying, some hug each other, and some just stare open-mouthed. A platoon of Latvian flags, large and small, has appeared on deck, and they twist and snap in the wind. The red-white-red flags were seemingly conjured out of thin air, but the men and women that hold them aloft have dreamed of this day for decades—in their mother's bellies, in Saturday morning Latvian school, at church, at Latvian song festivals, and at Jāni, when they wake with their throats sore and their heads pounding after a long night of too much singing and drinking of home-brewed beer. I count fourteen flags. Once again, the *Baltic Star* transforms itself into *Freedom Ship*. Once again we will be testing the authorities. With so many outlawed flags flying, will they allow us into port? Will we be turned back, or worse, arrested?

Soon, Kurzeme, Latvia's westernmost province appears in the distance. We are now past Kolkas rags and into the calmer waters of the Gulf of Riga. A group of musicians assembles on deck and begins to play familiar folk songs. But soon, both the music and the festive mood turn solemn, as the *Baltic Star* approaches the wide mouth of the Daugava River. Mother Daugava, as it is sometimes called, opens herself to welcome us. Stretching from the Baltic Sea across Latvia to Belarus, many songs sing its praises; I grew up singing those songs. We glide past the winter harbour and its once great shipyards, now littered with rusting hulls and idle cranes, past giant coal heaps where butter mountains and pork bellies once awaited shipment to the rest of Europe. I pray not to be disappointed, and turn from the desolate riverbank to behold the well-known, majestic skyline of the Old City upstream. Somehow, inexplicably, it is all very familiar, even though I have never laid eyes on any of it. My brain must have been transforming a lifetime of stories and songs and fuzzy images into a memory.

Suddenly, the familiar first chord of "God Bless Latvia" brings us to attention. Our national anthem is still banned in Latvia, but we sing with strong voices and glad but aching hearts. The wind snatches the words from our mouths and carries our song ashore to a throng of waiting relatives. As we near, I can see that they are singing with us. We repeat the beloved verses over and over, and begin to feel more confident, more secure in our decision to make this historic journey. Many of the elderly passengers, and some of the younger ones, too, are crying and singing at the same time. Cousin Mara has tears flowing down her cheeks, and Aunt Elza, mother's sister, is holding a handkerchief to the end of her nose. Father, Roland, and I remain dry-eyed. In our family, tears have always been discouraged, considered unseemly and a sign of weakness, even, at times, a too-obvious attempt at manipulation. "Stop blubbering" and "What use have tears?" are phrases I heard many times as I was growing up. Their echoes in my brain seldom allow me the release that a good cry might bring.

With surprising gentleness for such a large ship, the *Baltic Star* is nudged into position and secured. On the front of a long, low building, a sign reads *Jūras Pasazierstacija* (Sea Passenger Terminal) in Latvian and Russian. We have arrived at Andrejosta. On the dock below, under the watchful eyes of border guards, customs officials, and probably a KGB agent or two, relatives and friends shout and laugh and wave bouquets of summer flowers in the air. Some carry hand-lettered signs with the names of the unfamiliar relatives they are welcoming. For me, it has been forty-six years since I left Latvia, a baby in my mother's arms.

Our ship is to serve as a floating hotel for our stay in Riga. It is considered sovereign Swedish soil, and each time we go ashore or return, we will have to run the gauntlet of immigration and customs. This won't be easy for some, especially if they or their families have suffered at the hands of the Soviets. We know the rules, but also know that we will flaunt authority as much as we dare. In a strategy session the previous evening, my brother, Janice, Anitra, and others discussed how much and what we would declare; for us, the younger generation, there is no thought of telling the truth. "The communists don't scare me," I declared defiantly. My father shot me a warning look. "I'm Canadian, what can they do to me?"

"Don't expect the Canadian government to get you out of trouble," said Roland, who is now an American citizen.

"Tell me, when have the Soviets ever respected international laws? You, Ilze, were born in Riga, and they could still claim you as their citizen. Worse, you could be considered a traitor for having fled." Father made a fist and pointed his thumb downward to show what might happen to us if we were not careful. I thought he was overreacting, but decided to say nothing.

It is time to disembark. We form several lines, documents in hand. Outwardly, most of us are calm, but inside I suspect we all harbour fears and misgivings. As I wait my turn to go through customs, I try to recall the tricks I learned in my high school drama classes. I draw a deep breath and hold it for a count of eight before slowly exhaling. I could blame my wobbly knees on the twenty-four hours spent on board a rolling ship, but who or what is to blame for my pounding heart and dry mouth? All too soon, it is my turn. Without saying a word, I place my documents on the high counter. My Canadian passport will give me away when it reveals my place of birth—Riga, Latvia. Here, today, it is like an accusation. Will I be considered one of those foolish dissidents who escaped? My only defense, and I am not sure it will be admissible, is that being a baby, I had no choice.

The official first glares at me, and then studies my passport photo, before raising his dark eyes to stare intently at my face once more. When I notice that the olive-skinned, dark-haired official has a birthmark on his cheek that wiggles when he speaks, I suppress a nervous giggle. He turns my passport this way and that, and holds it up to the light to check for tampering. I look up too, and a shiver runs up my spine, when I realize that strategically placed mirrors afford him a view of my back and sides. I feel naked, as if he could see right through my light summer clothing. For a minute, fear almost makes me confess the actual amount of American dollars I am bringing in to Latvia, but before I do anything so foolish, I see that Roland and Janice have successfully managed their entry into the country. All thoughts of incriminating myself vanish. I surrender my passport in exchange for a pass, and the official waves me through. Father is right behind me, and I hear him say, a touch too loudly, "*Moskva,*" when asked his birthplace. He is now an American citizen, with an American passport that clearly states he was born in pre-revolutionary Moscow in 1907, but when my father feels defiant he pronounces Moscow the Russian way. I see the official suppress a smile and hear him say something to Father in Russian. Soon we are outside in the bright sunlight.

We make our way through the crowd to meet the relatives whose names I have by now memorized. My closest blood relative and the only one I recognize, is my cousin Janis Freimanis, the son of Father's sister Marija, who remained behind in Latvia. I had suspected there might be a family resemblance, but I learn soon that we are very different. Decades of foreign occupation have taken their toll on his posture and temperament. With a PhD in organic chemistry, he is a well-respected scientist, but his shoulders lack that western squared-off determination that clearly says, "Here I am, someone to be reckoned with." With him are his wife, Arija, their children and grandchildren, as well as others. We shake hands and hug, and I smile at them, but they are slow to smile back. I soon learn that Latvians here rarely smile and seldom laugh, especially in public. I accept their flower offerings, already beginning to wilt in the summer heat. My relatives are wary and curious, but we all realize that this is a historic moment for our family and, perhaps, for our country. I begin to relax, hoping we will understand each other and become friends. Regina, the widow of Janis's brother, shakes Father's hand and declares with great enthusiasm, "I have a surprise for you when you come to visit us in Valmiera."

Father's face sags into tired lines; he is not fond of surprises, since experience has taught him that surprises are as often as not, unpleasant.

Then, too, Father does not like displays of emotion; for too many of his eighty-two years he has worked at hiding his true feelings.

My brother Peter and his daughters finally make it through the crowd to greet us. He is a Canadian diplomat serving in Germany and has flown to Riga to be with us. His daughters, Alex, Kristi and Tammy, speak no Latvian and seem overwhelmed by the hubbub around them. Peter grins, shakes hands all around, and looks quite at home, although it is also his first time in Latvia. Peter turned two during our family's flight from Latvia in August 1944, aboard the ship that carried us on the dangerous waters of the Baltic to German-occupied Poland, the start of a long journey that changed our lives forever. I am glad to see Peter, as we seldom see each other any more. Since we became adults, we have never lived in the same city at the same time. Both of us have spent time abroad, he in the navy and later, in Foreign Affairs, and I following my husband around the world with his international career. I hope that the distance Peter and I now feel will soon melt away, so that we can become as close as we once were. He is so much like our mother in both looks and mannerisms. He lights a cigarette and blows out the smoke. "Welcome to Latvia," he cries, already feeling a sense of belonging.

The large knot of people soon begins to untangle and, smiling and gently jockeying for position, forms a long line. Soon, we will be a conquering army, marching triumphantly into Riga with our sad memories and unforgettable traumas tucked out of sight. We set out under the watchful and possibly envious eyes of the immigration officials and KGB agents and follow the Daugava River for a while. Ahead of us, like a beacon showing the way, the spire of the Dom Cathedral reaches skyward. Not far off are the octagonal, rooster-topped steeple of St. Peter's Church and the slender spire of St. Jacob's Church. It is a Christian trilogy that distinguishes the skyline of the Latvian capital. The Dom looks deceptively close, but Cousin Janis warns us that it is at least a half-hour walk. Roland looks worried. "Dad," he suggests matter-of-factly, "why don't you and I hop in a cab and meet everyone at the church?"

"No," Father answers curtly, and shrugs away Roland's offered arm.

"It's a good idea, Dad," I say, although I know it is impossible to change Father's mind once it is made up. I realize too, it is a matter of pride, and

Father is obviously determined to participate fully and on his own terms. I look around to see that we are somewhere in the middle of the long column. Up front, leading the procession are nine or ten ministers, men and women, the organizers of this trip. They are dressed in the black, flowing robes of Lutheran pastors, unadorned except for the heavy silver crosses that hang from chains around their necks. They are here to make both a political and religious statement. For them, the voyage is no mere outing, they plan to hold church services, Bible studies, seminars, sacred music concerts, as well as start a dialogue with fellow Christians. But all of us, by our very presence, are announcing to the Soviets that their days as oppressors are numbered. We overseas Latvians are here to join with our countrymen and women to reclaim our lost rights and freedoms: the freedom to worship, the freedom to assemble, the freedom to fly our flag, and the freedom to sing our national anthem—in short, the freedom to be free.

Despite the heat, some in our procession are wearing traditional Latvian dress. For the women, this consists of a thick, hand-loomed woollen skirt, gathered at the waist and secured with a wide woven belt; a loose, embroidered linen blouse topped with a woollen vest; and a homespun shawl spread over the shoulders or carried over one arm. Head-coverings are varied, from linen scarves and bonnets for married women, to metal crowns adorned with bangles and beads for unmarried ones. The men wear dove grey woollen trousers and vests, linen shirts and black, knee-high boots. Narrow, woven ribbons are tied around their necks. Latvia is a small country, about the size of Belgium and the Netherlands combined, but each district has its own style and colour of national dress. I look for and recognize the blue and red striped skirt of Vidzeme, my ancestral home.

Our procession ambles along the Daugava River that slices the capital in two, Old Riga on one side and Pardaugava on the other. Several bridges connect the two halves. Cousin Janis points out the landmarks as we walk. "That's Stalin's birthday cake," he says, pointing to a large, graceless building that resembles a multi-tiered cake. "Is typical Soviet architecture, meaning to inspire awesome and fear, I guess," he adds. I try to explain that our strip malls do much the same sort of damage to our small towns as communist architecture does to a skyline, but I fear I am not successful. Still, why dwell on the negative when there is so much beauty to look at?

We cross Gorkija iela, skirt Riga Castle, and suddenly, we are in Old Riga. The centuries have melted away, and we are back in a medieval world of twisted and narrow, cobblestone streets and crumbling, red-tiled houses in need of paint. The old city, a mere dozen years shy of its eight-hundredth birthday, looks its age. After the war and a half-century of neglect, Old Riga is in desperate need of a face-lift. Riga Castle seems abandoned, the nearby Powder Tower threatens to collapse any moment, and the once splendid Riga Opera House that my parents frequented has closed its doors. Even the mighty Dom Church is in trouble; its foundations are sinking. Some vestiges of Riga's proud past as a member of the Hanseatic League do remain, however, and this is what Father now sees. He walks stiff-legged and red-faced from the heat and long walk, breathing heavily, but with his eyes locked on his goal. He is not using his cane; it is draped over his arm and swings gently with every step, marking time like a metronome. No precious energy is wasted in conversation. I realize he is tired, and I worry he might trip on the sometimes loose, uneven cobblestones.

"Let's stop a minute," I venture. Father shakes his head. "Daddy, please take my arm. It'll make walking these uneven streets easier." He ignores me and pushes on. The sidewalk, narrow and broken in places, is no better. "Dad?" I cup his elbow, but Father jerks his arm away and nearly loses his footing. I am hurt at the rebuff, but I know I shouldn't be. Somehow, my aged father imagines himself a young man walking the familiar streets of his youth; he has no need of his daughter's arm.

Some hopeful signs of restoration stand out amid the decay and disrepair. Finished rebuilding their own war-destroyed capital, skilled Polish workers have arrived to give a face-lift to Riga's sagging facade. In return, and since there is little hard currency to spare, Latvia is providing Poland with much-needed grain. I breathe a sigh of relief when the narrow street finally opens onto the wide expanse that is the Dom Square and see that we are at the church. Father, Roland, Janice, and I slide into a wooden pew and look around as we wait for the organ concert to begin. Whether it is because the grand Dom has not yet been restored to full use as a church, or because it remains faithful to Martin Luther's teachings, there is not much to look at. The only bright spots are several stained glass windows set high in the wall.

"This is where your dear Mama and I married. August 1936," Father tells me, after he has wiped his face with his handkerchief. His eyes, brimming with emotion, look unusually soft. I fear he might actually break down and cry. "She was the most beautiful bride."

"I know," I whisper in reply. I, too, am overcome with emotion. It is hard to imagine my parents young and in love and on the threshold of a new life together. As they exchanged vows in the Dom in 1936, they could not have imagined the hardships they would soon be facing or how far they would stray from their homeland. In the photo album back home, their formal wedding pictures attest to an attractive mix of carefree confidence and shy wonder. "But this place is enormous. How ever did you fill it with guests?"

"No, no, it was there, in the side chapel," Father explains, pointing. He turns to Janice, "You know, this church was shut down by the Bolsheviks, who forbade all religion. Every church in Latvia was closed. I imagine the Dom stood empty, or maybe they used it for some sort of storage. Now it's a museum, and sometimes, because of its excellent organ, it's a concert hall, like today. Six thousand, eight hundred eighty-three—that's how many pipes the organ has, making it one of the largest in the world." We turn to admire the organ that is above and behind us, in the choir. "Not all churches were so lucky," Father continues. "Some in the countryside were turned into stables for horses and even pigs!" Suddenly, the organ music starts, filling the air with deep, rich notes that cause my insides to vibrate, making further talk impossible. We all fall silent, alone with our thoughts, and surrender to the music.

After the concert, everyone is relieved when Father agrees to take a taxi back to the ship. "Good idea, Uncle, but whatever you do, never climb in Russian taxi, only Latvian one," advises Cousin Janis.

"Why not?" Roland asks, his arm already in the air, ready to flag down a car.

"Yes, how do we know if it's Latvian or Russian?" I ask. Smiling to show I'm not serious, I add, "Will the driver have an *R* tattooed on his forehead, like Hawthorne's adulteress?" Janice chuckles, but my attempt at humour is lost on my Latvian relatives.

Janis hesitates and clears his throat. "When driver opens mouth to speak, then you will know." He is serious. In a nervous gesture, he pats down a lock of his hair that refuses to lie flat. His steel grey hair is thick and stiff, unlike anyone else's hair in our family. Father was already balding in his early thirties, and my baby-fine hair flies around in the slightest breeze. Janis looks uneasy, and is reluctant to say what he thinks outright; years of oppression have taught him to be careful. At last, he shrugs his shoulders and states simply, "Is the way things are." Father, understanding, nods in agreement.

With the fearless bravado of the young, Janis's twenty-five-year old daughter, Ligita, adds, "It could be dangerous. At best, he will cheat you." Ligita and her mother are dressed in what I am sure are new, made special for the occasion, summer dresses in coordinating colours.

Janis turns again to Father, "Don't worry, Uncle, I've taken holidays from my Organic Synthesis Institute and will personally drive you where you want to go. Of course, due to Soviet embargo, petrol is rationed, but I will do best I can. Arija, too, has taken leave from her kindergarten."

Arija, Janis's pretty wife, feels the need to explain further. "Very few Russian people have bothered to learn our language. But of course we Latvians, in our own country, must speak Russian if we want to work."

Janis flags down a taxi for us and exchanges a few words with the driver. Satisfied that he is Latvian, he motions for us to get in. We say good-bye and arrange to meet him again the next day.

That evening in the ship's lounge, we compare our first reactions and impressions of Latvia. When we get around to discussing the concert in the Dom, Father begins to reminisce. "Sitting there, it felt like my wedding was only yesterday, and yet, so many years have passed, and so much water has flowed out to sea along the Daugava." His brow furrows, as he concentrates on recalling precise details. "It was the kind of summer day that sent people out of the city to the sandy beaches of Jurmala." Father's memory is surprisingly good. He locates himself in time. "August 12, 1936. War was unthinkable, unimaginable, impossible. Erna—your mother—and I had planned to marry earlier, in the winter, but my dear mother, your Grandmother Alīde, went to her eternal rest. Yes, as you know, she spent the last year of her life in bed, unable to speak or move, paralyzed by a stroke. Out of respect, we put off marrying for six months. Even so, some thought our hastiness unseemly, but we didn't want to delay any longer—Erna, you see, was already twenty-six, and I had just turned twenty-nine. We wanted a family." Father covers his obvious embarrassment at this admission by raising his glass to his lips. "*Prosit*," he toasts.

Father glances at his watch. It is almost ten-thirty, but the light refuses to fade, and we look at him expectantly, willing him to go on. "Everyone was there, my father, and my sister Ede arrived from Denmark with her diplomat husband and two dark-haired daughters. My sister Marija and her doctor husband came from Jaunsvirlauku with their children. Juris, my only brother, his new wife, Zenija, and their two little girls came, as well as Juris's son, Valters, a gangly boy of thirteen from a first marriage. My sister Elizabete and her family, and my sister Milda not yet married." Almost as an afterthought, he quickly adds, "Of course, Erna's family was present also." Father's last comment is for the benefit of my mother's sister, Aunt Elza, and Cousin Mara, who are sitting with us.

How I wish my mother were still alive to share this perfect moment with us! I blink away angry tears that threaten to embarrass me, as I realize that she, of all people, should be here. Mother was more Latvian than any of us; her heart never left her country's sandy shores and gently rolling fields. All during the difficult years— during war, occupation, exile, and resettlement—she kept alive for us the songs, traditions, and riddles ("What has eyes but cannot see?") as she struggled to survive, to care for us, and then to start over, in a foreign land. After her marriage, Mother lived mostly in cities, but she remained a country girl at heart and at belly. She loved flowers, and when spring came, she planted radishes and tomatoes. Some of her tastes in food were peculiar and not shared by the rest of the family: pumpernickel bread slathered with bacon drippings, fried cottage cheese that turned stringy as it cooked, or thick, sour-smelling clotted milk. However, we all loved her baking.

Father's voice rises with emotion and calls me back to the present. I long to share my thoughts, too, but I hold back. As a Zalite, I am uncomfortable in expressing sentiments and feelings. We tend to state the obvious, to see things as either black or white, to make declarations that defy dispute. We don't want our observations examined, just confirmed.

"Erna wore a long, white dress," Father resumed "and I had rented tails for the occasion—"

"Jani," Aunt Elza interrupts in her gentle, yet persistent way. I am not sure if, even now, so many years later, she totally approves of her sister's choice for a husband. "Erna wore a fluid, ivory silk gown that splashed to the floor in a puddle around her feet. Covering her dark hair was a veil, longer than floor-length, that billowed around her like foam on water." Aunt Elza moves in Latvian literary circles; her husband, my Uncle Karlis Rabacs, is a writer, a rare combination of journalist and poet. In New York, they count many exiled writers and artists among their friends.

"Of course, of course. A woman's eyes are better at seeing those details," Father admits, then allows himself to smile. "Dress, gown, what's the difference? All I know is that she was beautiful." Father was a naval architect, a designer of ships, and long ago, before the war, had earned a degree in mechanical engineering from the University of Latvia. He possessed an engineer's mind, precise and calculating, and in the days before computers, he was skilled at using a slide-rule and set of compasses to transform complicated equations into smooth, curved lines on blueprints: the graceful outline of a hull, the snarled entrails of a heating system. He knew or cared little about fashion, and he was not up to arguing with his sister-in-law about fashion terminology or design.

"A gown paints a much more elegant picture," I venture.

"Hah, of course you women stick together. After all this women's liberation and such nonsense, it's turning out to be a woman's world. But let me finish. A crown of myrtle leaves, shiny and dark green, nestled in Mama's black hair; I myself had a sprig of myrtle pinned to my lapel. For luck," Father adds, aware of the irony. My parents' lives had been both lucky and unlucky. They were lucky to have survived the war; they were unlucky to have lost so much.

"A real handsome couple," says Roland, lifting his glass. Of all of us, he is the lucky one, the only one born after the war in Sweden. Roland most closely resembles Father, and now, in his early forties, his hairline threatens to recede. A fondness for sweets causes him to struggle with his weight, but his nose and mouth give him away—they are the Zalite nose and mouth, both just a touch too full. "Yes, for luck." The irony is not lost on us. "*Skol!*" he toasts in Swedish, and he takes a gulp of gin and tonic before translating for Janice.

"*Sveiks*," Father replies in Latvian. He casts a quick glance at Elza before he continues, hoping to avoid stumbling again into a woman's domain. He feels safe discussing flowers; his love for carnations and roses is legendary. "Your mother cradled a sheaf of fragrant, long-stemmed roses that matched her dress, gown, whatever you want to call it. They were creamy white roses, tied with a great big bow. After the ceremony Talavija presented her with an even bigger bouquet of white roses gathered together by a wide green, white, and gold ribbon—the colours of my fraternity. Ah, those roses. If I close my eyes, I can still smell them. They gave off such a perfume, not like the modern roses of today that may look perfect, but have the smell and feel of plastic. Yes, it was one of the happiest days of my life."

"Afterward," Father continues, "the wedding reception was on board the *Adonia*, that was tied up right here at Andrejosta, down a little way from where we sit. Incredible, isn't it?" He looks around for confirmation. "No longer considered seaworthy, the *Adonia* was used by the Riga Yacht Club for parties. You do know I was a member of the yacht club on Lielupe; that's where Juris and I kept the *Tobago*." The sailboat had been named for a former colony of Latvia when it had dreams of becoming a naval power.

"The celebration afterward was elegant and measured. Of course, some of the men threw back too much vodka—who could blame them? It was a celebration. The women's cheeks glowed prettily from the effect of the champagne, but it was not the Latvian three-day bacchanal of olden times. We danced. Mama loved to dance, especially the Strauss waltz, and she never seemed to tire. Your grandfather Peteris Zalite welcomed my Erna into the family in a very moving speech. My fraternity brothers in Talavija, especially Erna's younger brother, Janis Šķenders, embraced Erna into their midst. To his credit, my brother Juris, who scorned fraternities and all they stood for, kept his comments to himself so as not to spoil the festive mood."

"The caterers had prepared a feast—lox on dark rye, smoked eel, and other delicacies, and a mountain of shrimp. There was much more—herring, jellied meat; all was as it should be. It was late in the afternoon, but the sun still hung suspended in the western sky, when Juris picked up a long-handled dessertspoon and began to tap his glass. Tok, tok, tok. His face was wet with perspiration from dancing, and his mouth was twisted into a lopsided grin; Juris was tipsy and enjoying himself immensely. '*Bitter, bitter*,' he cried, and his table companions joined in. '*Bitter, bitter*,' all the guests sang in unison. Erna blushed, from embarrassment or excitement or the champagne—maybe all three—and turned to me with those forget-me-not eyes. Shyly, we touched our lips together."

"You kissed. Admit it, Dad," I cry. In my eyes, Father has always been a prude, uncomfortable when confronted by public displays of affection or emotion. I try, but cannot remember ever seeing my father and mother holding hands or kissing each other, even in the casual way most married couples do. He did not hug or kiss us, either, although I wish he had. "Go on, please," I add.

"We departed the next day for Sweden. End of story." Father checks his watch. "Oh, it's time for bed. Tomorrow's another day."

The rest of us are not yet ready for bed; outside, there is still enough light by which to read. Here on the amber coast, the northern summer day fades reluctantly. After Father retires with the usual admonishment of "don't stay up too late," Aunt Elza picks up the story of my parents' wedding.

"Your father didn't tell you everything," she begins, and sits forward in her chair. Aunt Elza is petite, delicate, and small-boned, unlike my mother who was taller, thick-boned, and more generously endowed. Now at eighty-five, wearing something black and voluminous made of a soft jersey, and wrapped in a black shawl against the evening chill, Elza appears even smaller than I remember. Her grey hair is gathered in a bun, and her eyes are soft and deep-set, lost in shadow; her nose is slender and straight, without my mother's characteristic bump. Except for certain facial expressions, the family resemblance is not obvious. Elza's personality, too, is quite distinct from that of my mother. Elza was the older, serious sister, and Erna the younger, freer spirit; Elza was the dutiful daughter who attended to her chores; Erna had to be roused from her bed by harsh words from Omama. Family rumours hint of the existence of a painting by Ernests Brastiņš, tucked away somewhere in the back rooms of the Latvian National Art Gallery, of three nudes – Elza, Erna, and Irma. I have difficulty imagining my mother or Elza posing nude. I am discovering my mother's split personality—one pre-war personality and a very different post-war one.

"It's true that the reception was the best that money could buy, but your mama broke more than one heart when she married. She was popular and so loved to dance—any excuse to go to a ball, to dance. The next day, Karlis and I were on board to see the newlyweds off. They were sailing to Sweden where Janis had a job in the shipyards. Göteborg," Elza passes a hand in front of her eyes, as if trying to wave off a dark shadow that threatens her memory. "If only they had stayed in Sweden and not returned in '38, Ernina could have been spared so much."

"What are you saying?" I ask.

"We can't change the past, so it's best to put it out of our minds, all those bad parts," Elza continues. "We strolled along the deck arm in arm, your mother and I, while Karlis and Janis walked ahead, arguing about politics, I imagine. Some others are there, too, I don't remember exactly who, but the mood is gay, not at all sad."

Now that I am in the same place my parents married then departed for Sweden, I see my parents in a new light, as excited, self-conscious newlyweds off on an adventure. My father, a naval architect and former sailor, probably wore white trousers, a blue blazer, a captain's hat on his head, and binoculars around his neck. They were his lucky Zeiss binoculars that led to the chance meeting with the woman who was now his wife. My mother was surely wearing something flowery that billowed prettily around her legs, absurd high-heeled shoes, and a hat that threatened to be snatched by the wind if she removed her hand from it. Father would be explaining something nautical to his new bride, but she would be too excited and a bit too worried to pay close attention.

Elza's voice interrupts my daydream. "All of a sudden the ship vibrated and a shrill whistle sounded, telling us it was time to disembark. From the shore, we were waving and shouting, "Bye-bye," when I heard the drone of an airplane that seemed to be getting louder and louder." Aunt Elza has my full attention; I have never heard this story. "Like a pesky fly at a picnic, this small, one-motor airplane, no bigger than a child's toy, swooped down low over the ship, and its shadow rippled over the people assembled on deck. A few passengers covered their heads, but most looked up to see the plane gain height over the Daugava, bank steeply, and head back toward the ship."

"The war was starting?" I ask, thoughts of bombings and air raids in my head.

"Oh, no. No, nothing like that. My first thought was Juris had concocted some stunt, maybe together with our younger brother. Your mother craned her neck to look up, holding on to the floppy brim of her hat, while Janis tried to locate the plane in his binoculars. His face had that serious look that was often mistaken for displeasure or anger." Elza takes a small sip of her mineral water.

"I just love this next part and would give anything to have seen it. It is so romantic," sighs Mara.

"Mara, you were not yet one year old and had been left in Omite's care. So we all watched open-mouthed and incredulous as the pilot tossed something out of a small window. As they tumbled from the sky, the dark clumps separated and turned into sweet peas and daisies and multicoloured snapdragons that landed on the ship, but mostly in the water. Stunned as I was, I couldn't help thinking of a familiar song, except it was the Daugava and not the River Gauja that carried the flowers in its bosom." Elza laughs softly and smiles. For a moment, no one knows what to say, but soon we are all talking at once, asking questions.

"Some onlookers clapped in delight, and children rushed to gather up the blooms, but Janis, no, he was not amused. Janis knew who it was, and the ridiculous display by one of Erna's former suitors left him with a bad taste in his mouth. You know he hated being made a fool of in front of his new bride and the other passengers."

"I think it's so romantic," says Mara.

"Well, Janis didn't. Erna must have been secretly pleased—who wouldn't be—but she couldn't let it show."

I couldn't help exclaiming, "It's like something out of a Harlequin novel."

"My sister opted for a solid, hard-working man who would look after her."

Roland added, as if to defend himself, "Romantic is good, but they don't always make the best husbands, you know."

"'One of these days the fool is going to kill himself,' Karlis said, on our way home." Elza pauses, "His words actually turned out to be prophetic. A few years later, Vidvuds was conscripted into the Luftwaffe by the occupying Germans and never lived to get married, have children...," Her voice trails off. "Yes, children—I call you children, you're all so young—that's how it was." The tragic postscript to Elza's story spoils our happy mood, and we soon decide it is time for bed. The sun has finally dipped below the horizon, and before it reappears all too soon, we want to get a few hours of shut-eye.

It is hard to get comfortable and I lie awake for the longest time. I recall other stories my Aunt Elza has told me on our too-infrequent visits to her home on Long Island. During the sixties and seventies she traveled to Latvia several times, and afterward, regaled us with stories that fed our cold war paranoia. The only way to get there was to fly Aeroflot to Moscow and then Riga. She had to stay in a hotel and could only meet her relatives in public places, in full view of an assigned watcher. Desperate for foreign exchange, the only shopping allowed visitors was at the state-run Dollar Store. "The Soviets hungered for American dollars, like a dog after a bone," I remember her saying. Any gifts, even used clothing, brought in to Latvia were subject to a heavy duty, so Elza wore multiple layers of clothing, and stacked wristwatches up her arm. These things were important and could be readily sold on the black market or traded for things that were sorely needed. The watcher must have been surprised at how long Elza and her sister-in-law Gaida or other female relatives spent in the ladies' washroom. It was hard to imagine my soft-spoken, ladylike aunt bundled up in too-large clothing and flouting the law. She was certainly generous. I recalled that, more than once, before boarding the plane to return home, she removed her warm coat and gave it to whoever was seeing her off at the airport. Her suitcases were empty, except for the odd gift she had received from grateful relatives.

In the morning, the dining room of the *Baltic Star* is abuzz with voices as passengers exchange experiences and plans. We feel that Latvia's struggle for independence is almost over. The city is full of choirs and dance ensembles that have converged on Riga from all over, some as far away as Australia. Our visit coincides with the Song Festival, and we are excited to be a part of Latvia's "Singing Revolution". I am beginning to realize now, that as with the struggle for women's equality, every action is political and every word carries a weight.

Our excitement is slightly dampened when we learn that one passenger did not disembark yesterday. An elderly Latvian-American, mentally reliving some wartime horror, could not bring himself to face the Soviet official who stood between him and Latvian soil. Neither could his friend and traveling companion convince him that it would be all right. "I do hope he finds the courage today," I say.

"How's it possible to still have such severe post-traumatic stress syndrome after all these years," Roland wonders.

"You were born in Sweden after it was all over," I say, stating something we all know.

"I guess he never really dealt adequately with his trauma," suggests Janice.

"Yeah, he never got any help in that way, and seeing the uniforms must have caused a flashback as real as the original experience," I add.

"That sounds like so much modern psychobabble to me. Life must go on, no matter what happens; choices must be made, no matter how difficult," says Father expelling his breath. "It's not healthy to brood on the past."

A while later, on our way to disembark, we are surprised to see Mara pushing her mother in a wheelchair. I open my mouth to ask what happened, as Mara puts a finger discreetly to her lips and continues on her way with my usually able-bodied aunt slumped in the chair. We follow, wondering what is going on. When we are safely through customs, my aunt explains that she has brought the wheelchair into the country without paying duty, and that the plan is to give it to her relatives. They can then sell it for sorely needed revenue. "I plan to return on foot, living proof of the miracle of the black market economy," explains Elza, a twinkle in her dark eyes.

"Won't they be suspicious?" I ask.

"No, no, they are not that clever."

Mara adds, "Our relatives plan to use the money for a new roof. This way, everyone wins—us, my relatives, and the person who buys it."

At that moment, I am surprised by how superior and better informed I feel when I compare myself to the Soviet customs agents, who are no doubt fed daily lies. All of us—Latvian-Canadians and Latvian-Americans—have, for years, dined on the image of corrupt, dim-witted, and out-of-step Russian bureaucrats, who are easily fooled, and now that image has been confirmed. "I can't believe it all went so smoothly," says Roland.

"There're still many days to go," admonishes Father, who dislikes tempting fate. "Just you wait. They could still have a card up their sleeves."

"No doubt," jokes Roland, "as long as it's not an ace."

I don't wonder at the animosity of Latvians against the Russians, but I am surprised by its intensity. It is the age-old response of the vanquished to their conquerors, of the downtrodden to their rulers. It is obvious that in all these years since the illegal annexation of Latvia into the Soviet Union, the wounds have not healed nor memories faded. Russians and Latvians live and work side by side, but like oil and water, they do not mix. To prevent schoolyard fighting, children attend separate Russian or Latvian schools.

On board ship, we are safe from harassment, but it continues in minor, irritable ways. Every day, a launch floats menacingly off our bow, presumably keeping watch for defections or other unwanted activity. Is someone eavesdropping on our conversations, I wonder? It serves as a stark reminder that although Latvia is teetering on the brink of freedom, it is not yet free.

Father does not seem at all surprised by this. It only serves to confirm his beliefs.

A few days later, as Father had predicted, the customs officials reveal their trump card. The unsettling news that the *Baltic Star's* documents are not in order spreads quickly through the dining room. We are told it will be impossible for anyone to disembark. Impossible. Disbelief and anger register on the uplifted faces. The room buzzes with questions. I cannot believe this is happening, but Father, who expected something like this to happen, takes the news calmly. We did not come all this way to sit on board ship. We have plans. But as we wait for the situation to sort itself out, there is nothing to do but drink another cup of strong Swedish coffee. Unused as I am to so much caffeine, the coffee only serves to increase my anxiety. Finally, a half hour later, the ship's first officer strides into the dining room to inform us that the impasse has been resolved. "Good news, you are free to disembark."

Father rises slowly from his chair. "I bet some vodka or maybe a bottle of perfume or chocolates from the duty free shop did the trick," he says.

A few minutes later, standing in line to go through Customs and Immigration, I overhear the whispered comment followed by suppressed laughter, "I guess they had to feed the monkeys some bananas." Although we liked to think so, the Russians were no fools. I think they knew all along what kind of petty subterfuges we were up to and decided to make the most of their opportunity.

"This is exactly why I opted for freedom just after you were born," Father tells me that evening at dinner. "Now you see why Mama and I, along with thousands others, risked our lives and those of our children. We were desperate to escape the clutches of the advancing Bolsheviks." He then launches into a brief version of a story I know all too well, the story of my birth.

***

I came squealing into the world, a big baby, as generously upholstered as the sofa that squatted in our front room, with similarly bowed legs but a less placid disposition. My grandmother, Marta Šķenders, or Omite, took one look at me and said to her daughter, "Thank God, Erna. She's a big, strong girl—good lungs, too. She's awakened the whole floor. And smart, hesitating the way she did. She knew better than to come into the world at a time like this." It was January 5, 1944, early afternoon, but the electric lights in the Abolin Clinic had already been switched on. The smell of ether and disinfectant lingered in the room. Outside, it was snowing, and the flakes settled gently on the window ledges.

My mother kept her eyes closed, but smiled weakly through her twilight sleep, "A little sister for Peteritis."

"What will you call this little dumpling?" asked Omite.

"Janis and I decided on Ilze Ingrid for a girl," said Mother, opening her blue eyes a crack to observe her mother's reaction.

"The name's as common as rye bread. Seems like every other girl born in Riga this year is named Ilze."

"We picked it years ago, when we hoped to start our family. It wasn't so common then," Mother blushed at the implication but continued, "and still, the name is perfect for the times we live in. A solid Latvian name, but it could also be German or Swedish. The Ingrid is Swedish."

"Shhh, Daughter. Better rest a bit before Janis gets here." Omite adjusted the homespun woollen shawl around her shoulders, got up slowly, and went to the window. The damp cold made her joints ache and complain like rusty hinges. "It's thick as porridge out there now."

Father arrived as soon as he could, his karakul hat in one gloved hand and a string bag of oranges in the other. His thick glasses, round and black-rimmed, were still opaque with frost, because he had hurried directly to Mother, stopping only to remove his galoshes at the front entrance. The shoulders of his heavy, black coat held a fine dusting of snow that was fast disappearing. Father bent over to kiss his wife's smooth, white forehead and patted her dark hair. I like to believe he smiled, but I cannot be certain; although I was an eagerly awaited child, I was an added responsibility in an unsettled time. Both food and heating coal were rationed in German-occupied Latvia, and the future was uncertain. Luckily, Father's job at the Riga Shipyards guaranteed our family much-needed ration coupons. After four years of war, much of Europe had been destroyed and countless lives lost. No one knew how it would all end, but one thing was certain: Latvia would go to the victor. Only a fool would dare hope that Latvia could regain its independence.

Father's sadness stemmed not just from the difficulties of raising a family in wartime, but also from the recent loss of his own father. My paternal grandfather, Peteris Zalite, had been laid to rest in the Meža kapi cemetery only a few days earlier. The death of my grandfather set Father free in a way he didn't want to admit—even to himself. He had worshiped his father and, for years, each decision had been predicated upon the question, "Would Father approve?"

During the long, dark nights before my birth, in our apartment on Tomsona iela, Father's preoccupations with his family's safety and half-formed evacuation plans filled his mind and robbed him of much-needed sleep. Even when he did sleep, his sleep was shallow, disturbed by murky dreams, and he woke without feeling refreshed. Thank goodness the baby has finally arrived, he thought. As soon as the weather grew warmer, he would move Erna, Peteris, and baby Ilzite out of the capital to the relative safety of the countryside. My father smiled wanly at his wife—he possessed the inexplicable ability to look happy and sad at the same time, as if he could never allow himself the luxury of feeling pure joy. He lifted Mother's hand, patted it, and said simply, "Thank you, dearest Erna. Thank you."

Two

Now, forty-six years later, I am finally seeing Latvia through my own eyes and am surprised to realize that the Riga skyline, pierced by three church spires, is as familiar to me as the skyscrapers of Manhattan are to a New Yorker. As I walk the narrow, twisting streets of the old city, I get a sense of dèja-vu. On the edge of a city park, stands the Laima clock. It predates the war, and surprisingly, still shows the right time. The clock was, and still is, a popular meeting place. Many of my parents' dates started at this clock. I am delighted when I come across the Laima candy store down a side street. The Laima chocolate factory survived World War II and the following years of occupation. I have tasted their candies before, when Aunt Elza brought them back for us from her earlier visits.

My heart beats quickly as I walk down Freedom Boulevard toward the forty-one-meter tall Freedom Monument. Built in the 1930s and dedicated to the fatherland and freedom, it is one of the most important landmarks of modern Riga and now, during Latvia's Third National Awakening, it remains as important a symbol as ever. It is to the peoples' credit that it survives today. Atop a travertine obelisk stands Milda, a slender figure representing liberty. Her outstretched arms support a trio of gold stars for the three regions of ancient Latvia. But even today, the Freedom Monument is far from free. Day and night, two Soviet soldiers patrol the base of the monument. They are not to be mistaken for an honour guard; they serve instead as a deterrent to patriotic demonstrations and to prevent Latvians from leaving offerings of flowers. Even so, I see that the base of the monument is strewn with brightly coloured, summer flowers, and I am heartened to see several people approach the monument and, without so much as a sideways glance at the soldiers, place their bouquets at Mother Latvia's feet.

As I walk, I am delighted to hear the Latvian language spoken on the street. It is such a novelty. Growing up in Montreal in the early fifties at a time when immigrants were labeled Displaced Persons, I used to cringe when Mother spoke to me in Latvian in a store or on the bus. In Latvia at last, I am delighted and relieved to learn that my relatives understand my Latvian, although I do occasionally catch them giving each other a knowing look when I mispronounce a word or use an English word instead of the proper Latvian one. My mother tongue provides plenty of opportunity to stumble, with its difficult soft *g* sound, an *l* that sounds more like a *y*, and a soft *k* that sticks in the throat like a lozenge. Perhaps Father feels vindicated for all the times he barked at us to "Speak Latvian!" when we were growing up.

To me the Latvian language is as convoluted as the streets of Old Riga, and it is just as easy to lose one's way. It is an inflective language, with two grammatical genders and German–influenced syntax. Each noun is declined in seven cases: nominative, genitive, dative, accusative, instrumental, locative, and vocative. A diminutive form of a noun is often used. Latvian uses a modified Roman script with thirty-three letters as well as a number of diacritical marks to lengthen vowels and soften consonants. Along with Lithuanian, Latvian is considered to be the most archaic of the Indo-European languages still spoken. No wonder it is an orphan with few living relatives. But still, it has persisted—in Latvia and abroad—despite decades of the Soviets imposing a policy of forced Russification.

I see everything more clearly now that I am finally here. The circumstances surrounding my birth were not quite as simple and harmonious as I liked to imagine, but it was one of the very few happy stories my parents told of the war years. In my adult years, I learned that 1944, during the German occupation of Latvia, was a desperate, dangerous, and hungry time for the people of my homeland. As Soviet troops gathered along its borders, preparing to invade and reoccupy the country, the Wermacht tried to hang on and continue its dreadful work. The Latvian nation was slated for extinction, both under the Nazis and under the previous Soviet regime. Many people, including most members of my extended family, were already familiar with Soviet atrocities and had made plans to flee first into the Latvian countryside and then out of the country. Possible escape routes were few and dangerous. Latvia trembled in fear on the shores of the Baltic, a once calm sea that had turned deadly, patrolled by German U-boats and dreadnoughts as well as by Allied submarines and warships. Battles took place in the skies over the Baltic, shredding clouds and lives. Escape by sea in small fishing vessels was possible, but it was extremely dangerous, and many lives had already been lost. To head east was unthinkable; to go west, by land and sea, seemed a preferable option.

My homeland's first, brief, intoxicating flirtation with independence had lasted a mere twenty years, from 1918 to 1939, but the experience had marked our people forever. Sovereignty and the right to choose was not something easily forgotten or lightly discarded. Spurred on by the wish to save his family from a terrible fate, Father chose freedom, as did so many other Latvians. They scattered like leaves before a storm, vulnerable, fragile, and easily trod upon.

At the start of World War II, the Soviets illegally occupied Latvia and installed a hated regime predicated on arrests, executions, and deportations to Siberia. This was followed by a process of transformation that was catalyzed by intimidation and fear, as well as by the open collaboration of some Bolshevik sympathizers. Russification, collectivization, and nationalization—of people, institutions, the economy, and agriculture—were the operative policies. Latvian President Kārlis Ulmanis was arrested and deported, and he died in exile; no one knows the exact circumstances. A terrible year of horror, arrests, and repression followed, culminating in the mass arrest and deportation of fifteen thousand Latvians in June 1941. Overall, the number of Latvians eliminated was probably double those deported. Intellectuals, politicians, and professionals were marked as *undesirables*. Some escaped arrest by hiding in the woods while the danger was greatest. Mother's brother, Janis, who had fought with the Latvian Legion, was deported to forced labour in Siberia and did not return home until many years later, his health destroyed. Father's cousin Varaidotis Pļaviņš, who was a magistrate, and his family—wife Olga and four of their children—were forcibly removed from their home in Valmiera on the night of June 13 to14 and deported to Siberia in separate boxcars. Varaidotis never returned, and no one knows his fate. Olga and her children suffered unimaginable hardships, but survived and were repatriated after the war. The other relatives who remained behind in Latvia were not singled out for such harsh punishment by the new Soviet regime, but they did suffer oppression and deprivation in many ways.

I have carried this sad family history with me. On this trip, my first one to a country I fled as a baby in my mother's arms, I hoped to undo a knot of conflicting emotions and gain insight into scraps of stories that have become entangled for me with folk history, epic stories, and songs. As Omite had done with old sweaters, I wanted to unravel a no longer serviceable notion, rescue its threads, and rewind them into a smooth ball from which I could create something new. I wanted to separate fiction from fact, but I soon realized this was not going to be easy; there was too much baggage, little of it physical, aboard this legendary Freedom Ship.

I am glad my visit coincides with the Song Festival. It brings us together and confirms our identity as a nation. It is to be a political statement as well. *Dainas* and folk songs are the very embodiment of our culture and reflect the soul of our people.

Except when they are singing or dancing, Latvians are for the most part a melancholy, taciturn people. Especially in the winter, they turn inward, keeping their thoughts and feelings to themselves, no doubt preoccupied by their tragic past and difficult present. But during the long days of the brief northern summer, when all of nature seems to shout at them from earth and sky, they undergo a miraculous metamorphosis. Women emerge like butterflies from their chrysalises, shedding dark, heavy coats and clumsy boots to flaunt their gaudy, gossamer garb of summer. Men abandon jackets, gloves, and ties and head for the countryside. The melancholy songs they sang during the winter—songs that told of loss, hardship, oppression, and slavery—disappear and are replaced by happier melodies and lyrics that extol nature.

I toss and turn that night on my narrow bunk, struggling with thoughts and feelings that are new to me, among them a kind of survivor's guilt. I personally have not suffered very much, although growing up in foreign lands I often felt deprived and out of place. Now I feel as if I am playing the part of someone else, an actor on a stage. How or what should I really be feeling? Alternately, I am bold and timid, sad and happy, full of hope for the Latvia's future one moment and in the next, pessimistic. These are not feelings I am able to share with my father, but my cabin mate, Anitra, echoes my thoughts. "We can be happy and optimistic if we don't over-analyze but accept things at face value," she suggests. "No one can change the past. Haven't we seen how optimistic the Latvians themselves are? With the Berlin Wall gone, their freedom is virtually assured."

We spend the next day together, and my optimism returns when I see that the street names have already begun their transition from Russian to Latvian. Leniņa iela is now Kalķu iela that becomes Brīvības bulvaris that ends at the Freedom Monument. During the years of German occupation it was called Ādolfa Hitlera iela. Bouquets of summer flowers are everywhere, tucked into baskets on the way to work, intended for display in store windows and on shop counters, at ticket booths, and even on kiosk shelves, fighting for space amid the cigarettes and magazines. Daisies, red clover, and fragrant sweet peas mix with flowering timothy and orchardgrass. "Remember how we used to weave crowns out of those same flowers?" I ask Anitra. We are returning from the Central Market, where we have toured the mostly empty stalls, and are walking in the park that flanks both sides of the city canal. Wearing crowns of flowers in our hair or bedecking ourselves with long necklaces made from the orange berries of the mountain ash and pretending it was amber, were just small parts of the idyllic summers of our youth spent on Ile Perrot. It was a small island detached like an afterthought from the bigger island of Montreal.

"Yeah, those were great summers," Anitra replies with a lopsided grin, before slapping me on the shoulder, "but who was the cry baby when her crown fell apart or her necklace broke, spilling beads everywhere?"

Before I can reply to Anitra's teasing, I am unexpectedly forced off the sidewalk by an aggressive, oncoming pedestrian. "Hey, watch it," I say and turn to look, but the man strides away with no hesitation or apology. "Did you see that?" I ask.

"That," declares Anitra with conviction, "was a Russian. No Latvian would be so rude."

"*Yah*, what nerve. My relatives warned me, and they were right. Next time, I'm not going to step aside. I'll show them I'm not one of the locals who can be pushed around."

"The Russians resent us visitors," says Anitra. "They must feel threatened by the changes happening so fast, the new ideas from the outside, and returning Latvians carrying wallets they imagine to be stuffed with dollars."

"I wish."

Anitra, a psychologist, suggests a simple experiment. "Let's play chicken and see." After a few more encounters, we abandon our little game and sit down on a wooden bench to rest and decide where to go next. For a while, we amuse ourselves playing another silly, but less hazardous game. As each strolling couple or group draws near, we scan for clues to their nationality: style of dress, shoes, facial features, and posture. Latvian or Russian, local or foreigner, friend or foe?

"Definitely Russian," I state as two young women approach, wearing short skirts and too-high heels with their hair and lips coloured bright red. I cling to the stereotype that Latvian women are more modest in their dress and wear sensible shoes. But mostly my decisions are based on body language—the Latvians have the more submissive posture of the vanquished, while the Russians sport the confident look of the conqueror. As they pass, we strain to catch a fragment of conversation. Often, to my surprise and even perverse delight, we guess correctly.

After a while, we tire of our little game and decide instead to shop for gifts for our families back home. We exchange rubles for inexpensive souvenirs. The price in dollars depends on where and for how much we have changed our US dollars into the local currency. The official exchange rate is fixed at 1.8 rubles for each dollar. But for statistical purposes, the risible rate of 0.56 rubles per US dollar is maintained, in order to capture hard currency and to inspire confidence in a currency that was daily losing value. Although it is illegal, most Latvians are eager to exchange their rubles for dollars. At the money exchange, I transform my dollars into rubles at the happy rate of eight to one, and were I brave enough and willing to venture down a back alley, I could obtain a rate of ten or even twelve to one. But I am cautious by nature and want to stay on the good side of the law. I am further cowed by the knowledge that, when we leave, we are expected to present official receipts for any money we have exchanged. This amount should tally with the amount of American currency we declared upon arrival and that which we have remaining. We doubt that the customs officials will bother to do the calculations, but we do not want to risk any unnecessary problems when it comes time to depart.

Rubles in hand, Anitra and I search for a coffee shop in Old Town. Since there doesn't appear to be any in sight, I ask a passerby who points us to a brick building with no sign and a closed door. He assures us it is a government-run restaurant. "Remember," says Anitra, "no private enterprise allowed." I knock on the heavy wooden door, wait, and knock again. After a few minutes, a dark-haired, sloe-eyed fellow opens the door a crack and pokes his head out. He says something in Russian and slams the door before we can ask anything more.

"I guess that means they're closed," I say, looking at my watch; it is eleven in the morning. "Customers are definitely not wanted—they only serve to create unwelcome work." Although we are inconvenienced, we are more than happy to confirm the abject failure of the totalitarian economic system.

"Now that's one for the textbooks, title: *Why Communism Failed*," says Anitra. We look at each other and burst into laughter. It is all too bizarre, especially the realization that our attitude toward communism has been ingrained in us from an early age by our parents. We can analyze that later, we decide, as we unashamedly enjoy the moment.

Still thirsty, we head toward a sign proclaiming the *Universalveikals*. It turns out to be a large, shoddy department store that sells faded dry goods, Woolworth-quality jewellery, candies, and food. We see a line-up and head over to investigate but are disappointed to discover it leads to the sausage counter. We look around for amber but find none and soon leave, disappointed. These days it seems that even amber, worn by Latvian women the world over, is out of the reach of ordinary citizens at home. Finally, Anitra and I, hungry, thirsty, and somewhat dejected, return to the ship for lunch.

But there is little time to brood or rest. Our itinerary is so packed it could have been prepared by an overly ambitious, spiteful tour operator. It is part tourism, part history lesson, and part family reunion, and often the three are rolled into one overwhelming experience. This afternoon, we are accompanying my father to visit his parents' graves. Cousin Janis and his wife, Arija, will drive some of us in his Žiguli, a Russian-built car, and the rest of us will follow in a taxi. Cousin Janis's car has been unmercifully battered by the neglected roads, is in need of repair, and occasionally emits a death rattle, but he is lucky to have it at all, along with the petrol to make it run.

Janis is an attentive host, full of nervous energy and the desire to connect with his overseas relatives. He wants us to understand the Latvian reality, present, past, and future. It is a tall order for such a short time. Although a scientist by education and training, Janis is now in politics. He is a recently elected deputy of the Latvian Saeima (Parliament) and serves on its Foreign Relations Committee. For years, as a founding member of the Latvijas tautas fronte (Latvian Peoples Front) political party, he has worked actively and unflinchingly toward the goal of an independent Latvia, while at the same time continuing to serve as a director at the Organic Synthesis Institute. His institute, like many others, is under fiscal pressure to become self-sufficient by producing marketable drugs such as birth control pills and other hormones. As the USSR continues to disintegrate, and with it the value of the ruble, research money is becoming scarce but Janis's new political career leaves him less time to ensure the Institute is financially sound.

We disembark at the cemetery entrance and head for the flower stalls. Father moves slowly from vendor to vendor, examining the flowers, remembering, considering. Forty-six years have passed since he last visited his parents' graves, and only the best will do. Finally, he sighs, selects a bouquet of white lilies and carnations, pays, then lifts the blooms to his face to inhale their perfume. He is satisfied. Flowers in hand, we first stroll along an avenue lined with linden trees in full flower. I sneeze, non-stop. At the entrance to Brāļu Kapi (National Military Cemetery), Cousin Janis explains that this cemetery honours the Latvian Riflemen and other patriots who fought and died during Latvia's 1919 struggle for independence. The war graves are watched over by the statue of Latvia with two fallen brethren at her feet. Each sculpture is a work of art. Brāļu Kapi has the reputation for being one of the most beautiful military cemeteries in the world and rightly so. However, its allure is tinged with sadness. In my homeland, sadness and beauty always seem to be intertwined, suffering made into art.

"In 1945, after you had already fled," Janis tells Father, and I detect a slight accusatory tone, "the Soviets threatened to take away statues, but we made protests and demonstrations and this prevented from happening." How brave, I think to myself as I realize once again how little many outsiders know about what went on in occupied Latvia. Cousin Janis distinguishes for us the memorials erected by Latvians and those of the communists; the former are to be revered, while the latter are to be ignored. At the nearby grave of Jānis Čaksta, the first president of independent Latvia, my cousin removes several flowers from his bouquet, and lays them on the granite pedestal. "All these years, Soviets forbid to put flowers or light here candles, at this memorial, but no, it never stop Latvian people."

Arija nods in silent agreement. "The Cheka (KGB) hid in bushes and snapped photographs so later, they able identify people with flowers," she adds helpfully, causing Cousin Janis to lift his hand in a dismissive gesture. Though still a neophyte politician, he knows it is good policy not to say more than is necessary. But Arija is friendly and open and wants us to truly understand what they went through. I wonder, too, if she wants us to feel a tinge of guilt for having abandoned our homeland.

There is little time to wonder as we follow a wide, dirt path that leads from the national cemetery to the Meža Kapi (Forest Cemetery) where Peteris Zalite and his wife, Alida, the grandparents I never knew, are buried. Cousin Janis's sister, Mirdza, lies there too, having succumbed to tuberculosis at the age of forty. The rest of us stand back, silent, and observe as Father lowers his stiff body down on one knee and gently places his bouquet of white flowers at the base of the black granite that is inscribed with the names of his mother and father. He traces the names with his fingers, but says not a word. We wait, silent, in the verdant surroundings, breathing in the heady scent of mock orange and honeysuckle. A bird sings in a nearby tree. Father shows no outward emotion and says nothing. Slowly, he struggles to his feet and once upright, leans both arthritic hands on his cane. The effort of getting up has flushed his face pink.

"Shall I take a photo?" Janice breaks the silence. She has been quietly recording the event, but now wants to get all of us lined up on either side of the tombstone.

When she is satisfied, we turn to go. Cousin Janis retrieves a miniature rake from behind the stone and smoothes the course, damp sand as if it were a Japanese garden. Our footprints are gone and only our limp flowers remain as testament to our brief visit. As we retrace our steps, questions that I hesitate to ask crowd my mind. I don't want to appear ignorant in front of Father and the relatives I scarcely know. Not for the first time, I silently regret not having been more interested in our family history while I was growing up. Like most teenagers and many young adults, I was preoccupied with myself and with my friends and thought little about unknown relatives in a faraway country that could not even be found on a map. Seeing my relatives' graves make me realize how much my brothers and I have missed out on, not knowing grandparents and others who were real people who led real lives and who were not merely inhabitants of water-stained photo albums or faded picture books. They were people who lived, laughed, and loved, and did their best to survive in a chaotic, ever-changing world. I am thankful we are together at last, the living and those sleeping in the earth of a soon-to-be-free Latvia, and I can begin to understand and know more.

***

Latvians have always been tied to the land. Long before my grandfather Peteris Zālīte became a teacher and his children studied to become engineers and schoolteachers and pharmacists, we were a family of peasant farmers from Jumurda, in Latvia's midsection. The land was part forest, part open meadow with low, rolling hills, meadows, and lakes. If he was lucky, my great-great grandfather Juris Sahlīts (later Latvianized to Zālīte) plowed the heavy soil with the help of a horse; if he was unlucky, he hitched himself up to his wooden plow and strained and hauled until his eyes bulged and the arteries in his neck stood out like thick, blue ropes. A wet spring could have killed him. Fortunately, that did not happen. The fields eventually dried out enough, except the ones down in the hollows, and he sowed oats, rye, and barley for himself, his family, and his animals. Ilze, his wife, planted a kitchen garden of potatoes, onions, carrots, beets, and cabbages to see the family through the winter. Like the nature they were a part of, my ancestors' lives turned with the seasons, as much dependent on the sun and rain as their crops. On the shortest night of the year, in June, Latvians threw down their rakes and hoes and celebrated nature with wild abandon. The women gathered grasses and wild flowers by the armfuls and filled their homes. They clipped tender young branches from the sacred oak to plait large, floppy wreaths for husbands and male friends—anyone named Janis. Even today, it is the most common male Latvian name. For the midsummer celebration, farm wives curdled milk to make Jāni cheese, throwing in handfuls of cumin seeds for flavour. The men brewed a yeasty, dark beer that slid down their throats like sweet syrup and brought forth lusty song. On those midsummer nights, no one slept. Giant bonfires built in the sun's image burned all night, in order to lure back that all-important celestial body. Couples in love and those emboldened by the brew and unaccustomed gaiety, melted into the nearby woods in search of the elusive flowering fern, rumoured to bloom only on that one special night. On Jāni, Latvians could celebrate with complete pagan abandon; Christmas and Easter celebrations, tempered by the Lutheran Church, were much more sedate.

***

Later on, during one of our onboard get-togethers, during which I never fail to learn more about my past, Cousin Valters Zalite provides us with more details.

Valters adjusts his thick glasses—he has inherited the Zalite trait of poor eyesight—and begins. "As a young boy our great-grandfather, Andrejs Sahlīts, witnessed the dawn of change in the Latvian countryside. It's amazing really. When news of revolutions elsewhere finally reached the ears of the downtrodden Latvian peasants, they too began to protest until finally, the time had come for long overdue and much needed land reform. You can imagine their joy. Finally, they would be allowed to own a piece of the land they had been working for centuries."

He looks around at the attentive faces and continues, "Land surveyors appeared suddenly in the countryside, as common as spiders after a rain, and scurried here and there with their strings and measuring sticks and notebooks. But immediately, there was a problem."

Oh, no, I think, unsure of what lies ahead.

"How could they register the parcels when the peasants had only one given name and so many the same?"

"Janis, Andrejs, Peteris, or Juris," Irma offers.

Valters continues, "There were hundreds of serfs with the same name, living and working on farmsteads that belonged to the privileged descendants of Teutonic Knights. So they took inspiration from what they knew best, the countryside around them, and became Andrejs Plaviņš (meadow), Peteris Zālīte (grass), Juris Zariņš (branch), or Karlis Ozoliņš (oak). The Latvian ending *is* was added to German names such as Beikman to become Beikmanis."

"What about Irma's maiden name?" Roland asks. "It doesn't sound very Latvian."

Irma looks at her husband and smiles. "The name, Dumbrovskis, came about in a curious way. Before going to register his name, my ancestor confided to his neighbour that he liked the name Ošenieks, after the robust ash tree that stood in a corner of his yard. Well, the neighbour beat him to it and took the name for himself, and when my ancestor got to the registry office, he was told he would have to choose another name, as Ošenieks was no longer available. Of course he was annoyed, maybe even angry. He didn't know what to do."

"Remember," interjects Valters, "these were not educated people."

"Yes, it was a dilemma for him, with so many good names already taken."

"'Well now, what about Dumbrowsky?' the clerk suggested, impatient to get on with it. He didn't want to waste more time than he had to with what he considered to be ignorant peasants. He dipped his quill in the inkpot. I guess he was anxious to get back to the city, so when my ancestor hesitated, thinking Dumbrowsky didn't sound all that Latvian, the official chided, 'Come, come. Why, it's even better. Dumbrowsky's a decorated Polish general.' The clerk, feeling more important than he had a right to, lowered his pen to the paper, and made a downward stroke. It mattered little to him what these serfs called themselves."

Valters takes it upon himself to finish the story. "Only later, in independent Latvia, was the name latvianized to become Dumbrovskis.

"Our family name wasn't always Zalite, was it Dad?" Roland asks.

Father slumps in his chair, looks tired, and answers slowly. "No, until the thirties my father still signed school documents as Sahlits."

"Oh, I much prefer Zalite," Janice adds and flashes a smile at her father-in-law, "but without that little line on the *a*."

"Me, too," I say. "But sometimes it would have been nice not to be at the end of the alphabet."

"Well, some things we can't choose," Father says and moves to the edge of his seat. I see that he is about to bid everyone goodnight.

"Don't get me wrong, it's a very nice Latvian name."

"Solid, very solid," he agrees and with a wave of his hand, bids everyone a good night.

Three

In the morning, my brothers and I accompany Father on a tour of his old haunts. A taxi whisks us to our first stop, the house on Gertrudes iela where our teenaged father had lived with his parents when the family returned from Moscow. We gather on the sidewalk, and Father points to a first floor window. At that very moment the window is flung open, and a woman asks us what we want. "We're returning Latvians," Father explains. "Many years ago, I lived here." The woman beckons us to come on in. We look at Father, but he is already moving toward the door. Once inside, Father explains that what used to be a spacious apartment with two separate entrances (one for the servants) has been divided by the Soviets into several smaller units. His former kitchen and dining room are now in one apartment, and Father's old room is in another. We peer into the small room that had once been Father's bedroom.

"It was really quite a spacious place when we lived there," is all Father says once we are back on the sidewalk. After a short walk along Lāčplēša iela, we arrive at a building that once was the home of Talavija, Father's fraternity. I admire the ornately carved wooden portal while my father and brothers discuss whether to take a closer look inside. When the Soviets annexed Latvia they wasted no time in banning the fraternities they considered nationalistic organizations. They also took over their properties. A plaque on the building announces that it now houses the Soviet Army's Baltic Division's Economic Section, a sort of American PX, that provides special goods for senior Soviet Army officers stationed in the Baltic. Peter decides to enter.

Father's glasses glint in the sunshine when he looks up. "You know, negotiations are already underway between Talavija and the government. Soon, this place will be Talavija's once again."

Peter rejoins us, shaking his head. "If that happens, I hope they've got lots of money. It's in really bad shape." Father looks crestfallen. Talavija has been, and still is, an important part of his life. His fraternity brothers are his lifelong friends.

Our next stop is the University of Latvia where Father studied. We tour a few empty lecture halls, and Father is suddenly tired. He sits on a bench while my brothers and I walk across the street to examine a statue of Krišjānis Barons. As we stroll back under the lindens, I see that a young woman has stopped in front of Father, and they are conversing. She waves good-bye, and Father nods in return.

"What was that all about?" I ask.

Father looks up at me in surprise, but decides to answer. "I told her we arrived on the *Baltic Star*, that we were returning Latvians—"

"God, I hope she didn't ask you for money," Roland interrupts. "Latvians still believe the streets of North America are littered with money."

"Or that it's a *Lejputria* where food falls from the sky like manna from heaven," adds Peter.

"Nothing like that. She was polite, though somewhat naïve. She asked me if everything was the same as when I left fifty years ago!"

"Wow, she has no idea what's been happening, here or anywhere else. What did you say?"

"I'm afraid I wasn't very helpful." Father twists his handkerchief into a rope as he speaks. "I told her 'yes and no', but she didn't really understand. Ha, I'm not sure I do either. I think now that I'm here I'm seeing everything the way it was fifty years ago. Poor thing, she hasn't known any other life but this."

We return to the ship for lunch and to give Father a chance to rest a bit. During the meal, Father is in a pensive mood. "You know, I've been through so many changes in my life; I hope this, Latvia's transition to freedom, is the last one I have to experience."

"It's the best," I say.

"Even before I was born, your grandfather Peteris Zalite had already lived through so much change. But with change came possibilities. One of those possibilities for my father was education. That's what got him off the farm in Jumurda and into school and a lifelong career in education…"

Peter takes advantage of the pause. "Didn't he study in Tartu?"

"Yes, Tartu Teacher's Seminary in what's now Estonia. You know my father was much like me in many ways."

"You mean you are much like him?" I venture.

"Don't interrupt, Daughter. My father also was the youngest son and he grew up during the First National Awakening, an event that, just like a tattoo, marked him forever.

"Awakening? It sounds like something out of Rip Van Winkle," I venture, a little surprised at how open Father is.

Father ignores my comment and sets down his knife and fork. "It took place from the 1850s to the 1880s," he explains, none too patiently. "It was like a mini-Renaissance—you know what that is I hope—a time when Latvian literature and nationalistic thought flourished and found voice in books and newspapers. People started to think, why couldn't Latvian be used in business or taught in the school? Why do we worship in German and sing German hymns instead of Latvian ones?"

When Father stops to catch his breath, Roland speaks up. "But your mother was German."

"Yes, of course, but that's not the point. All the power and money remained in the hands of Baltic Germans, the descendants of the Teutonic Knights who brought Christianity to Latvia. Latvians were finally speaking out, people like Krišjānis Barons." Father looks around to see if he needs to explain and decides he does. "Krišjānis Barons, the patriarch of Latvian folk songs. He's the one who collected *dainas* (quatrains), folk songs, fairy tales, legends, proverbs, and riddles, all that, and he urged Latvians to be aware of and to treasure their heritage. After all, most were farmers."

"Tell us about Oma," I plead, "your mother."

Father's eyes mist over and he begins in a shaky voice. "My mother, Alida Charlotte Taube, was a teacher too, at the German Orphans' School, where they met. I guess, in her youth, she was a pretty, dark-haired girl, slender, and with gentle eyes. She had a way of looking at you…yes, regular features and a nice straight nose." As he continues, Father's voice grows stronger. "You know, she was born in St. Petersburg, the daughter of a Baltic German piano tuner and builder. His company was called Balodis. That means dove, *taube* in German." Father examines his hands, and then clasps them together. "I've always wondered if the

Balodis pianos didn't somehow become Baldwin." He shrugs, "It doesn't matter anymore anyway."

"I'm gonna check that out," Peter says.

"She lost both her parents when she was still young, so she became an orphan. Luckily for all of us or we wouldn't be here, the Baroness von Brevern took Mother in and raised her in her home in Haapsalu. But Mother had to become self-reliant, and there weren't many choices for women at that time, not like today. So she studied to become a teacher. That's how they met. Soon after marrying my father, she stayed home to raise us six children, but you know all that."

"Yeah, but wasn't she thirty-three when she married?" Peter asks, the best informed of all of us. "It's amazing she still managed to have six kids."

"Seven actually, one died a baby. Yes, it was like that, one every year, and it did take its toll, although of course, I didn't realize it at the time. Mother was devout, and on Sundays, she would gather us children around her and read Bible stories, or we'd sing German hymns. She was quite musical, with a lovely singing voice. She taught all my sisters, one after the other, to play the piano, but when I said I wanted to learn, they all laughed."

"Why?" I ask.

Father shrugs, the reason lost in the mists of time. "I suppose because I was a boy, or maybe because my feet couldn't reach the pedals. I don't know. Or maybe Mother was just plain tired with so many mouths to feed. During the war, the first one, when we were living in Moscow, some of our Latvian relatives were sent to live with us. I guess I was seven at the time. That made twelve people around the dinner table, and even though Mother had servants, there was still a lot to do. My father was always out, either working at two or three jobs trying to make ends meet, or trying to help the Latvian refugees that were arriving every day. He was always on some committee or other." Father moves the food around his plate, thinking. "But she managed to get out once in a while, to sing and play at a private party. She was quite popular that way. German *lied*, light opera, French chansons, and Latvian and even Russian folk songs—she had a large repertoire. Sometimes, around the house though, she sang sad songs, remembering her parents and how she felt and all. Or maybe her husband had been impatient with her. He asked a lot of himself, but expected no less of others."

"Sounds like a fellow Talavs," Peter says, "with his motto 'Work makes the man'."

"No, no he wasn't. On his return to Latvia, he enrolled in law school at the university but had to drop out, for he had too many other obligations. Still, the motto sounds a lot like the words my father lived by, 'Work is the soul of life'."

In many ways, my father was much like his father. Both were strict disciplinarians, and both expected their orders to be obeyed without question. No talking back. No questioning authority. Growing up in Montreal, if I ever complained that a teacher had been unfair, my father showed no sympathy and always sided with the teacher. "You're a child, at school to learn, and you should do as you are told," he would say. I had no recourse but to shed tears of anger and frustration in my room. My only consolation was that Father wasn't quite as harsh as grandfather had been. "On your knees," Grandfather had barked at children who dared to disrupt his lesson.

We have reminisced too long and down our food quickly. There is no time for a rest. Cousin Janis has invited us to his apartment this afternoon and is no doubt already waiting dockside.

"We're in luck as situation is changing," he tells us as we walk to his car. "Only few years ago, was impossible to invite visitors inside my home. But," he turns, to address all of us, "today is different." As he drives, Janis points out some of the sights along the way, but always with one eye on the road to spare his car the worst of the holes. We pass the national theatre, the art gallery, and further on, an unassuming, square, brick building. "Now that," he declares, "is the tallest building in Latvia!" He shoots a quick glance sideways at Father to see his reaction.

No one says a word. We don't quite know what to say, as we have all seen taller buildings. Is it a joke, I wonder, and lift the corners of my mouth in anticipation of the punch line? Father ventures to admit the obvious, "It doesn't look all that tall from here."

"That building we just pass is home of Cheka, the secret police." He shivers.

"KGB?"

"Just so. KGB, Cheka, is all same. It's most tallest, because from basement you can see Siberia!"

I don't know if I should laugh or cry. I guess even black humour is better than none. I see that Father's mouth is set in a thin, straight line, and he is struggling to contain his emotion.

The mood in the car suddenly shifts. It is no longer carefree and lighthearted the way a sightseeing excursion should be; it has become somber, and we all feel the tension. My cousin's feeble attempt at humour underscores how different our experiences have been and how difficult it will be for us —those who stayed and those who fled—to really understand one another. Although Janis was only nine at the time and had no say in his parent's decision to stay, I begin to sense that he feels like the real patriot. I wonder, is he judging us now, finding us to be less loyal or not Latvian enough? Or did we not suffer enough? Funnily enough, I have heard a similar but contradictory argument voiced by Latvians in North America: that those who fled were loyal to their roots, having worked hard all those post-war years to preserve a language and culture that was under assault. Weren't Latvian schools, Latvian churches, and Latvian associations proof enough? I realize this is not a subject to be raised now, if ever, but I don't want to be made to feel guilty for having lived, studied, and worked in the west. It is not a choice I made, but I am grateful for it.

Janis tells us that we are nearly there, and he turns onto a street that is lined with five-story brick apartment buildings, all of similar, uninspired design. After carefully maneuvering his Zhiguli around two giant potholes, he parks, and we get out. A few children are playing ball nearby, and they stop to stare at us. Janis holds open the building's door and we crowd inside. There is no vestibule and no elevator, and when the door closes, it is dark; there are no bulbs in the light sockets. A small, dirty window above the door provides the only light. I take shallow breaths of the fetid air. I tug at Roland's sleeve, and when he turns to me. I see that he is worried, too. Father lives in a Florida bungalow and is not used to climbing stairs. The Freimanis family lives on the top floor.

My cousin waves his hand dismissively, "Bad smell is neighbour's cats," he tells us before hurrying on ahead. The common areas in his building are dirty and neglected, an unwelcome by-product of the totalitarian system; common areas belong to everyone, so no one looks after them, "the tragedy of the commons" someone once called such a situation. I warn Father to be careful so as to not trip on the torn linoleum.

As I slowly ascend behind Father, I wonder if I would have risked using the elevator had there been one.

On every landing Father stops to catch his breath and to allow his heart to settle down. Mid-way up, he pops a tiny pill into his mouth and holds it under his tongue. I am relieved when we reach the top. Arija opens the door, and the aroma of baking greets us. The apartment is clean, cozy, and well furnished, but with only four small rooms—a living room, kitchen, and two bedrooms—it is tiny by western standards. They share it with their daughter Ligita, her husband, Oskars, and their two young sons; it is impossible for young families to afford a place of their own. Five of us squeeze together on the sofa, and the rest sit on wooden chairs brought in from the kitchen. Arija disappears for a moment and returns with a plate of *piragi* that she places on the low table in front of us. Ligita follows with a tray of coffee cups. The two small boys observe us timidly, from the safety of their father's side. We offer our gifts, and the boys try out the small cars I give them. Cousin Janis happily uncorks the bottle of duty-free cognac Father has brought for him. Haltingly, we feel our way, eager to get to know one another better without bumping into anyone's sensitive spot.

"I have two boys also, but quite a bit older," I tell Ligita, and I raise my arm to show how tall they are. "They're in university, back home in Canada." Immediately, I regret having used the word *home*. I know they think I should consider Latvia my real home.

"Do they speak Latvian?"

"No, unfortunately, they do not," I answer, and know I have disappointed her. "You know, my husband is Canadian, and he would've felt left out." It is not a good excuse, or even the whole truth, but I am suddenly tongue-tied and on the defensive. I suspect the real reason is much more complicated than that. Perhaps I felt that my own Latvian language skills were not good enough to teach others, or perhaps it was partly due to a delayed teenage rebelliousness. Marrying a non-Latvian meant I no longer had to speak Latvian. After the bilingual service, during our wedding reception at Victoria Hall in Montreal's west end, my Aunt Elza had declared that my new husband was a "nice young man, but it was too bad he was not Latvian". I remembered being momentarily taken aback, but I soon forgot her words until much later. No doubt my parents must have been disappointed as well, that one of the nice, obedient, studious, Latvian boys from a good family had not ended up as a son-in-law.

It is important to stay away from controversial or painful topics. Roland asks Arija if, now that the world was opening up to them, she plans to study English. As a scientist who has traveled abroad to international conferences, Janis already speaks English.

"Not at all," she answers, her round face serious. "Now is time for all overseas Latvians to return home to help in the rebuilding of their country. So much help is needed."

Roland lifts his eyebrows in surprise, and he throws a quick glance at Janice; this had never occurred to him. "Gee," he smoothes back his hair, "I don't think I could get work here, or if Janice would even consider it." Janice is snapping pictures, but stops and smiles when she hears her name.

"In practical terms, it would be very complicated," I add. "For starters, what would my husband do? He knows only a few words of Latvian."

It soon becomes obvious that my cousin shares his wife's opinion. "He's an agriculture specialist, no? We could use his help. Years of collective farms have put agriculture to ruin."

"Perhaps, if I were a bit younger," Father offers wistfully, "I might consider returning, but my health…."

"Nonsense, Onkul, you don't look old at all," Arija counters. "Our wholesome food, not food in boxes, and exercise—oh we do a lot of that—walking, climbing stairs," Her colour deepens. "To say nothing of the rejuvenating effects of living in your very own country, just imagine what that could do."

"I really don't think Latvians here would appreciate outsiders returning to take away their jobs," says Roland.

Cousin Janis is quick to respond. "Of course we don't want that, but you could bring money and expertise to create new jobs, together with us here. Why soon, all of confiscated property will be returned to owner," he adds.

"So I've heard, but I myself didn't own any property," Father says. "You may recall that Erna and I lived in a rented apartment on Tomsona iela."

"Well, I, for one, am optimistic about the future. I'm tired of shortages and line-ups just to buy the daily necessities—sugar, sausages, bread."

Arija pours more coffee and asks her daughter to bring something from the kitchen. Suddenly I realize what a sacrifice it must have been for her to buy all the delicacies she is offering us today.

Ligita's husband, Oskars, a shy man, speaks for the first time. He works in a bicycle factory, and in his spare time, to earn extra money, he repairs bicycles. He hopes that his family will someday be able to move out and have a place of its own. "We even have an answer to the petrol shortage," he says. "In Latvia, the most common form of transport is the bread driven machine."

"Bread machine?" Roland looks up from stirring his coffee.

We all look at Oskars while he gazes intently at his hands. "Yes, bread. Man, or woman for that matter, fueled by bread, can walk or cycle anywhere!" He allows himself a modest chuckle.

It is meant to be a joke, but his words ring all too true. I smile, more from surprise than from mirth. "You should be in advertising," I tell him. "That's a good one for Raleigh or Schwinn."

Ligita returns with a glass jar of something olive-green and oily that resembles a child's muddied tempera paints. She hands the jar to her mother.

"Look what we have for you, Onkul. *Kaņepes*!" exclaims Arija, holding up the container. I stare in dismay, as she smears what looks like axle grease on a thin slice of pumpernickel.

Father accepts the bread and explains to the rest of us, who look puzzled, "It's just like peanut butter, but made instead from ground hemp seeds."

"Marijuana seeds!" I overhear Roland whisper to Janice. "I'm gonna try it and hope I don't get drug tested on my return to the US." He takes a small bite and considers the taste.

"It's about the only thing is no shortage of. The Russians, with their so refined tastes, are not fond of peasant food." Arija gestures with a finger held to the end of her nose, then blushes when she realizes what she has just done. She bends to refill Father's cup and offers him sugar. "But sugar," she laughs without mirth, "that is other story. I'm very lucky to have sugar today. When the nomenclature—you know who they are," she looks around. "That is factory manager, *kolhoz* overseer and top men of party. When they meet quotas and have a rest, they come here, to Jurmala, for holiday. The very first thing they do—before unpacking or sticking a big toe in sea—the very first thing is they run to the nearest store and buy up everything in sight. Especially sugar, which is scarcer than palm trees on the taiga. Then, kilo by kilo, they mail it home." Arija's voice is becoming strident, and Janis interrupts.

"*Nu, nu,* Arija," he soothes. "You're forgetting…it's useless…." He sweeps the fingers of his right hand through his grey hair, which remains separated in four, even rows like neatly planted corn. Arija's sudden, unexpected outburst makes him uncomfortable; it's too much like hanging laundry out in public. "Why don't I play a melody while you show Onkul Janis some photos?" He gets up and moves over to the console piano and, after flexing and shaking his arthritic fingers, begins to play.

I barely hear the music, for my mind clatters with the noise of half-formed questions, possible explanations, and first impressions that need to be mulled over. It is a bit like being on a first date with someone you barely know and feeling awkwardness set in with several hours left in the evening. Hopefully, the universal language of music will help this situation. I try to concentrate on Janis's fingers as they move up and down the keys. Overall, despite a few misunderstandings and the sensitivity of some topics, the visit goes well and helps to solidify our friendship. Father quietly takes Arija aside and offers to take her to Dollar Store, while my brothers and I invite everyone to join us for a lunch at the Hotel Riga.

Four

The next morning, Father, Roland, Janice, and I take a taxi to Jurmala, a seaside resort some twenty kilometers west of Riga. We plan to spend some time with Peter and his daughters, who are staying in a posh seaside hotel. Father is eager to see the place where he spent many happy, carefree, summers, while growing up. Jurmala was once the amber jewel in the czar's crown and later, when Latvia became independent, a place where Latvian families holidayed during the brief, northern summer. After World War II, Jurmala was taken over by the Soviets and it was off-limits for ordinary citizens. Over the years, heavy industry polluted the coastline, which was closely guarded and constantly patrolled. The sanatoria that Latvia had built for its tuberculosis patients and war veterans became the sole domain of the party faithful. No longer needed as sanatoria, they were transformed into luxury hotels and spas for the deserving communist elite, as well as the nascent Soviet capitalists. Latvia, with its year-round open harbour and its fertile soils, boasted the highest standard of living among all the Soviet republics. By breathing clean sea air, warming their tired bodies on Jurmala's white sand—as fine as talcum powder—and drinking pure spring waters, the members of the politburo hoped to rid their bodies of the factory poisons they themselves had created.

Jurmala has the air of a resort village. It is dotted with quaint, somewhat dilapidated, wooden houses surrounded by picket fences and adorned with fragrant flowering shrubs. The pace is livelier here than in Old Riga, and I spot several restaurants that are actually open. But the resort, with little Latvian about it, seems foreign. I study the unfamiliar faces of the party faithful that have arrived here from the far corners of the Soviet Union. Men with straight, black hair, olive skin, and dark, almond-shaped eyes are here to spend their rubles. Jurmala is the most European-like destination accessible to the *nomenklatura*. While

I observe the passersby with a critical eye, Father studies the wooden houses in a vain attempt to recognize one he might have stayed in. There are not many left, and those that remain are in need of paint and repair. Even the once lush gardens cry out for weeding and pruning.

"Every summer, after we returned from Moscow, my father rented a house somewhere around here," Father remembers. "Hah, all together, we were quite a crowd. Ede and her daughters spent their summers here as well, sailing over from Copenhagen. Only after my brother and sisters married did they rent their own small houses nearby. We played tennis and sailed and swam. You could swim then; it wasn't polluted like it is now." Father smiles briefly, as he remembers, "Your mother was pretty good at volleyball." It is hard for me to imagine. I never witnessed her playing a sport or even walking for pleasure. Father swings his cane at a clump of weeds growing through a crack in the sidewalk and almost loses his balance.

Peter walks ahead, with his arm around his daughter Kristi's shoulder, with Alex and Tammy right behind. Our pace is slower, and we stop frequently so that Father can look around, but I suspect it also gives him a chance to catch his breath. When we reach the sand, we stop.

"Look," Father waves his cane like a wand, "over four hundred kilometers of coastline—nothing but pure sand, fine and white as sugar—and what do you see? A handful of swimmers braving the polluted waters."

Father decides to sit on a bench while the rest of us kick off our shoes and trudge through the loose sand to the water's edge. Here, the sand is wet and packed hard, making walking so much easier. I scan the shoreline with the hope of finding a piece of amber that has washed ashore. Once, twice, I bend down, only to be deceived by a shiny, wet stone glistening in the sun. If I am lucky enough to find a chunk of fossilized tree resin, it will have waited forty million years for me to claim it. The sap that once flowed beneath the bark of pine trees protected them from attack by insects. Now it often preserves ancient life—flies, seeds, spiders, or pollen, even bees. As a young girl, I loved to hold my mother's amber beads, round and yellow as egg yolk. Unlike agates, they felt warm against my skin. "Amber has trapped the sun's energy," Mother told me. "That's why it feels so warm and shines like gold." Today, the beads are mine. I recently learned that amber has other properties, as well.

Yesterday, in the Dollar Store, a saleswoman tried to convince me that amber possessed the power to heal. As proof, she took a necklace made of clear amber from the case and placed it on a black cloth. "Do you see the small bubbles inside the beads?" she asked. "Yes? They are fossilized tears of the gods. Is very good medicine."

I give up my fruitless search and look up to see Father waving for me to come back. It is time to go. As I draw near, I realize that he has been sharing stories of his past with his granddaughters. Too bad that, like my sons, they live so far away, and he doesn't get to see them very often.

"Then the war changed everything, and I decided to leave, give it all up for freedom, not without risk, mind you." Father shades his eyes with his hand, and looks around. "Just look what they've done. Instead of families like before, the top brass of the politburo is here. Those *zhuliki* are sleeping in the softest beds and stuffing their bellies with delicacies undreamed of in their own miserable republics."

"Dad, I don't think my girls are familiar with those words—*politburo* and *zhuliki*," says Peter. "Why don't we go have some lunch now? I've brought over my own delicacies from Germany."

"Clever boy." Father lets out a low moan as he rises slowly from the bench. I give up trying to brush the fine sand from my feet and shove my still-sandy feet into my shoes. Then, two by two, we retrace our steps along the dirt path that is lined with wild rose bushes and guarded by tall pines. I stamp my feet, as much to remove the sand as in annoyance that my dream of finding amber has eluded me.

Soon, we are back on the sidewalk and Roland, who is walking ahead with Janice, suddenly stops and points at a clumsily hand-lettered sign in a store window. He translates for his wife and for his nieces. "'Merchandise for display only—not available for sale'. Isn't that weird?" The place looks more like a dusty museum than a store.

"Arija wasn't kidding when she told us that the Russians come for a holiday and clean out the stores," says Peter.

"Back in their own republics, there are shortages of everything, especially luxuries," Father declares. "For sure, communism is one experiment that has failed. Kaput. *Finito*. Hah, I could have predicted that back when I was a frightened, hungry ten-year-old fleeing Moscow after the revolution. Just like an army that can't march on an empty stomach, the proletariat won't work if there's nothing to eat," Father declares. I'm not surprised. He is a staunch republican and a wholehearted Reagan supporter.

"Look, that restaurant must have food." Peter points to a line-up of people. Since our arrival, we have learned that if there is no line-up outside of a store or restaurant, there is nothing worthwhile inside. "Can you believe last night, when I tried to buy a beer, they had run out?"

"You're kidding," says Roland. "Total disaster, that."

"Yeah, but don't worry, I've got a couple of bottles in my room. Cheese, ham, and real meat sausages, too."

After lunch, we return to the ship so that Father can rest; I plan to shop for gifts to take home.

The following day is taken up with the Song Festival, beginning with a procession, and ending with the main event, a choral concert of massed choir. We soon become separated from the others and I stand beside Father, part of the crowd that has gathered along the festival parade route to cheer on the choirs and dance ensembles as they pass by. With growing pride and pure amazement I wilt under a bright sun as forty thousand Latvians stride by—they are men and women, young and old, all in national dress. They are the Song Festival participants. Each choir or dance ensemble shows off a banner announcing its name and city of origin. Each participant, man or woman, carries a bouquet of wildflowers or a bunch of grasses and leaves, and as they walk, they wave at the onlookers, who clap and cheer. Many choirs are singing, and the crowd joins in. Pride and excitement shine on their faces, and it reminds me of the parade of nations at the start of the Olympics, except here, there is only one nation, one purpose. The procession is truly without end, and eventually, Father's stamina gives out. He finds a nearby bench and is content to sit for a while, and to just listen, from a distance.

Late that afternoon, we board a special bus bound for Mežaparks, north of the city. We are on our way to the choral concert. We hope to meet Peter and his daughters at the concert, as well as other relatives, but when we get there, I soon realize this could be a hopeless task—our seats are not numbered, and the open-air amphitheatre is packed. Spectators are arrayed on backless benches that fan out on a gentle slope opposite giant bleacher-like scaffolding that holds the twenty thousand singers of the massed choirs. We find seats in our assigned section, and Roland and I decide to cruise the aisles in search of our brother.

We are in luck and soon spot Peter. As I draw near, I can see that something terrible has happened to him; he has a black eye and a crooked, obviously broken nose. "What happened?" I ask, trying to hide my distress. Peter's smile is lopsided, and he appears to be in real pain.

"You've had an accident?" Roland asks.

Peter waves a hand, as if shooing away a pesky fly, "No, no. Nothing like that. Some Russian left the imprint of his boot on my face." A few of his teeth are loose, and his words come out slurred.

"You look like shit," declares Roland.

"Your poor eye. It's all swollen. Have you seen a doctor?" I demand. Even when he was young, my older brother was never much of a fighter. He is now a diplomat, a peacemaker, good at reaching consensus by words and negotiation. But it is obvious that whoever did this to him was in no mood to negotiate.

Slowly, painfully, Peter relates his story. "Yesterday, I went with a friend to the Hotel Latvia. It's one of the few places in Riga where you can get a drink at night. When we got to the second floor lobby, I saw a Latvian being shoved around by two Russian thugs. I looked around for security but didn't see any, so I decided to go over myself. Big mistake," he tries a grin, but his mouth is too sore.

"Remember, Janis warned us," Roland reminds him.

"Yeah, but I thought I'd help the guy out by just being there or saying something and they'd stop, but I hadn't said more than 'Hey' when I was knocked flat. Then they kicked me in the face. I don't remember much after that."

"Jeez," says Roland, and lets out his breath. "That's horrible. But it's such an upscale hotel."

"Why didn't someone stop them? Hotel security?" I blink back the tears.

"Nope, but I've since learned that they don't interfere in fights between Latvians and Russians. They figure they're grudge matches. I was lucky, though. The friend I was with is a doctor, and she called an ambulance."

"You look awful," I say, meaning to show sympathy, but it sounds accusing.

"Thanks, Sis. Makes me feel a whole bunch better," Peter says, and gives me a brotherly pat on the shoulder.

I feel my cheeks grow hot. "Seriously, you've got to do something. Shouldn't your nose be in a cast or bandaged?"

"Of course not. My nose and teeth will just have to wait until I get back home to Germany in a few days. My biggest problem is I can't eat properly. Good for the waistline, I guess," he says, and pats his non-existent belly.

We go to find Father, who is equally shocked, and Peter tells his story again. "Son, have you reported this to the police?"

"No, Dad, and I don't plan to—what could the police do, anyway? It's just that the Russians in Latvia feel especially threatened now that we're taking our first steps toward independence. And as you know, they too are resentful of outsiders and supposedly rich Latvians from overseas, who will be clamouring to get their family properties back," Peter draws a shallow breath, "and then kick them out or take away their jobs."

Father thinks for a minute, then replies, "I doubt if they've thought it through like that. They're just hooligans, always were and still are. But please, please, be more careful. You don't want to mess with the Russian mafia."

Peter manages a crooked laugh, but winces in pain. "You still see the red menace everywhere."

"Yes," Father replies, "it's a part of our history. My history. That Russian bear has always had its hungry eyes on Latvia, especially the Gulf of Riga." Father lets out a deep sigh. "Too bad that, when Janis warned us about the Russian taxi drivers, he didn't mention how dangerous it was to be out at night."

"I was *inside* the hotel, Dad. Don't worry, Dad. I'll be fine. Really." The concert is about to start, and Peter returns to his daughters.

Seeing my accomplished brother in pain, with his face disfigured, made me lose some of my earlier optimism. It wasn't fair that my brother, the diplomat and peacemaker, should get hurt. Handsome and intelligent, Head Boy, or Eagle Scout, he won awards without trying. Growing up in Montreal, he had given my parents what every Latvian mother and father hope for: a child to boast about. I take Father's gnarled hand in mine and squeeze it gently, "Don't worry, Dad. He'll be okay. Peter's tough, a survivor."

"We all are, Daughter," Father replies, and pats my hand.

All of a sudden, a loud hum fills the air like a giant swarm of bees, as the singers start to limber up their vocal chords. First and second soprano, alto, tenor, and bass, their voices vibrate in an ageless, mystical *Ooommm*. Folk songs are my homeland's prayers, its collective memory, its history and lament, even its armour during times of siege or occupation. The refrains can be as poignant as the end of summer, or as happy as sunlight dappling white birches. Music is the voice and mood of my people, with one recurring theme, love of their country, and tonight is a night for unrestrained patriotism, for celebration. High up on a specially erected platform and looking no bigger than an insect, a white-gloved conductor stands; with a leap and great sweeping motions of his arms, he starts up the twenty-thousand-voice massed choirs. Sweet notes burst from the singers' mouths. The conductor sways this way and that, and the music follows him. He spreads his arms wide, and then lifts them, and the melody swells, filling the night with music. The audience is enthusiastic, rivaling the best rock concert crowd. We clap and cheer and shout bravo, over and over.

The concert carries on with lengthy clapping and many encores, and after several hours sitting on a hard, backless bench, Father has had enough. He is tired and wants to go back to the bus, with its more comfortable seats. I am loath to leave, but I offer to accompany him. Once comfortably seated, Father dozes off. As I am about to return to the concert, his eyes open, and he is wide awake. "That business with the Russians," he shakes his head in disbelief. "I've spent my whole life fleeing the Soviets, and here we are again on the merry-go-round."

"Don't worry, Dad," I offer, lamely. My father has been through a lot in one lifetime. He was born in Moscow in 1907, in the fading years of Imperial Russia. He was the youngest son, especially cherished by his mother as her last baby. Until the chaos and upheavals that resulted from the Russian Revolution of October 1917, the Zalite family led a quiet, comfortable, middle class life. Peteris Zalite worked at two or three jobs to support a large family, and Alida stayed home. The children went to school, attended matinees at the opera or theatre, and they all spent summers in the countryside, in a rented dacha. Life was good. It all changed when Czar Nicholas II and his family were brutally murdered, and Lenin rose to power.

"I've seen so much harm done by the Soviets, and I've been running from them all my life."

"I know, Dad."

"You don't know. I've never really talked about it, but this, tonight, seeing Peter, it's all coming back. So much chaos and needless suffering. And hunger. You know, an immediate result of the October revolution was that food disappeared from the stores. Landowners lost their fields, and agriculture production stopped. In the spring, the fields did not get planted. Of course, that meant hunger and eventually, starvation. Especially in Moscow. That's why, in the summer of 1918, my father took three of us smallest children, Elizabete, Milda, and me, and also my brother's three children, who'd been staying with us, back to Latvia. Somehow, we managed to make it across the German-Russian controlled border safely."

"Wow, you were ten, old enough to remember."

"Yes, but I didn't speak Latvian very well. I was good at Russian and German and had a little, badly accented Latvian. I believe it was my father's ability to speak all three languages, Russian, German, and Latvian that helped. All six of us children went to live on the farm in Jumurda. My father returned to Moscow alone, crossed again without the proper papers, and made it back to what was left of his family in Moscow, as well as his job." Father cups his hands to see out of the window better. I know he wishes the concert would end, so he could get back to his bunk on the ship.

"Even back in Latvia, it wasn't easy. That part of the countryside had seen fierce fighting during the first war. With six more mouths to feed, we all had to help. As the youngest, I was sent to work as a shepherd boy for a neighbour's few remaining animals. At harvest time, I got a sack of peas—that's it. Oh, but I was so proud when I brought that sack home. No one cared that most of the peas were infested with maggots; we ate them gladly. Yes, those were hard times." Father leans his head back against the seat and closes his eyes for a moment. I don't know what to say, but mumble something. "Then, in the fall, my father made that same crossing again, bringing Mother and two more children. He went back once more to be with Marija, the oldest, who had started college and worked as a nurse."

I take Father's hand and hold it. It is unusually warm, and I can feel his pulse beat fast in his wrist. "Opaps was quite a hero."

"Yes, he was, but he didn't think so. He was just doing what he had to do for his family. The problem remained, how to get back to Latvia and his family. Finally, in 1920, when the Latvian War of Independence against Soviet Russia ended, and Latvia declared its independence, he saw his chance. Patriotic Latvians inside Soviet Russia were eager to return home to their newly independent country, and the communist sympathizers in Latvia didn't see much of a future for themselves here, so even before the peace treaty was signed, a cross-border exchange was set up. My father and Marija were part of that exchange."

"Wow, you never told us all that."

"I'm sure I did, but you and your brothers weren't interested," Father reproaches. "Many prominent Latvians were on that train, some even in the same wagon. When they reached the eastern border at the Zilupe River, a one-for-one exchange was made. It was very strict. It so happened that there was one communist sympathizer too few, and the border guards held my father back. It was tense for a bit, but he was finally released and allowed to cross the temporary bridge that spanned the river, and so into Latvian territory. It was May 25, 1920, a date none of us ever forgot. All those exchanged had to undergo a brief quarantine and go into a *pirts* (Latvian sauna), then in Riga there was another quarantine. But finally, my father and Marija arrived safely and with all the Moscow furniture."

At last, we hear voices, and soon the bus is filled with happy people, talking and humming snatches of songs. A sigh of relief escapes Father's lips, and he settles back, closes his eyes, and waits for the bus to take him to the ship.

Five

Cousin Janis picks us up at the dock in a rented van the next morning. I feel as if I have hardly slept: all through the night, folk songs bounced around in my head, rattling my dreams. We are on our way to Valmiera, to visit Regina Freimanis and her family. She is Janis's sister-in-law, the widow of my deceased cousin Alvils. As we cross the bridge and head northeast, there is little traffic on the two-lane highway. "Is due to gasoline rationing," Janis explains. We travel through a picturesque landscape that alternates between open fields studded with Monet haystacks and dark, dense forests. I cry out in delight when I spot my first stork, half-hidden from view in its nest atop a pole. Soon, I see many more, and it becomes obvious that the large black and white birds have returned in great numbers. They patrol the meadows or swoop low over the wet spots, in search of frogs and other delicacies. These are the same fields and meadows, interspersed with bogs that hide ancient Viking remains. This is the Latvia of my ancestors. But as I continue to look out the window at the passing landscape, I see that something is not right. The grain is thick with weeds, and many fields are overripe, begging to be harvested.

"Where are the farmers, and why are they not bringing in their crops?" I ask. There is no activity or din of machinery to disturb the quiet morning.

Somewhat embarrassed, Janis explains, "The farmers have not petrol for their tractors. You see Russia's economic blockade of Lithuania affects us also. Gasoline is rationed, only twenty liters each month, even for farmers."

"That's not much," Father says.

"Of course, it does have upside," says Oskars, who is driving. "Since refineries close down, air and river pollution is less. Result is many stork."

For a time the highway follows the course of the Gauja River, whose treacherous waters and sandy shores have, according to song, claimed many a betrayed lover. The current is strong, and the water is clear but dark, like strong tea. Now and then, the river cascades over a rock shelf that has been eroded by the fast flowing river. Thirsty willows, poplar, and birch grow along the river, and on higher ground stands the occasional, sacred oak.

Cousin Janis names the crops as we whiz by: flax, winter wheat, barley, and rye. "I've seen quite a few potato fields," I add to his litany.

"Ah," Janis says, "the only root crop you can drink."

"Vichyssoise?" I venture, and my biochemist cousin's face contorts into some semblance of a grin.

"Vodka! Best Russian vodka made of potatoes."

We laugh, and Father nods in agreement. During the years of Soviet occupation, when money was scarce and almost worthless, vodka was the currency of choice. It was more precious than gold, and with a bottle or two, you could obtain medicine and other necessities of life.

Valmiera is a medium-sized city of low, wooden buildings, famous for its theatre. Regina welcomes us warmly and introduces her children and grandchildren. She is a tall, slender woman, with soft brown eyes and faded brown hair framing a long face. Soon after our arrival, Regina takes Father aside to show him the first of several promised surprises. "Look, what I have here, a chest of drawers and the oak desk from your apartment!"

In an effort to remember, Father furrows his brow and purses his lips. He shifts his weight slowly from one foot to the other. He has lived in so many different places, and in the course of a long life, has acquired and abandoned more furniture than a secondhand dealer. "From you and Erna's last apartment, on Tomsona iela," Regina prompts. It is obvious that the furniture means more to Regina than it does to Father; she has lived with it all this time, dusted and polished it, and waited for the day when she could delight its rightful owner.

"Was this really mine?" Father wonders aloud, but shows little emotion. "It's...it's been such a long time," he murmurs and, in a characteristic nervous gesture, takes out a handkerchief to wipe his forehead.

"Yes, yes, look closely. Remember? You left the key with Marija. She managed to claim these pieces from your apartment before it was collectivized."

"It could be," Father allows, but without much certainty.

The smile vanishes from Regina's face. "Not could be, but *is*," she insists. Many times since she first learned in a letter that her uncle was planning a trip to Latvia, she has rehearsed this encounter in her head and imagined surprise, disbelief, recognition, and finally, thankful acknowledgement; no *could be* formed any part of it. Regina runs her hand along the wood grain of the desk and opens a drawer. Then, carefully and with both hands, she extracts a large, cloth-covered photo album and places it on the desk. "Please, sit down, Onkul. Here is your album. You left it behind when you fled in 1944! Yes, all these years. Look, I've even managed to save the cover from moths. See, it's the cover that Erna embroidered. Her engagement gift to you."

Father is, at last, visibly overcome and accepts the offered chair. The sight of Erna's finely stitched handiwork in tones of ochre, beige, and green, moves him almost to tears. *Erna, why did you leave?* he demands silently of his departed wife. But the ancient text is silent, muted by centuries of progress and change. He had never planned to live out his last years alone, always insisting he would be the first to go. When we were young and living in Montreal, my parents often argued over who would be the first to die. They must have known it was upsetting to my brothers and me, but at times, death must have seemed a welcome respite from everyday hardship and disappointments. Father uses his crumpled handkerchief to wipe away the tears that threaten to spill from his eyes. He does not want to worry Regina with an old man's thoughts, so he forces himself to return to the present. "It's very nice, but how did you get it?" he asks politely.

"You gave it to Marija yourself, that long-ago day in July, when you pedaled all the way to Jaunsvirlaiku to urge her to flee Latvia. Thousands were leaving, and you planned to do so also."

"Yes, I remember now. The very last time I saw my sister."

"You know, she always thought of you, her little brother, with such fondness. Well, you almost convinced her, but Fricis would not hear of it. The family was staying. Marija told me that before you said good-bye, you gave her the album for safekeeping, along with the key to your

Riga apartment. Only one week later, with Jelgava in flames and the Red Army marching on Riga, you made that incredible night bicycle ride to Bene. That was quite something."

"Ah, yes, I'll never forget that bicycle ride," Father recalls, his brow furrowed with the effort of remembering. "That could only have been accomplished by a young and desperate man. I had to get to Erna and the children. It was the only way."

"Such a dreadful time," Regina agrees. "Even though we were all afraid, and so many of our family and friends were leaving, both Fricis and Alvils felt their place was here, and we respected that. No matter what happened, which side won and which side lost, good doctors would always be needed. They were quite certain they wouldn't be harmed, and they were right."

"Yes, they must have been very respected doctors."

"They were."

"Good, good. But even in staying, Fricis knew he was taking a risk," Father insists. "That last time, he showed me the shelter he'd dug in the garden."

"The bomb shelter," Regina repeats as she remembers.

"Well, fortunately no harm came to my sister and her family," Father concedes and turns to observe Marija and Fricis's descendants talking nearby.

"Maybe if more people had stayed, things would have been different for us," ventures Cousin Regina.

Her words sound like a reproach, and they put Father on the defensive. He expels a breath through partly closed lips, like the sound of a balloon deflating. "Nonsense. What could a few thousand badly armed men, women, and children do against Soviet tanks and artillery? Like your father-in-law and husband, I did what I thought best for my family."

Regina is not happy with the turn the conversation has taken, and decides to end it. "Jani," she says, turning to her brother-in-law, "please help me with the drinks, and let's give our uncle a moment to look at his photos in peace." She hesitates at the door. "Onkul, after lunch Inguna has offered to play the violin if you like. She's so thankful for all the violin strings you sent over the years. It was impossible to find any here."

Left to himself, Father lifts the corner of each page carefully, as if he is uncovering a long-buried treasure. He says nothing, but now and then his facial features rearrange themselves, and perhaps a hint of a smile plays the corners of his mouth. He removes his glasses and brings the album to his face to check on some detail, all the while wishing he had one of the magnifying glasses he keeps handy at home on top of the TV Guide Magazine or on his desk. He pauses at a photograph of Erna and him on the steps of the opera. These, the early years of their marriage, were the golden years. Life was full of possibilities, and war was unthinkable. Even after war had been declared, and foreign troops—first the Russians, then the Germans—invaded Latvia, he had managed to cling to the naïve hope that life for him and his family could evolve in a normal way. He had continued to work and, as his parents had taught him, had deferred to whoever was in authority on everything except technical matters. Album in hand, Father's thoughts reach back to 1938.

***

He and his wife, Erna, were newly wed and living in Sweden. He was happier than he had ever been before, both at work in the shipyard and at home in a small, rented apartment. Each day he traced smooth lines across a vast expanse of blueprint that remained tightly rolled up at either end and made parts of ships magically appear in perfect detail. At the end of the day, he returned home to Erna and a hot meal. He so adored pancakes, and once a week, Erna whipped eggs, milk, and flour into a thin batter that spread out on the hot griddle like melting ice cream. The fillings varied. Sometimes the crepes concealed leftover shredded beef, moistened with broth; other nights they held mushrooms in a sour cream sauce; or for dessert, a sweet strawberry preserve. He was a dutiful worker and for the most part, concentrated on his drawings, but sometimes his thoughts wandered. He liked to picture Erna sitting in an easy chair by the window where the light was best, embroidering or, after she disclosed to him that a child was on the way, knitting. Blissfully happy, Janis was unaware that his wife was lonely and homesick.

Even though she sorely missed her mother and sister, Erna put aside her wish to return home and concentrated instead on preparing for the baby and on learning Swedish, something that her husband urged her to do. She did not like to disappoint him when he quizzed her on what she had learned. Often however, Erna's thoughts strayed from the page of grammar to the growing baby that stretched and kicked and made its presence felt. When the unthinkable happened, and she lost the baby, she blamed herself. Almost thirty, she feared she might never bear a child. Erna's grieving was deepened by the fact that her husband pretended not to be affected and buried his head deeper in his blueprints. It only made matters worse when he reminded Erna that his own mother had married at thirty-three and had borne seven children, one each year.

When the opportunity presented itself, Janis decided to resign from his job in Sweden and return to Latvia, to the western port city of Liepaja. Either political innocence or the optimism of youth, maybe both, blinded him to the signs of war about to break out on the continent. Not long after they settled in to their apartment in Liepaja, a city where the wind blew constantly, the war broke out. A confusing political situation gave the Soviet Union the excuse it had been looking for, and in June 1940 it illegally invaded its three small, independent neighbours, Estonia, Latvia, and Lithuania. The people in the three Baltic Republics awoke one morning to find their town squares filled with soldiers and their streets barricaded by tanks. All resistance was immediately and brutally quelled. The Latvian government wanted to avoid bloodshed and urged cooperation by its citizens.

Janis felt he had no real choice but to continue his work in the shipyards. Besides the occupation, he had more personal concerns. In spite of mud bath treatments and endless soaking in mineral springs, the years passed, and Erna failed to conceive. He worried, too, about the welfare of his oldest sister, Ede, who had been widowed a few months earlier. Janis wrote to Ede in Copenhagen inviting her and her two young daughters, Rita and Milda, to come and live with them. He promised to find her work in the factory and assured her that his four-room apartment was big enough for all. "Erna and I would be very happy if you would accept this proposal. We live a lonely life. We have no children, and I really want to help bring up your two girls. My dear Edite, I beg you to accept my invitation. You won't be a burden—there will be no talk of that—but exactly the opposite, our lives will have greater meaning, and it will be warm and cozy living all together. Your girls can go to school in Liepaja." The letter contained only passing reference to the recently changed political situation: a law had been passed obliging Latvian citizens living overseas to register before November 1 at their respective

Soviet embassies. Janis continued to persuade, "All our relatives stand behind my proposition."

Edite declined the invitation. In the rational way that their father, Peteris Zalite, had taught them, she did not allow her heart to rule her head. She decided to remain in Denmark and struggle to educate her daughters on her own. It proved to be a wise decision, one that perhaps even saved her life.

Latvians everywhere remember 1941 as The Year of Horror. The occupying Soviet army and the Secret Police purged the country of anyone they thought might oppose them. In one night, from June 13th to 14th, fifteen thousand innocent persons—entire families, including children—were rounded up and forced onto heavy trucks that lumbered to the nearest railway station. Then soldiers loaded them into boxcars—four hundred ninety boxcars in all—that rolled east into the depths of the Soviet Union. Weeks later, sick and starving, the people were dumped without pity or provisions onto the Siberian taiga. About the same time, the German army invaded the USSR. They pushed into Riga on July 1. Suddenly, a new regime replaced the hated Soviets, but, for most, the horror did not end. The Holocaust in Latvia began with the murder of Latvian Jews and continued with the killing of European Jews shipped to Latvia for extermination. During the Nazi occupation, special campaigns killed about seventy thousand Jews, as well as two thousand gypsies. As with the Soviet occupation, some Latvian collaborators were also involved in the executions. The Nazis conscripted more than two hundred thousand Latvian soldiers. About half of them perished in battle.

Soon after the German occupation began, still living alone and still childless, Janis and Erna moved to Riga. He was transferred to the now German-controlled Riga Shipyards. Although food and petrol were still strictly rationed, they both hoped that life would be better for them in the capital. Erna welcomed the change and hoped she would be less lonely. As for Janis, he believed he understood the German mind with its need for order and discipline. After all, he was the son of parents who were both educators and who had instilled in him a respect for authority, along with a sense of duty. Further, the Germans were no strangers to Latvia. As far back as 1201, during the Second Crusade, when Bishop Albert brought Christianity to Latvia and founded the city of Riga, the German nobility and clergy had ruled *Letland.* For years, the ruling barons profited from the abundance of amber on Letland's shores, and the nobles extracted more than their due from the toil and sweat of the peasants. As part of the Hanseatic League, Riga had flourished as an important commercial center. Janis and Erna now hoped that a new German occupation would prove to be the lesser of two evils. Janis's work in the shipyards assured him of food rations and a place to live; also earned him exemption from military service.

When, after nearly six years of marriage, Erna gave birth to a dark-haired, blue-eyed baby boy, Janis's eyes filled with tears. He suggested they name the boy Peteris after his grandfather, and Erna happily agreed. The added responsibility of providing for his new son spurred Janis to work harder and to wish all the more for an end to the war. What glorious times the three of them would have, he thought.

However, the year following Peteritis's birth brought Janis new worries. His own father's health was deteriorating, and every day the old man's cough sounded worse. The war raged on in Europe and elsewhere, and Latvia's future hung on the war's outcome. When he learned of the failure of the German invasion of the Soviet Union in the bitter winter of 1943, Janis dared hope for an Allied victory, but at the same time, feared the consequences. Only fools, Janis thought, could cling to the belief that a postwar Latvia would ever be free again. He was not optimistic by nature and could foresee nothing but disaster, reprisals, and a settling of scores.

He was frustrated by the lack of information, but when *Voice of America* broadcast the news of Third Reich defeats, a Soviet offensive into Latvia changed from a worrisome possibility to a frightening probability. He needed a plan. Flee or stay? Both options were dangerous. Janis leaned toward fleeing to the west, but this choice was complicated by his father's advancing lung cancer and his wife's condition. Erna was now expecting another child.

One overcast Sunday in the autumn of 1943, Janis hopped on his bicycle and pedaled to Jurmala, in hopes that the exercise and the sea breeze would clear his head of all troubling thoughts, so that he might make the right decision. He leaned his bicycle against a bench and looked around. The beach was almost deserted. After untying his laces, he pulled off his shoes and socks and pushed his toes into the sand. Then he walked down to the water's edge where the sand had been sculpted into ripples by the action of the wind and waves. His eyes searched the horizon for an answer, and while he found none, he felt calmer. He knew the Baltic well; he had sailed the coast many times with Juris in the *Tobago*. But that had been in a better time, that brief golden interlude between independence and this war. The Baltic was now patrolled by dreadnoughts and submarines and sprinkled with deadly mines. It was dangerous, but it still offered an escape route. He was not a risk-taker, especially now that he had one child and another on the way. He would rely on his brains. They had never failed him.

Janis retrieved his bicycle and pedaled back to the city. He did not go directly home but instead, knocked on his brother's door. Juris, who was an engineer with the Department of Highways, opened the door. "Come in, come in. You look half-frozen."

"Thanks." Janis rubbed his hands together in an attempt to warm them. He welcomed the offer of a glass of tea that Juris's wife, Zenija, served from the samovar on the sideboard.

"Brrr. It's more like December than October out there."

"Thank goodness it won't be long now 'til the heat's turned on," Zenija said.

"I've been to Jurmala and back, looking for an answer," Janis confided to his brother once they were alone. "I'm really worried about our father. The medicine doesn't seem to help much, and he's gone downhill quickly, ever since last winter, when he lacked the breath to blow out the candles on his cake."

"*Nu*, what do you expect? Seventy-five candles is no joke. Why, I thought the ceiling would catch fire!" exclaimed Juris.

Janis set his glass down hard, spilling some of the milky tea. He resented the fact that his older brother still treated him like a child, even now that he too was an engineer and had a family of his own. Juris had always lived at a faster pace. Already married once before while still a student, he had divorced, and married Zenija. From his first marriage, he had a twenty-year old son, Valters, who was also an engineer and skinny as a surveyor's pole, and he had two little girls by his second, more glamorous wife.

"Seriously, Juri, it's not easy to make plans with our father so sick and my Erna in a delicate condition. Father insists he's not going anywhere. If we all leave, who will look after him?"

"Of course, I'm worried, too, but I'm not losing any sleep over it. I don't think Marija and Fricis plan to leave. The Reds will never harm a doctor."

"I've been thinking about the alternatives. None of them come with any guarantee," Janis said.

"You really are a pessimist."

"Not at all, I'm a realist," Janis answered, "and up to now, no one has ever handed me anything on a silver platter."

"Right now, the least dangerous option seems to be Germany," said Juris. "Whatever happens, there'll be rebuilding to do, and they'll be wanting civil engineers. I really think it would be less risky—not totally risk-free, mind you—but less risky than trying to make it across the Baltic in a wooden tub like our *Tobago* or on some leaky fishing trawler."

Janis had to agree. Although he was at home on the sea and on ships, had worked as a naval engineer, and had spent his year of obligatory military service in the navy, he respected the sea, especially now. "The Baltic's too dangerous. Our shores are constantly patrolled by sea and air. What's worse, it's been seeded with mines that float just below the surface, as invisible as jellyfish. And believe me," he added with a wry smile, "an Allied mine is just as deadly as a German one."

"Actually, I've already looked into the possibility of sending Zeny and the girls ahead to Germany. Maybe that's the answer for you, too. But I'll not run, unless it becomes absolutely necessary. No, sir, after all, my heart's here," Juris clamps a fist to his chest.

"Right now I'm staying put, doing what I'm told, nothing more," Janis said. "But if the Soviets invade, and it looks pretty likely—you know how they are—for certain, they'll be downright dangerous." This sobering thought silenced both brothers, and they could hear high-pitched girlish laughter in the next room, reminding Janis that there was another reason for his visit. "Don't say anything to Zenija yet. It's too soon, really. But Erna and I have been thinking we'd like Zenija to be godmother to our next child."

"She'll be pleased about that. You know, it makes me so happy to see my Zeny and your Erna such good friends. Well, well, this calls for a little celebration." Juris got up and gave his brother a pat on the shoulder, then crossed over to a large oak desk, pulled open a drawer, and extracted a bottle. He took down two small, gold-lined, silver goblets from a shelf, and filled the cups until only surface tension kept the vodka from spilling over. With a perfectly steady hand, he handed one to Janis. "Prosit. To the future, uncertain as it is."

"Skol. To our health and our families," Janis replied, and both men downed the fiery liquid in one gulp.

"Brrr, good stuff, that," Juris grimaced.

Janis nodded agreement, unable to speak. The raw alcohol burned his throat, and he shivered, not from cold this time, but from the fire it ignited in his belly.

Over the next few months, their father's health continued to deteriorate until finally, in December 1943, at the age of seventy-nine, Peteris Zalite closed his eyes on a turbulent world. "Life has been good to me personally," he whispered to his family who gathered at his bedside, "but I've witnessed enough cruelty and suffering for two lifetimes."

***

"Dad," I say, as I lean over his shoulder to see what he has been staring at for so long. It is a large photograph, in black and white, depicting a winter funeral. Everyone in the picture is bundled up, and there are no fresh flowers, only fir boughs piled high atop and all around a fresh grave. "You really should come outside and see the garden," I say, and gently close the album. "It's yours now to take home."

Regina's garden is different from any I've tended back home. There is no idle lawn begging for attention, and little that is purely decorative. Her garden is completely devoted to edible plants, with hardly any space wasted. It includes peas, carrots, string beans, strawberries in raised beds, currant, raspberry and gooseberry bushes, gnarled apple trees boasting small, green fruit, and some flowers destined for a vase. The plants in this garden must earn their keep. The children have followed us outside, and they are intrigued by our reaction.

"What's so interesting?" asks nine-year-old Lauris, "They're just vegetables." He is neatly dressed in shoes, cotton pants, and an ironed shirt. No jeans or sneakers for him or for any of the other children. The girls all wear summer dresses.

"Oh, everything. I just love the smell of sweet peas, don't you?"

“I’d rather eat peas than smell them,” Lauris answers, and snaps off a young pod.

“Hey, didn’t Oma tell us not to pick them?” one of the older girls admonishes Lauris. Her blonde hair is pulled back from her round face and neatly braided.

We are saved from further transgression when Roland calls us in for lunch. The adults sit together at one long table, and the children occupy a smaller table set up in the room next door. A Latvian feast awaits us, much like the food my mother used to serve her guests. Plates of roast pork, crisp oven-browned potatoes, and a mound of sauerkraut studded with brown flecks of bacon and caraway seeds are on the table. Everything shines with pork fat. For the health conscious, there is a dish of boiled garden vegetables. Regina offers a toast to our happy gathering in her home, and we sip sweet, pink Riga champagne and homemade, red currant juice.

Since Regina’s son, Juris, speaks English, he is seated beside Janice. Between bites, he tells her that he is an astrophysicist. “But soon, I will be without job. You know, all these years the Cold War has drained Soviet Union of the money and now, there’s only little bit left for basic research.”

“Yes, that’s what Janis told us also, for his research,” Janice says.

“Yes. Yes, everywhere same is happening. And free Latvia will have differing priorities. Is very much neglect for so many years. You have seen the roads?”

Janice nods in agreement, then helps herself to a slice of meat.

“In the Soviet Union, science and scientists, considered part of the intelligentsia, have always been under some suspicion, but now we have become liability. Looks like is end of road for many of us,” adds Cousin Janis, not without bitterness.

“Except maybe for arms and the space race,” says Father. “People might be hungry, but there’s always money for that.” A shadow crosses Father’s face. “Not counting the newer suburbs in the outskirts, what I see is the Riga of 1940.”

“Mothballed for fifty years,” suggests Regina.

“Not quite. Then, it would have been better preserved,” Father counters. “But I must say, I was rather pleasantly surprised in many ways. The architectural elegance of many of its buildings remains—the opera house, the university, the ornate Jugendstil facades of Albert Street, the apartment buildings along Freedom Boulevard…."

"Janice and I love the Art Nouveau architecture. Let's drink to it and to Freedom Boulevard," cries Roland, lifting his glass, "for reclaiming its rightful name. No more Lenin Street."

"That's just symbolic. I don't think the transition will be as simple or as painless as replacing a street sign," Father says.

"Sadly, all too true, Onkul. We still fear a crackdown," adds Cousin Janis. "The Soviets have too much at stake here, what with our year-round Baltic ports, their military bases, and their equipment to spy on the rest of Europe, even their factories. Like the amber they hauled back to Russia years ago, Latvia still has what the Soviets want."

"Well put, Janis. We're all like fossilized flies, trapped for years in the communist resin, paralyzed, not able to move!" Regina's younger son cries out, his face pink and his shyness banished by several glasses of sweet wine.

"My personal hope is that our total freedom will be negotiated politically. No bloodshed. That's what we in the Saeima have been working toward. But even there, we have the hard-liners to contend with," Cousin Janis says. "But no more politics. How about instead a toast to my dear sister-in-law and this wonderful meal she has prepared?"

"To your health, Regina," I join the chorus, and once again raise my glass to my lips. My cheeks are burning, and I feel lightheaded, so I allow myself only a tiny sip.

That same evening, after we have passed through the now familiar and necessary boarding routine and are back aboard the *Baltic Star*, I invite Father and Roland to join me in the bar for a nightcap. I am anxious to hear the story of how our family escaped.

Father consults his watch. "It's getting late, and it has been a long day—"

"Just a club soda with lemon."

"Please, Dad," says Roland.

"Why this sudden interest?" Father asks, but when he sinks into a comfortable armchair, I know we have convinced him. I take out the scribbler I have been using as a diary and turn to a fresh page. This time, I plan to record every place, name, and date, so I won't forget or get the details mixed up. My husband and sons will be interested, too.

Father wipes a handkerchief across his mouth and begins. "I suppose I should start with the bicycle ride—the ride of my life."

I smile to myself, as I write *velosipedu* in Latvian. I can clearly see the origin of the word from velocipede. As Father speaks, I make notes in Latvian, with the occasional English word thrown in for my own clarification. My spoken Latvian is improving every day that we are here, but my written Latvian is rudimentary at best. Growing up in Montreal's east end, my brothers and I would have had to make a two-hour, cross-city bus ride each Saturday morning to attend Latvian school in the west. We did not do that and the result is poor grammar and dubious spelling. As I write, I sense that the diacritical marks—the macrons, carons, and cedillas—that I sprinkle above and below the letters do not always land where they should.

Father takes a single, folded sheet of graph paper from his inside breast pocket and smoothes it out on the low table in front of us. It is almost impossible for him to explain anything without the help of paper and a pencil. "You, Ilzit, were only four months old and little Peter not yet two years, when I took you out of the city to Bene." He draws several straight lines on his paper and bows his head, so that, for a moment, I fear he has fallen asleep. "An occupied city with shortages of food, everything, is no place for children. I arranged to settle the three of you in an empty schoolroom in the countryside. Mama was not too pleased that there was no running water or inside toilet, but it was for the best. Food would be more plentiful, especially in summer." Father's grey eyes moisten, but he continues, "I told Mama that soon, very soon, the lilacs would be in flower. "You know, in Riga, food was rationed, long line-ups for everything. I was lucky to work at the shipyards, where we were given a hot midday meal. We drove out of the city, Mama in the front with you, Ilzit, in her arms, and Peterits perched like a Kaiser in the back seat, high atop a soft bundle."

"What kind of car was it?" Roland wants to know.

"An Opel Kadett, black and shiny. My very first car." Father shrugs, but there is pride in his voice as he adds, "Hard to believe now, but in those days not many families owned a car."

"And you returned to Riga," I prompt.

Father nods. "Back to work. But you know, I visited as often as I could, by train mostly, as gasoline was rationed. Toward the end, I left the car in Bene. Fortunately the mail was still fairly reliable, so Mama and I kept in touch by letter." Father turns to me. "I knew when you got your first tooth, when you sat up by yourself, and how much you liked the sweet, wild strawberries that Mama picked. All that summer, the news was not good. For more than a year, and especially since the German invasion of the Soviet Union failed in the winter of 1943…."

Father stops talking and watches me jot notes in my book. "But that's history you learned in school. It's getting late, so I'll go straight to my bicycle ride."

"Tell me anyway," I plead, not wanting to reveal the gaps in my knowledge. How could I make Father understand that the history I had learned in high school meant nothing to me? It was as anonymous as a newsreel, as remote from my life as Timbuktu.

Father adjusts the lead in his mechanical pencil and squares the paper in front of him. With nothing more than the equations in his brain and formulas he found in books and manuals, Father could transform simple measurements, origami-like, into three-dimensional ships that sailed the world. He sketches quickly, surely. A few lines and circles, and the shipyard appears at the mouth of the Daugava River, the besieged city of Jelgava to the south, and Bene far to the west and south. With a steady hand, Father draws a double-headed arrow and the number *100* between the arrows.

"More than one hundred kilometers stretched between me and Mama. As the fighting drew closer, I feared being permanently separated from my family. I did not want that. For weeks, rumours of an imminent German collapse had been circulating among the workers, but that day, the news that reached us in the German-controlled shipyard was particularly distressing. The Russians were amassing to the south of Riga in order to cut off the rest of the country from its capital. Like wringing the head of a chicken, blood would flow. Already it was feared that Jelgava had fallen. All day, with long, serious faces and armloads of documents, my supervisors rushed back and forth and conferred behind closed doors, fearing the worst. I could barely concentrate on my work; my head was spinning. With one half of my mind, I was calculating torque, and with the other half, I was formulating a plan. By four that afternoon, I had made my decision."

It is a warm evening and not yet dark. Few people are around, as most are attending Song Festival events—concerts or the theatre—or visiting with relatives. I am eager to hear the whole story, yet filled with dread; Mother never really overcame her wartime experiences. Father taps his pencil, looks closely at his drawing, and then erases part of a line to redraw it nearby. Showing on his face is the effort needed to recover the exact details that had been buried in the sands of time. The lines across his forehead deepen, and his eyes narrow. I turn my notebook to a fresh page.

"The Opel was in Bene for safekeeping, and I had only my bicycle. When the six o'clock whistle sounded, I clipped my pant leg securely out of the way, swung my leg over the seat, and pushed off. I set my course toward the sun, just beginning its downward arc. My two-wheeler was sturdy yet heavy, and it seemed to weigh ever more as the night wore on. Soon it felt as if someone had stuck weights on my ankles. My thighs burned. Slowly, the sun dipped below the western horizon and ignited a red glow in the sky. It was the strangest night. I could see two sunsets, one in the west where it should be, and another one toward the southeast, where Jelgava was burning. The Germans burned the city as they left. Along the way, I came across pockets of a chaotic and frightened German army in retreat. No one seemed to be in charge. More than once, ashen-faced soldiers stopped me and demanded to know where I was going, but fortunately, they did nothing to stop me. They knew their game was up."

"'To Bene,' I gasped, whenever I was questioned. My lungs screamed for air. 'My wife, children are there.'"

"'You're too late,'" the soldier shook his head, not from sympathy, mind you, but disbelief. "'The Bolsheviks are already there.'"

"Ilze, Roland, I'd never heard more terrible words. It was like an arrow had pierced my heart, and for a moment, I thought it had actually stopped. But what choice did I have? Turn back? Never. The roads were jammed with cars and trucks and wagons. People walking. Latvians were fleeing. The Red Army was advancing. German soldiers were retreating." Father pauses, gathering the courage to continue. "It was chaos. Soon, the checkpoints I passed yawned empty. Silent sentinels."

Father draws his hands across his eyes, as if trying to erase this terrible image. "I think the moon had risen by now, as I was able to make out dark clumps in some of the fields, accompanied by the stench of fresh blood on the night breeze. I hoped they were not corpses, but farm animals, slaughtered by their owners to keep them out of the mouths of the Soviet army. I remember that as I turned south, to Bene, I was surprised to hear the flap of a wing and birds chirping, as if it was the dawn of a normal day. Then daylight and the full extent of the horror were revealed.

We sit in silence for a while. It is obvious from Father's face that his head is filled with vivid, awful memories with which he does not want to burden us. Although I know the ending of Father's story, the tension in my body grows until the pain in my jaw forces me to unclamp my teeth, to speak out: "What you did was so courageous."

"I was only doing my duty to Mama, to my children. Whatever happened, we would be living with the consequences the rest of our lives."

"So brave, but Dad you should've told us before," Roland reproaches gently.

"We talk of people voting with their feet. That night, I voted with my whole body." Father consults his watch and shifts in his chair, as if about to get up.

"Please, Dad. Finish it," I beg. "The part where you find us."

Father takes sips of his soda water while he considers. "I don't know where I got the strength, but I finally reached the turn-off to the schoolhouse." His voice catches in his throat for a moment, and he coughs into the handkerchief he has been twisting through his fingers. "The classroom was empty, the nearby farmstead deserted. No one. My heart fell to my feet."

"But you found us." I cannot wait to get to the good part of the story.

"Yes, Daughter, I did." Father pats my hand. "I soon found Mama crouching between the hilled-up rows in the potato field with Peter hiding in her skirts and you, Ilzulite, sound asleep in a willow basket. Another hamper with some food and clothes lay nearby." Father's grey eyes, behind thick lenses, look bigger and darker than usual in the soft light. "Mama's blue eyes were big as saucers, and at first I thought she doesn't recognize me. Panting and sweating, I must've looked like a wild man. 'Where are the others?' I asked Mama, and sank to the soft earth beside her. 'Gone,' she answered in a flat monosyllable. 'Gone.' Just like that. The others had fled, and Mama and her babies were the only ones left. I felt sick with anger, but soon calmed down as Mama told the full story. The others had urged Mama to go with them, to flee. But she was right. How could she run anywhere with two babies and baskets and nowhere to go? How would I have found her?"

"Mama knew you would come for us." I swipe at my eyes with the back of my hand and look at Roland. Lucky Roland, I think, he knew only peacetime.

"Poor Mama," Roland says.

"My actions might seem brave now, but really, what else could I have done? Abandon my family? The war broke apart so many families. Do you remember Vitols, our church organist in Montreal? He escaped, but his wife and children remained behind in Latvia. I could never let that happen to me."

Father retrieves the wedge of lemon from the bottom of his glass and squeezes it, then wipes his fingers on his handkerchief. The liquid is satisfyingly tart. "Fortunately…no, not fortunately. By design, my Opel was still locked in the shed, but first I had to dig up and install the battery. You see, I had hidden it," Father taps his head with his index finger to signify his cleverness, "and a can of gasoline. Then we drove west, toward Liepaja. My God, the docks at Liepaja were in total chaos. So many frightened people, Latvians and Germans, running this way and that, yelling, crying, shoving, and pleading. Some were offering their life's savings, just to get on a ship, any ship, to get away from the Red menace. It didn't seem to matter where the ship was heading, so long as they could get away. We were lucky, though. Since I'd worked in the Liepaja shipyard, I knew some of the directors personally, and I managed to secure passage for the three of you on a ship bound for Gdansk."

"German occupied Poland?" asks Roland. "From the frying pan into the fire."

"Only three of us? You sent us on alone?" I ask, in disbelief. But my words come out as a reproach. "Wasn't the whole idea to stay together?"

"Of course it was, but I had to go back. You see I had not been released from my work." Father holds out his hands in what looks like a gesture of helplessness or a plea for understanding.

I am momentarily too upset to be charitable. "To save your good Zalite name, you sent Mama and us on alone? Is that why?" I am in the grip of hot, justifiable anger. I knew something of how much Mother had suffered during that time and of how seriously ill we had all been.

Father slams both palms onto the table. "Don't talk to me in that tone. You wanted to know what happened. I don't have to justify my actions to you. I did what I had to do, that's all. I'm sure Roland understands that a man doesn't just abandon his work, his reputation, all that he stands for. *Darbs cel viru.* Work builds the man, our Talavija motto. I believed in that, and I have always lived by those words. My reputation, my knowledge, that's all I had left to build our future." Father's words slow down as his anger fades. "You know I needed to obtain a certificate that would allow me to transfer to another shipyard. It was the only way to survive. Without work you had no place to live and no ration coupons. No work, no food, simple as that." He picks up the paper he has been using to demonstrate and slaps it with one hand.

"Isn't war a failure of signed contracts?" I ask. I know it is useless to argue with my father, but I foolishly persist.

"Keep to subjects you know something about," admonishes Father. Soon, calm returns to both of us. "My work and my professional reputation, that's what got us out of the camp before anyone else, to Sweden, and three years later, to Canada. And don't forget, it was my profession that saved me from being conscripted into the army of the Third Reich. It kept us together." Father notices that I'm about to say something. "Please don't interrupt anymore. It's getting late, and I'd like to finish. I told Mama I would apply for an immediate transfer to Gdansk so we could be together. It was the only possible way." At that moment, Father looks all of his eighty-three years.

"Anyway, I got you on board, kissed Mama good-bye and shook Peteris's hand. 'You are a big boy now, I told him, and have to help Mama.' Then the whistle shrieked, so I turned and hurried down the gangplank. You know, it was the next day, August 6, that little Peteritis turned two, aboard a ship that hugged the coast to stay clear of Allied submarines and British dreadnoughts."

"Why, Peter was just a baby," I wheeze, short of breath and thinking back to my own son at the age of two. I have almost stopped breathing.

"Sorry," I say, as Father shoots me a look that tells me I have interrupted him again.

"I went back. I was afraid the roads would be impassable and much too dangerous, so I parked my Opel on the dock, locked it, and pocketed the key. It was the very first car I ever owned, and it wasn't easy to abandon it like that. But that night, I boarded a ship that was heading for Riga with supplies. The Germans were preparing for a long siege, but the end came quickly. That's it. Now you see how it was." Father is on his feet now, a bit unsteady due to fatigue and the lateness of the hour.

"How come you never talked about this before, when we were growing up?" I ask, trying to keep my voice even and free of any hint of reproach.

Father steadies himself on the back of Roland's chair. "It's not something Mama and I talked about much, but I'm sure I mentioned it. But really, why dwell on the past? What good does it do anyone? It all happened so long ago." Father is about to go, but hesitates. "Actually, Ilze, you're not the only one surprised that I returned to Riga. My coworkers threw up their hands in disbelief, but my director showed his appreciation by promising to get me a transfer and passage to Poland, as soon as possible." Father considers a moment, and then he sits back down.

"While I waited, I spent the evenings going through my files, keeping only the most necessary documents. I would be foolish to try to take too much. A small packet of photographs, some silver wedding gifts, a few precious mementos from my father and, most important, his portrait. You know the one; it's always hung in the living room. Carefully, I removed the nails that held the canvas secure in its heavy wooden frame and rolled it up, paint side out the way you are supposed to. It seemed the wrong way to do it, but anyway, that's what I did, and it survived intact. I wrapped it first in a sheet and then in the blue and red oilcloth that I removed from the kitchen table. I remembered also to take my new, navy woollen suit with the striped pants that came from the finest men's tailor in Riga. It was heavy and took up space, but I thought, you never know when such a suit might come in handy for my laying out. At least your father would have been a respectable corpse!"

"Please, Dad, don't say things like that." My eyes are swimming in unshed tears.

"Facts are facts. Those desperate days, I often walked around with the feeling that I had a rubber band stretched tight around my chest. Well, the Germans held on to the capital for two more weeks, before finally capitulating to the Russians. Those weeks gave the army time to bulldoze a western corridor and throw down railroad tracks, connecting Riga and Liepaja. With their backs to the sea, it was an alternate, overland escape route. My director finally signed the certificate of transfer I had requested to the Schichau Shipyards in Danzig (Gdansk). Without that piece of paper, it would have been impossible for me to get anywhere. That last day alone in our Thomson street apartment, waiting for the night when it would be safer to travel, I wrote Mama a letter that I never sent, but carried with me."

My beloved wife,

In case fate has decided that we never meet again, I wish to thank you for each year, day and hour that you gave me. Still in force are all the words when we first got acquainted: Beautiful is each day you gave me, Marija Luize. Thank you for the strong son and cuddly little one, bring them up to be upright and tell them about their Daddy.

Your life's companion, Janis.

"Marija Luize?" I asked.

"Yes, after a popular song at the time. I locked the door, and lugging two heavy suitcases, I boarded a tram for the train station. Fortunately, black night had not yet fallen, and a feeble light entered the building through the open doors and the empty windows. I found my assigned car and fell into a seat. I had plenty of time to catch my breath and calm my wildly beating heart. We waited for several hours, until total darkness, and only then did the train emerge and slowly steam blind-eyed toward the west. Without lights."

"Without lights, so you would not be bombed," states Roland.

"Just so, Son, that's how it was." Father seems very tired, as tired as if he had rushed to the train station with his heavy bags and dragged them up the metal steps and into his car a moment ago. "The train slithered slowly along the uneven rails, up and down like a snake on a littered forest floor, with many stops, but we arrived. I looked for my car at the Liepaja docks, but of course, it was no longer there. It was a silly thing to do; what good would it have done me to glimpse it one more time? Already, it was part of the past…."

"My all-important piece of paper got me a berth on the next ship bound for Danzig." Father ventures a small, ironic laugh. "Well, as you can see, the ship made it, and I reported to the director of the Schichau Shipyards, as soon as I arrived. Well, goodnight everyone. I suggest you get to bed, also. Tomorrow is another day."

"Wait a sec. That can't be all. How did you find us?" I ask. "And how did we get to Germany?"

"That story will have to wait. All that talking has dried out my mouth, robbed me of my breath. Goodnight."

Roland and I are left limp and breathless, as if we were the ones who had been pedaling all night, fleeing danger. We are filled with a new admiration for Father, but one that is mixed with disbelief and incomprehension. Were such acts of courage so commonplace during the war that they could be easily forgotten, set aside like discarded belongings that were too heavy or cumbersome to drag along? And how did Father's story now change the supposedly fixed reality of our childhoods, that our parents were actors in their destiny, not just spectators or props to be shifted about on a world stage? Certainly, Father appeared to us in a new light, as did Mother's lifelong health complaints and feeling of dislocation. I wondered if I might have felt differently as a child growing up between the two worlds, Canadian and Latvian, had I known? I ponder this as I try to relax and give myself over to the gentle rocking of the ship.

Six

In the morning, Anitra and I prepare to go our separate ways. She will meet her relatives in Bene, at what is left of her grandmother's farm. "I haven't felt like this since my high school prom," Anitra confides. "I don't know how they'll react to me." She slices a banana onto her muesli, and it causes her to remember. "Yesterday, visiting relatives, I gave this boy, seven or so, a banana, and he barely knew what it was!"

"Hard to imagine," I offer.

"Yeah, well, he ate it very slowly, savoring every bite, and when he was finished, instead of throwing away the peel, he shoved it in his pocket—the *peel*, for crying out loud. Said he was keeping it to smell later, so he'd remember the taste. The peel," she repeats, hardly able to believe it herself in the retelling.

This morning my family and I have plans to visit Gaida Šķenders, the widow of my mother and Aunt Elza's brother, Janis. I have heard a few stories about Gaida, and I am eager to meet her in person. A trained medical doctor, she nursed her husband when he returned in 1947 from forced exile to Siberia, a sick man. For that, Mother had always been thankful. Gaida and Janis married in April of 1950, but they had little time to be happy together. The Stalin era was a time of fear and suspicion and unwarranted accusations against ordinary Latvians, with the result that my Uncle Janis was imprisoned on various trumped-up charges and sent away again, this time to brutal, forced labour in the far-off Sakhalin gold mines. When he finally managed to return home in 1968, he was a physically and spiritually broken man. A large part of Mother's sadness during my youth stemmed from these events back home, events that she only read about in letters.

The taxi rolls to a stop in front of a large, two-story, white brick house with leaded glass and bow windows. It sits on a quiet street, not far from a lake and a forest, in the Riga outskirts. An unpainted wood fence encloses a small flower garden. We enter and walk to a side door.

Although it is Aunt Gaida's house, the very house that my uncle built and the one that cost him so dearly, my aunt now occupies only two rooms and shares the kitchen with a sister and other family members. "Please enter. Come in." Like most Latvians, superstition does not allow Aunt Gaida to extend a hand of welcome across the threshold: to do that would be inviting bad luck. Laima, the goddess of luck and fortune, dwells somewhere beneath the sill and must be shown respect.

I step inside to shake hands and kiss my aunt's cheek, its skin soft and cool; it is the healthy skin of a much younger woman. "Little Ilzite," she says, using the diminutive, affectionate form of my name. Gaida is now retired and supplements her meager state pension by working as a cosmetologist. She is a living testament to the effectiveness of the creams and lotions she concocts for her clients.

We crowd into the small vestibule, then climb a flight of stairs to a bright and airy sitting room. Aunt Elza, Mara, and my brother Peter are already waiting. Peter's daughters have decided to follow their own program today; the young have little interest in excavating the past or visiting family graves. Oil paintings jostle for space on the walls, and stacks of books perch precariously on side tables. Knickknacks and other treasures fill any remaining empty spot, while potted plants bloom on the window ledge. The low coffee table is already set with an assortment of plates and cups.

Aunt Gaida ushers Father to the most comfortable chair, and as he slowly lowers himself, she says, "*Nu*, Jani, this is almost like a Talavija meeting." Uncle Janis was also a fraternity member. During all the years of the occupation, when such meetings were forbidden, and even after her husband's death, fraternity members used to meet in secret, in their home. Gaida gazes with special fondness at Peter, looking past his battered face, and sees the face of her departed husband. Apparently, my brother resembles him. "I feel so honoured to finally be able to receive everyone in my home," she tells us. "In the past, Intourist, hungry for foreign exchange, made visitors stay at hotels and eat in restaurants. Then, too, I guess they didn't want the rest of the world to discover what miserable, cramped apartments we lived in."

"Undermines the propaganda war," adds Mara.

"There's no getting around it—neighbours were recruited to spy on neighbours," says Aunt Gaida, with a shake of her head. "Just terrible."

"After the first time, being followed didn't bother me so much. Oh, but how I wish I could have convinced Erniņa to accompany me, just once." Aunt Elza does not look directly at Father as she speaks, but blame is implied. Father did not approve of trips back to Latvia during the Soviet years, insisting that by spending dollars on the obligatory Aeroflot flight, Moscow layover, and hotels in Riga, you were bolstering the communist regime. As a consequence, after our escape in 1944, Mother never saw her native land again.

Mara shifts in her chair and accepts an offered canapé. "Those watchers made it harder for my mother to hand over the goodies she'd brought with her."

Aunt Elza's deep-set eyes flash, and her normally serene features become animated. "Sure, but there's always ways to get around authority."

Father does not participate in this exchange, since he could never condone disrespect for authority.

"Peter, would you open this?" Aunt Gaida hands him the ubiquitous bottle of Riga champagne that never fails to add to the already festive mood.

While Peter makes his way around the table, I look from him to the framed portrait of a young Uncle Janis on the opposite wall. At home, Father has a very similar portrait of Peter on his study wall. The two, Peter and Janis, do look alike. Both photographs show young, confident, dark-haired men, wearing white Talavija caps on their heads, gazing unblinking into the future. They could easily be mistaken for brothers instead of uncle and nephew with a generation between them. I remember clearly my mother's love for her younger brother and her desperate sadness at his imprisonment, exile, and illness. Around the time that my brother and I were preparing for our confirmation in Montreal's Latvian Lutheran Church, Mother brought out a sepia photograph taken on her brother's and her confirmation day. She must have been sixteen or seventeen, and Janis is two years younger. They pose as if in a wedding portrait: my Uncle Janis wears a dark suit, and my mother manages to look both elegant and angelic in a white, ankle-length dress. Each cradles a large bouquet of flowers.

I try to remember what I have been told of my Uncle Janis's bravery. As soon as he graduated from the University of Latvia in the spring of

1944, he was conscripted into the army and sent to defend the western province of Kurzeme against the invading Bolsheviks. He was wounded in the fierce Christmas fighting, and doctors later removed eleven pieces of shrapnel from his leg. When the Latvian Legionnaires and the German army finally capitulated, my uncle and thousands of others were forcibly taken to Siberia. Somehow, more than two years later in 1947, he managed to return home.

"Prost. To your health," I hear Father say, and I am shaken from my gloomy thoughts by the familiar toast. I lift my glass and stand up, so that I can reach over and click glasses with each family member. It is a familiar, comforting ritual. We exchange gifts, and I am embarrassed by Aunt Gaida's generosity. She is the relative who used to send us the books containing out-of-focus photographs of Latvia's monuments and landscapes, as well as art books by well-known Latvian painters. All these years, she has been holding her end of the invisible thread that ties us together, a thread whose existence I was not really aware of until today, but which bound me and the rest of my family.

"Please help yourselves," Aunt Gaida says, and hands out small plates. The coffee table groans with the weight of delicacies, even caviar, upon it. As I wonder how she has managed to obtain so much food, I hear her extolling to Roland the benefits of the barter system. "My clients don't have a lot of money, so they pay me what they can, sometimes it's half a sausage, other times a box of chocolates, or a couple of tins of sprats. In summer, it's something from the garden. Actually, it works out better than rubles, and I don't have to stand in long lines to buy what I need."

Aunt Gaida sits back in her chair and smiles. "It's almost like the old days, when Janis was alive and Mama, your Omite, too. We so enjoyed getting together with my parents and sisters, drinking a glass of beer and singing. Each of us had a favourite song. Omite's was 'At This Time in the Evening'. Gaida hums a few notes, and Elza joins in. I know the song; it was Mother's favourite, too. According to the song, when Death appears in the dark of night, the singer offers him a glass of beer. In exchange, a grateful Death grants the singer eternal life. That message is entrenched in our Latvian psyche: we can drink and sing our troubles away, or at least postpone them for a while. Over the years, the Latvian Song Festival, especially the one that we have just witnessed, with its massed choir of twenty thousand voices, has been one such expression of my people's longing for their troubles to go away.

"Do you remember, Elza, that one time I visited you in New York?" Gaida asks. Elza nods. "It was in winter, in '79 or '80, I believe. All that snow and those incredible tall buildings."

"Skyscrapers," Elza interjects.

"Just so, skyscrapers. We greeted the New Year in the apartment of Rudzitis, who was at that time the managing director of *Laiks*, the Latvian newspaper. It was there, after so many years of silence, that I could finally sing 'God Bless Latvia' in full voice, without fear. And I did, until the tears flowed down my cheeks. It was wonderful."

After the stories have all been told, and we have had our fill of champagne and coffee and the delicacies spread out before us, we sing a few songs. I am happy to hear that Father still possesses a strong, clear baritone. Then we set out on foot to a nearby cemetery, where Uncle Janis and his mother and my Omite, Marta, are buried. Gaida tells us she feels lucky to live close to the cemetery, so she can properly tend to their graves once a week.

"Isn't she great," I confess to Peter, as we stroll through the well-kept, peaceful graveyard.

Peter agrees, "This is the first time we've met, and yet she's so familiar to me."

"Me, too. Gaida's so warm and motherly, what a pity they didn't have children."

"I guess that's to be blamed on Janis's imprisonment and exile to Siberia. When he returned, he was too sick. It's just like many of the childless Latvian couples we knew growing up in Montreal—the war robbed them of the opportunity to be parents. Fewer headaches for them." Peter laughs, and I realize he's referring to his teenage daughters.

I think of the Apse, the Lapins, the Paegli, the Grins, friends of our parents; all of them childless. "Maybe it wasn't the war, so much as being immigrants in a new country and without job prospects that stopped them."

"Could be. Luckily, Gaida was able to express her nurturing instincts in other ways."

"How's that?" I ask, curious that Peter would be aware of such instincts.

"By becoming Talavija's spiritual mother, for example," says Peter. "When her husband was alive, and even after he returned from Siberia an invalid, their home was the fraternity's secret meeting place." We stop and wait at a fork in the path, unsure of the way. Peter walks quickly; he is tall and gaunt, fueled by a nervous energy that is the product of an overactive thyroid coupled with an equally agile mind. He picks up a smooth stone and bounces it on his outstretched palm. "That time Gaida spoke about, when she visited Elza in the US—you were already living overseas—she smuggled back into Latvia the forbidden symbols that meant so much to the fraternity, the silver pins and ribbons. Did you know she sewed several meters of the Talavija white, green, and gold ceremonial ribbons into the waistband and hem of her skirt?"

I didn't know, but I'm not surprised. It was something she would do. A nightingale announces our arrival at the carefully manicured gravesite, but falls silent as we arrange our flowers on the stone. Aunt Gaida carefully lays down the lily stem that she plucked from her garden. Father steps forward to have a closer look at the inscription, while Aunt Elza wipes her nose on a tissue. Mara wraps an arm around her mother's slender shoulder. Seeing them together, I can better appreciate my mother's sadness, and only wish that I had somehow managed to acknowledge it, instead of always feeling inconvenienced by it. In graveyards, forced to confront our losses, we tend to focus on our regrets.

In silence, we retrace our steps, and once on the main street, we flag down several taxis to take us to the Raina kapi, the cemetery where my Grandfather Aleksandris is buried.

***

The day Mother received the news of her father's death stands out in my memory. It was an unusually warm September day, and the back door remained open while we ate. Outside, birds were singing, and on the clothesline, a few sheets flapped gently in the evening breeze. Father returned home from work and handed Mother a blue airmail envelope that had been sent to the post office box that he used for corresponding with Soviet Latvia. Those first few years in Canada, Father did not want the censors back in Latvia to know our home address. Mother recognized her mother's handwriting and eagerly slit open the envelope, while we helped ourselves to the food. Suddenly, the paper started to tremble in her hands, and Mother hurried from the room. When she came out a while later, her eyes were red from crying, and in her hands was a small photo of her father. She leaned the sepia-coloured photograph against a vase and lit a white candle beside it, but said nothing. For a while, I studied Opap's face but, apart from sympathizing with my grieving mother, I felt little emotion. My knowledge of my maternal grandfather was scant. I knew a bit more about my maternal grandmother, Omite, to whom I was told I owed my life when it was slipping away in the makeshift shelters and jerry-built assembly centers set up for us homeless exiles. She had been with us for a while in Germany, but soon after the war ended, and Omite saw that we were safe and in the hands of the Allies, she decided to return to Latvia, to her husband, to await the return of her son, Janis, from forced exile to Siberia.

More than twenty years passed before I met Omite for the first time since she had left us in the camp and returned home. It was in 1970. I was married and had a son, Peter. Mother and Elza had arranged for their mother to visit them in New York, where they both lived at that time. When Omite arrived, except for the determined set of her mouth, she resembled neither her photograph nor my mental image of her. I don't know who I was expecting to meet, an aged grandmother or a cross between Florence Nightingale and Superwoman. But there she was, a small, nondescript woman in a too-large winter coat. When she later removed her hat and coat, everything about her was soft: her gently rounded body, her cloud of white hair, and her skin so delicate the veins underneath shone through. In our family, Omite's bravery was legendary. In times of danger, over the course of her long life, she had stood up to bullying border guards and ignorant young soldiers following orders. She had even defied the puffed-up officials of old Imperial Russia.

***

The sun has hidden its face behind a dark cloud, and I can hear some far-off rumbling. I bid a silent good-bye to Opaps Alekandris; we have had only the briefest relationship, and I have no idea when I might be back to visit his grave again. When I was growing up, I used to envy my classmates their grandparents who always seemed to be buying them presents or taking them to the circus or to the Ice Capades. Most of my Latvian friends lacked grandparents. The one or two ancient grandmothers that I occasionally met were bent, shadowy figures, not quite right in the head, who spoke no English, and rarely ventured outside. I could not imagine any of them suggesting an afternoon at the Ice Capades. One friend's frail grandmother possessed a drawer full of colourful, hand-knitted mittens, and if she heard us at the front door getting ready to go out, she would emerge from her room with a bouquet of mittens in her hand and urge us to put them on. The weirdest part was that she did this year-round, no matter the temperature. Another grandmother, brought to Canada from Soviet-occupied Latvia in the mid-sixties, hung herself from the exposed pipes in the basement while her daughter and son-in-law were at work.

"A penny for your thoughts," Roland says, as he falls in step beside me.

"I was thinking how dramatically the war changed the structure of Latvian society in exile, as if a great big knife had sliced through it, cutting off the older generation," I answer.

"That's a bit dramatic. I remember old Mrs. Miežinskis across the way. She was always good for a cookie or two, and for a while, even matches," Roland says, with a mischievous smile.

"Yeah, until you nearly burned down the apartment. But we really missed out, not having grandparents. I'm glad it didn't happen to my kids."

We reach the street and say our good-byes to Gaida, who promises to come to Andrejosta to see us off the next day. Our time in Latvia is coming to an end.

The next morning, after throwing my belongings into my suitcase, I count my dollars. It is a challenge to reconcile the amount I have left with my exchange slips and receipts for purchases made. I am now fuzzy on the dollar value I declared upon entry and even more uncertain of how many dollars I have exchanged informally. At breakfast, everyone at our table is animated, discussing strategies and giving advice. Only Father is calm, having recorded every transaction in his diary. As we sip the strong coffee, a rumour reaches our ears: the customs officials are planning to be thorough in their job of examining our exit papers. My hand is unsteady as I mop up the last drop of sweet syrup with a bite of pancake and bring it to my mouth. "Don't worry, Sis," Roland tells me. So instead of worrying, I go up on deck to snap the Riga skyline one last time. I am relieved to see that the launch, once parked in mid-river off our stern, is no longer there. That can only be a good sign.

The morning passes uneventfully, and soon our relatives arrive at the dock to bid us good-bye. They bring parting gifts of flowers, tomatoes, and strawberries from their gardens. Janis's son, who works as a forest ranger, has woven a sturdy willow basket for each of us. Arija proudly distributes jars of homemade preserves, and Cousin Janis tucks a bottle of Latvian Balsams into Father's hand. Aunt Gaida is here also, bearing more gifts. Sincere promises to write and to return soon are made, and soon it is time to leave. I give each relative one last hug and walk slowly to the immigration shed to meet my fate. I square my shoulders and hand over my papers. The official shuffles through them with little interest and asks me only a few questions that I have no difficulty answering. Then he stamps my passport. This, I think, is a sure sign that things are changing. I fall in step with Father, and we board the *Baltic Star*, our freedom ship and banana boat.

For the first hour, the ship sails smoothly across the protected waters of the Gulf of Riga, but soon the wind picks up, and the ship begins to rise and fall with the waves. I step out on deck and see that the Baltic is restless, with whitecaps visible in the distance beyond Kolkas rags. I realize these are the storms that Arija was telling me about, storms that churn up the water, lifting the amber from the ocean's depths to wash it ashore. Some other lucky person will discover it. I go back inside and sit at a table to write in my diary, but I soon give up; my thoughts and feelings are as turbulent as the waters through which we are sailing.

After dinner, the captain announces that we can expect heavy seas and rough weather tonight. The impending storm has already emptied the dining room, and only a few hardy souls remain at the tables—Father, Roland, and I are among them. Father, who does not suffer from seasickness, announces that it has become a fad, created so drug companies can sell more pills. Totally at ease, he can't fathom how others might feel.

Even as children, my brothers and I had been all but forbidden to feel seasick, so I am relieved to feel no ill effects. However, it doesn't stop me from worrying. "The wind seems to be picking up," I venture timidly.

"You shouldn't blow things out of proportion," Father says. "I've been in a lot worse." Father always took a reasoned measure of things, and frowned on exaggeration or excess in emotion, action, or talk. This is one of the few times I can appreciate his attitude, for it helps to calm me. "We should get some rest now," Father suggests.

I go to my stateroom and lie down, but I don't rest. Being prone feels much more unnerving than standing or sitting. The ship rocks back and forth, and I rock with it; my feet rise up and my head dips down, then my head rises and my feet fall. One minute, the blood rushes to my head, and the next, it pools in my feet. I am uncomfortable, but I do not get sick; after all, I am my father's daughter.

"Anitra, you asleep?" I call softly, after I hear my cabin mate groan.

"What do you think?" she answers, obviously displeased at this turn of events.

I give up trying to sleep and sit up, dangling my feet over the edge of my berth. "How'd everything go?" I ask. We have not seen each other for the last few days. "Did you see the farm?"

"Yeah, I did. Seeing grandmother's place was emotional, both happy and sad. It used to be a productive farm of ten rotations, and now it's practically a wasteland." Anitra leans out to look at me, but a sudden lurch of the ship causes her to withdraw. "After fifty years of neglect, the farmhouse is barely standing. There's still no running water -- only a pump in the yard and an outhouse. Imagine, in 1990? My mother's relatives first regarded me with suspicion; they thought I'd come to reclaim the property and kick them out," Anitra says, with a hint of a laugh.

"And will you?"

"Reclaim it or kick them out? I don't know. I guess I'll first wait to see if real freedom returns."

"Even parts of Riga still have outhouses. Someone told me that some apartment buildings have a common toilet on each landing." I am glad to be talking, as sleeping would be impossible. "Don't remind me of *small houses*," I groan, using the polite Latvian term for outhouse.

Anitra disregards my request and recalls the early summers in Ile Perrot, where both our families had small cabins. "Your brother Peter and Cousin Val were the worst, sneaking up on us to peek through the heart-shaped cutout in the door."

"Yes, they were terrors, almost as bad as the spiders and other bugs. Sometimes," I confess, "I slipped into the woods across the street to pee. Luckily, their fascination didn't last too long."

"They behaved themselves whenever your Father was around. But worst of all was the need to use the outhouse at night. Inside, the scratching and the squeaking and the pitter-patter of little feet—you were never alone in there—and outside, the ghostly sighing of the wind in the trees. I was so glad when we got proper plumbing." Anitra is sitting up now, knees to her chin, white-knuckled from grasping the sides of the bed to keep steady.

I begin to feel queasy and regret having eaten, when suddenly, like a rogue wave, an intense feeling of nostalgia washes over me. In this dark, closed space, it is as if Anitra and I are once again back in our summer cabin during a summer storm, with the wind blowing and rain lashing at the windows. We share so many childhood memories, but as adults we have grown apart and live separate lives in different cities. Our children have only met once and do not really know each other.

"How come you never changed your name to Anita?" As a teenager, I had often wished I had a less European-sounding name. Ilze was as common among Latvian women of my generation as Mary or Jane was for Canadians. While a student at McGill, I had not planned to join a sorority, but to please my father, I did join a Latvian sorority, Daugaviete. Four of its seven members were called Ilze.

"Oh, I tried it, but it wasn't me."

"Did you know that Peter, in a short-lived teenage revolt, used his middle name for a surname and became Peter Roman?" I offer as a lame apology.

It is light outside when the storm finally begins to abate, and the ship's arcing motion lessens. My muscles tired and bones aching, I stretch out full length and hope to sleep for a few hours. I have a full day's sightseeing in Stockholm ahead of me. "Good night, Anitra, sleep tight. Don't let the bedbugs bite," I recite the well-known verses in Latvian.

"Good night, Little Hen," Anitra answers, using the pet name I dislike.

"Good night, Flower," I add.

So many years have passed since our parents called us Little Hen and Flower. Even more since Father found my mother, brother, and me hiding in the potato field on Anitra's grandmother's farm in Bene. Did Father do the right thing in putting his family on the ship and then returning to Riga? Would our lives have turned out differently if he had gone with us and helped us through the worst parts? I am uneasy thinking such thoughts, and I try to push them aside. The unsettled weather that is rocking the ship is also playing havoc with the usually calm waters of my mind. This pilgrimage to Latvia, during what is already being called its Third Awakening, has also served to awaken in me the need to ask questions without knowing if I have the courage to hear the answers. How did my family survive during the lost years, those same years that are also the first years of my childhood?

I manage a few hours of shut-eye, and when we dock in Stockholm, the sun shines in a blue and cloudless sky. It is as if the storm was just a bad dream. A gentle breeze stirs the flags as we say our good-byes. Although he is older than most of the other disembarking passengers, Father appears fresher, more rested. He must be the only passenger who got a good night's sleep.

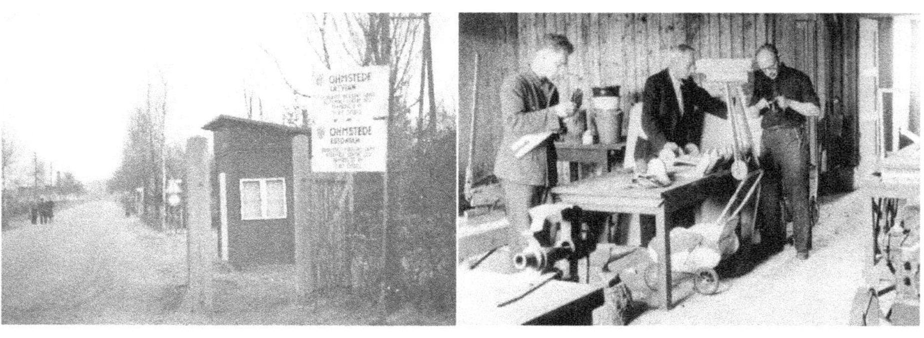

(left)1945 The main gate of Camp Ohmstede, Oldenberg, Germany.
(right)1947 The Zalite Workshop in Camp Ohmstede, Oldenberg, Germany

1947 Germany. Father, Mother, Peter and Ilze, with Uncle Valentine, Aunt Milda and cousin Valentine.

GERMANY

Seven

My trip to Latvia awakened in me a desire to know more about my past and that of my family. It did not help that we lived so far from each other and, at times, on different continents. At the earliest opportunity, I visit Father in his Florida bungalow to find some answers. We sit opposite one another, Father's paper-strewn kitchen table between us. He is meticulous in his record keeping, and I see ample evidence of his everyday life that has not yet been filed away. In orderly rows sit a calendar with important dates filled in, bills paid and bills pending, correspondence waiting to be answered, a grocery list, and squared off neatly in one corner next to the telephone, his Last Will and Testament and Living Will. Father moves some of his papers aside and sets down a clean sheet of paper in front of him. In his right hand, he holds the pencil stub that he has just retrieved from his shirt pocket. Without this magic wand, he is unable to tell his story.

"I'm not really sure what you are hoping to learn, so I guess the best place to start is the summer of 1944. You were just a baby," Father recalls, a far-off look in his eyes. "Only the truly desperate would seek uncertain safety via the dangerous, mined waters of the Baltic, but I felt it was our only option, and my work at the shipyards made it possible. So you see, that's how Mama, Peter, and you escaped to German-occupied Poland—by ship. After an uncomfortable, but—thank God—uneventful voyage, your ship landed in Danzig. I wasn't there, but you can imagine the chaos. The Germans already had their hands full with the war and with their own repatriating countrymen, and they didn't know what to do with the thousands of Baltic refugees fleeing communism. They simply were not prepared. So Mama and her two babies were shuffled from one overcrowded assembly center to another: a drafty school gymnasium, a damp church basement, and a dingy community center, all equally bad. At each shuffle, Mama, who with two little ones should have received some kind of priority treatment, was dealt the worst cards. Yes, the last to arrive got the worst spot, the leftovers. No one helped her."

The words catch in Father's throat, and he stops to examine what he has written on his paper. "You studied genetics, so you'll understand. It was survival of the fittest. To get food, even food unsuitable for your small bellies, they expected Mama to work. But how could she? She couldn't leave you alone." Father closes his eyes for a moment, and I feel bad for having stirred up these long-suppressed but still painful memories.

"Well, it was to be expected. You got sick first, then Peter. You had no proper food, no diapers, no milk, no medicine, nothing that a sick child needs. Within a week, all three of you had a fever. Then you were moved again, this time to an over-crowded refugee center in Berlin. Mama managed to send me a telegram, to my director in Riga, but he only gave it to me once we had arrived in Schichau." Father considers a moment before continuing, "I guess the s*chweinehund* was afraid I would leave, and he needed me. I'll never forget what it said, the words are engraved on my brain." Father massages his temples in small circular motions, as if trying to erase the painful image. "I still have it, filed away somewhere. The telegram is in German, dated August 15, 1944, two weeks after I put the three of you on the ship in Liepaja."

Please inform that the wife of engineer Zalite is in refugee center in Wilhelmshagen in Berlin. Frau Zalite says that both children sick and personal presence of husband is required.

"My God, it's a real miracle, then, that you found us," I say. I jot down something quickly in my notebook, but my hand is shaking and the writing is almost illegible; I will have to reconstruct it later. "The chaos and desperation in Poland and Germany must have been tremendous."

"Everywhere, but what d'you expect? A war was going on. The Third Reich was collapsing, and what didn't collapse by itself was bombed or burned to the ground. Of course, at the time, we didn't know the full story—the horrors we know now—and like everyone else, we just struggled to survive however we could. When I read Mama's telegram, I felt as if the director himself had stabbed me in my heart. The pain was so great, and I couldn't breathe. But sometimes anger has its uses; it gives you strength. I knew I had to find you. When I got over my initial shock, I started to worry. Was Mama still in Berlin? How would I find her?" Father looks at me with soft, grey eyes, magnified behind thick lenses.

"The trains were crowded, no real schedules. When a train did move, it was at a snail's pace, stop and go, stop and go. Like that." He makes a chopping motion with his hands. "Fortunately, my documents were in order, and I also had a letter from the director at the Schichau shipyards stating the reason for my travel. Although my papers didn't show it, I was half Baltic-German and spoke the language without error. You know my first words were German, spoken at my mother's knee." Father's pained expression softens, while for one brief moment, he recalls the face and voice of his mother. His face has the far away look of someone remembering a long lost love, a look I have never before observed on his face. I realized in that moment, such is the power of a mother's love; it is lifelong and transcends even death.

"Well, Daughter, Berlin was another shock. Even with a map, it was nearly impossible to find my way, but I finally managed to get to the Wilhelmshagen refugee center." Father's voice drops, until I can barely hear it.

"You found us?" I whisper.

"Yes and no. People remembered her. '*Ah, Frau Zalite. Ja, ja. Mit zwei kleine kinder?*' asked the official, consulting a long list."

"Yes, Erna and Peteris and Ilze," I repeated as clearly as I could, "I'm here to take them with me. We've been assigned a place to live."

"'Ah, Herr Zalite, let me see. They could not stay, nein. We are not a hospital….'"

"Where are they?' I demanded, trying to keep my voice calm.

"'It says here… hmm let me see, I believe they are somewhere in Küstrin (Kostrzyn).'"

"Küstrin? On the German-Polish border? I saw in him all those infuriating characteristics of a low-level official seeking his own advancement. Fortunately for us, the Nazis kept good records, and he was able to come up with the name of the woman who had appeared like an angel and taken you into her home. I had her name and the name of the district where she lived. That was all. No street name. No house number. With my heart in my hand, I made my way to Küstrin. All afternoon, I walked up and down the streets of the district, fortunately not too big, asking for the woman. But most people were close-mouthed and distrustful, unwilling to talk to a stranger. A shopkeeper finally recognized the name and directed me to the house. I'm ashamed to admit, but I cried with relief when I found you."

"Do you know the woman's name?" I ask softly.

"No, it's lost to me now, but God knows who she is."

A more demonstrative father might have hugged his daughter at such a point, but my father, the product of strict upbringing, sits at the table, hands crossed in front of him, unable to show his true feelings. The habits of a lifetime are hard to overcome.

"Whatever her leanings, she was a good woman," I say. "It takes more than war to erase basic human kindness."

"She may have been kind, but she was no pushover. It was getting dark, and you were too sick to travel, but she told me I could not stay, that I must find another place to sleep. So I soon found myself out on the street, but feeling somewhat relieved. Dead tired, I trudged along, looking for a place to spend the night. I wasn't too worried. I had some money, could speak the language, and carried a certificate allowing me to move about. I found a hotel, but when I showed the clerk my Latvian passport, he called me an *Auslander* and kicked me out into the street like a stray dog! That's the kindness of strangers for you," says Father.

"Why'd he do that?"

"Following rules, I guess. No room at the inn for non-Germans. Maybe he was just keeping his scarce rooms for his fellow Germans. Of course, he never stopped to think that, like him, I was just trying to survive. All I could do then was go back to Schichau and return for you when you were well enough to travel."

I suggest that we take a little break so that I can prepare a fresh batch of juice. Out in the back yard, the lawn consists of clumps of grass protruding from the sandy soil, but Father's fruit trees are heavy with ripe oranges just waiting to be picked. I go outside into the welcome sunshine and pick a basketful, wash them, and squeeze a dozen. I pour myself a glass and hand another to Father. The juice is still warm from the sun, and I drink it down in one go. I have never tasted anything so delicious. Father takes his time, and we talk of other things until he is ready to resume his story.

"As soon as I arrived back at Schichau, I reported to the director. After signing some documents, he showed me to my new desk. I was just getting my bearings when the sirens started, and along with everyone else, I hurried to the shelter. Oh, how I hated that now-familiar sound. Well, that same day, my first at Schichau, the Allies started to bomb Danzig and had the shipyards in their sights. The bunker shook and rattled, and the dust settled on us like snow. It was hard to breathe. Several hours later we emerged in one piece, but badly shaken. Schichau was gone. Kaput. Gone. All that remained was twisted steel and rubble. Believe me, it looked like the end of the world, and I could see the fires of hell, all orange flames and black smoke. I tied my handkerchief over my face and picked my way slowly through the debris, the broken glass crunching underfoot like gravel. When I finally found the director, he told me he had no choice but to release me from my obligation. I was free to find other work. Free! Hah! I was free to starve or die in the street. What did it matter to him? I needed work, I told him. I needed a place to live, food coupons. Without work, I could not take care of my family."

"You never told us anything, Dad. Nothing. All the years we were growing up." I don't mean for it to sound like an accusation.

"What should I have said? That war is hell? Or that life is hard? That we were like dry leaves scattered about by the winds of war? Does that sound any better? No, no, a child doesn't want to hear things like that from her father."

"But it would have explained so much."

"Explained what? I always provided for my family. You and your brothers had everything—a home, food, school." Father shifts in his chair and sighs, letting go of his anger. "Well, I'm telling you now. Isn't that good enough?" It is obvious that this stirring up of past, painful memories is causing both of us a lot of anguish. He suddenly looks small and powerless, and I regret having questioned him.

"Should I go on, or have you heard enough?"

"Please, Dad, go on."

"Well, I went to Swinemünde (Swinoujscie) and found work in a small, privately-owned shipyard, Willi Klotz. To work was to stay alive, and it was my profession that saved us. A good marine engineer in wartime is always in demand, like a beautiful woman at a ball." A faint smile lifts the corners of Father's lips. "There's no shortage of dance partners. Ships get damaged and have to be rebuilt, refitted, made seaworthy in a hurry, and sent back out. By this time, many German engineers had been conscripted into the army. Luckily, being Latvian and not German, I wasn't called up. As soon as I was hired at Willi Klotz, I visited city hall and was assigned an empty apartment near the seaside, next door to a cemetery. Good, I thought, so Mama can bury me with little trouble. My heart pains were getting worse, more frequent now—it was all that stress, running from one place to another."

"That's from rheumatic fever, isn't it?" I ask.

"Yes, I came down with rheumatic fever in my youth, and it left scars on my heart. The house at the seaside was not ideal: it was damp and drafty, and the wind that blew relentlessly in from the sea rattled the windows something awful. Instead of feeling that my life was back on track, I was disturbed by my own dark thoughts...," Father pauses, but his eyes do not meet my gaze. "I thought 'what's the use' and 'when will this nightmare end,' thoughts I had no business thinking. I pulled on my galoshes and gloves—I'd never removed my hat and coat—and trudged along the shore. Though the sea was wild, the walk calmed me. It was a familiar sea, the same amber coast that stretched north to Liepaja, then to Ventspils and curved around Kolkas rags to Riga. I longed to sail home, but the winds and tides of war were against me. It was impossible to go back. Calmer now, I went back inside, lit a small fire, and was finally able to get some rest."

"My poor, brave Dad," is all I manage to say.

Father clears his throat and looks at me, considering. "Yes, well, no braver than most. A few weeks later, I got news that Mama was better and could travel, so I borrowed a truck from the shipyard and drove to Küstrin. And so, the four of us returned to Swinemünde, not exactly the safest place to live. Swinemünde, you might know, was the jumping-off point for the Luftwaffe bombing sorties to London. But they say you can get used to anything. After a while, I didn't even bother to look up when I heard the roar of airplanes overhead."

"Swinemünde, isn't that where I was christened?" I ask. Growing up, I had studied the few small black and white snapshots in our album taken at my christening, searching for clues about the child in the white dress. I learn little from the photos; I am just a ghostly white blur in my mother's lap.

"Yes, by a Latvian minister who was also a refugee. Afterward, we even managed a little celebration with a few friends." Father shakes his head in disbelief, "I'd forgotten, it was all so long ago."

"For a few brief months, our lives were almost normal. I went to work, and Mama looked after you and Peter. A good thing, too, since we needed time to recover. Ilzite, your eyes were sunken, and your bones stuck out like a ship's ribbing. You needed proper food and vitamins, but as we had neither, we made do with what was available in that last terrible winter of the war. Mama's sister Elza and her three children, along with Omite, were in Küstrin, to the south of us, but Karlis stayed in Berlin, where the Latvian press was still operating. That Karlis, a poet and idealist. I'm still amazed to this day how someone can feed his family using only words and ideas."

"Sure it's possible. Sometimes words can be as effective as bullets," I add.

"True, true, but the results of my work are concrete, useful." Father taps the table with his fingers to emphasize his words. "Anyway, I sent a letter to Elza asking for Omite's help, and I'm grateful she came. Carrots and onions, that's all there was. Every morning Omite grated carrots and onions and squeezed out the juice, which she then spooned into your mouth."

I must have made a face, but Father went on. "She had a way of distracting you with songs and funny noises until the bowl was empty." Father chuckles softly, and the worry lines across his forehead momentarily disappear. "The carrots turned your skin orange, and the onions gave you gas, but you got better."

How lovable I must have been, I thought, a sallow-skinned, farting baby!

"The other challenge we faced that winter was to keep warm in that old, drafty house by the sea. To supplement the ridiculously small amount of coal that was my allotment, I brought extra coal home from the shipyards in my briefcase. 'Good, I see you've brought home work again,' Mama would say, almost merrily, as I washed the black soot from my fingers. I admit it to you now, but it was not something I approved of then. Because I spoke both Russian and German, the director at Willi Klotz put me in charge of a group of about a hundred workers, mostly Polish and Russian. They were a sickly, gaunt, miserably dressed lot of men whose names I never learned. Ruski 75 or Polski 38, that's how I knew them." Father raises his hands to his face and after removing his bifocals, rubs his eyes as though trying to erase an image from his brain. "Here I was, without a country, with barely enough to eat, but when I looked at them, my heart burst. Compared to them, we were lucky. I had work, a place to live. We were together. We celebrated a Christmas of sorts, then the New Year, and your first birthday." Father scratches his head, then smoothes down non-existent hair. "Mama asked me if I could bring a lump of lead home from the shipyards, just so we could see what the future had in store for us. So, on New Year's Eve, I heated it up in a tin can and poured the molten lead into a cup of cold water where, with a sizzle that sounded very much like a sigh, it solidified. All three of us, Mama, Omite and I, peered into the cup at the strange shape curled up at the bottom. It meant nothing to me, but Omite, she was the one who could see things in the lead."

"I always thought you didn't believe in fortune-telling, just the power of logic."

"Of course, I don't believe in all that hocus-pocus. That night, it was really more of a game. I don't remember now what exactly it was that Omite saw, but it must have been good news since we all survived."

"Things weren't going well for Hitler and his Wermacht, and every day, the Allied front kept getting closer, moving west. I really was afraid of being sandwiched again between the Germans and the Russians, like in Latvia. Then in early 1945, my worst fears were realized. Instead of spring showers, Allied bombs rained down on Swinemünde. I was at work when the sirens sounded and could go into a bunker, but Mama was at home in the house by the sea, next to the graveyard. Mama and Omite described to me later how a stray bomb woke the dead, and whole skeletons leaped into the air from their graves before landing again on the frozen earth, a tangle of bones. So, you can see, Daughter, that war is hell, even for the dead." Father savours his little joke for a while; it breaks the unbearable tension of his story. I have nothing to say and for a moment, write nothing. "The windows of our house were shattered, but miraculously, my little family was unhurt."

"Not hurt, only shell-shocked," I remind Father, who looks at me as if he doesn't understand what I'm saying. Perhaps, like seasickness, he doesn't believe in being shell-shocked, either. "Now, I get it. That's why Peter and I stuck our heads between our legs, even in Sweden, when we heard the drone of an airplane overhead."

"Do you want me to go on?"

"Please, yes."

"Luckily, even though shipyards are beacons for bombs, Willi Klotz didn't get a direct hit. I emerged from the bunker a bit dazed, and all around me, Swinemünde burned like the fires of hell, like Jelgava earlier, maybe like Moscow, when I was ten. I rushed home with my heart in my mouth, my tongue hanging out, afraid of what I would find. As I said, you weren't hurt."

"We needed to move west, always west. It was a refrain in my head, like a Latvian *daina*. We gathered up a few belongings and crossed by ferry to Ahlbeck to stay with the Ullises. Poor Omite; she never had sea legs. She was green as a cucumber, even before the ferry left its moorings. For a while, we stayed with them, Arturs, a very pregnant Irma, and the little boy, Janis."

Good grief, another Janis, I think, trying to count them in my head, but I don't dare interrupt.

"Irma was Mama's foster sister, and also our Peter's godmother, not a blood relative at all, but as close as a sister could be. Arturs Ullis had something of the Wild West in him from watching too many films, I guess. I sometimes called him a cowboy, but he referred to himself as an entrepreneur."

Father reaches back in his memory to retrieve an interesting tidbit that makes him smile. "Mama, Elza, and Irma—that was quite a formidable threesome. When I was courting your mother, I had to win all three of them over before she would say yes. Anyway, Ullis was one of those go-getters, who could convince you that black was white and white, black. He had a knack for profiting from a bad situation. For my part, I don't believe in miracles—God gave us brains so that we could do what was needed, help ourselves—but somehow, cowboy Ullis had driven his truck, with its Latvian plates all the way from Latvia, south through Lithuania, across Kaliningrad, and into occupied Poland." Father makes a map with his pencil as he speaks. "Would you believe he bribed his way past checkpoints and across borders, with bottles of vodka! Those bottles were good for petrol, too."

"With the city in ruins, Willi Klotz couldn't continue in Swinemünde, so he decided to close shop and evacuate to Libeke (Lubeck), where he hoped to continue a small branch of his shipyard. He asked me to take charge of the ship, along with his personal belongings. I said yes and was entrusted with the ship's papers and the necessary travel documents. I was to deliver the ship to his colleagues in Libeke. It was a reasonable plan, not too dangerous, I thought.

"When I asked Ullis to take my family with him in his truck and meet me in Libeke, he thought about it for a moment, then grabbed me by both shoulders. 'Jani!' he shouted, spittle landing on my glasses, 'This is it! Our chance! You've got the papers! Forget about Willi Klotz and Libeke. Think about the future! You're a sailor, aren't you? Let's hightail it across the Baltic to Sweden!'"

"'Arturs, don't talk crazy,' I said, and pushed him away. It's funny; we each thought the other crazy and almost came to blows. But what he was proposing was illegal, as well as dangerous. I'm no pirate, and I can't just steal a ship. Willi Klotz trusted me, and I'd promised to deliver it." Father laughs, his face slightly flushed. "That was Ullis."

"Fortunately, Ullis calmed down, and when he saw I'd never go along with his crazy scheme, he agreed to take you to Libeke. It was our only option, I thought, to keep moving west."

"With God's help, the ship steamed safely into Libeke harbour, and Ullis was there with his truck, ready to load it up with Willi Klotz's food and such. My first thought had been 'how nice of Arturs to meet me at the dock,' but when he charged up the gangplank, and started to help himself, I had to call for help. I tried to block his way, but he pushed me aside as if I was nobody. 'Come, come, Jani, be reasonable, the children need food.' 'Go to hell,' I said. 'Don't be such a miser,' he said, 'we're hungry.' I couldn't allow it. The owner had entrusted me with his property, and I'd given my word. 'That's not mine to give away,' I shouted, trying to wrestle a sack out of his hand. When he saw he was outnumbered, he backed off, but ever after there was a cloud over our friendship, though we never spoke of that incident again. Years later, I told Mama about it, because she wanted to know why I couldn't get along with Arturs Ullis."

"We stayed together in Libeke until it was taken by the Allies. And when the Allied soldiers advanced, Arturs and I followed behind the US convoy in his battered truck with the Latvian license plates and a small Latvian flag flying. We were relieved the long war was finally over. When the convoy stopped for the night in a small German town, we stopped too. The locals hung white sheets out their windows to signify their surrender. It was pretty spooky, let me tell you. One American soldier making the rounds noticed our truck, 'Hey Buddy, whacha think you're doin'?' Arturs heard the word *buddy* and offered his hand. Then we were searched like common criminals. The soldier took my pocket knife."

"That's when we were taken to Camp Ohmstede?" I ask, trying to rush to the end of Father's terrible story. I want to hear the "and they all lived happily ever after" ending.

"Soon. But first, we were processed like cattle in an overcrowded camp in Hamburg. Then we were sent to Camp Ohmstede in Oldenburg, in the British-controlled sector. The Ullis family stayed in Hamburg, where Irma gave birth to Karlis. That's how they ended up in the American zone. Funny, isn't it? Arturs Ullis did so want to see the American west, and that's where he eventually ended up: in Oregon. Finally, our future could begin, but I wasn't optimistic. I felt I'd already lived more than a lifetime and that mostly in hardship. I was tired to my bones. And for the very first time in my life, I had no job."

The effort of remembering and speaking tires Father, and he goes to lie down. I am left to mull over what he has just told me, and to try to make sense of my scribbled notes.

Eight

Our story is not unique; there are as many stories as there are victims of war. However, knowing it means more to me than I ever thought it would. I know, too, that our story did not end there. When the war ended and the Allied armies took control of a defeated Germany, they gathered up the stateless refugees who had washed up there, like flotsam after a shipwreck, and placed them in displaced persons camps. The refugees who ended up in the British zone, like us, eventually had the option of resettling in England or Canada, while those who ended up in the American zone had the opportunity to immigrate to the United States. I think back to our time aboard the *Baltic Star* and to what Aunt Elza told me about her family's escape from war-torn Latvia.

***

Aunt Elza's voice is soft, but she still possesses the penetrating gaze that looks like it could etch glass. "That same summer of 1944, when you were in Bene, Karlis sent the children and me to stay with his relatives in the countryside. That's how I came to be in Zante near Tukums while he finished up in Riga. Latvia, of course, was falling to the Soviets, and like many others, we'd decided to leave. But I so wanted to see Riga one more time before we left. Who knew when we'd be able to return?" Elza squares her shoulders as she admits she was wrong. "Of course, looking back, there's no justifying my foolish act; Karlis made that perfectly clear. Jelgava had already fallen, and the Russians were dug in not ten kilometers from Zante. The trains were no longer running, but I managed to beg a ride on a truck carrying farm goods to Riga. Like the innocent I was, I went straight to my husband's office to get the key to our apartment. I thought he'd be glad to see me, but when Karlis saw me, he turned white as a sheet of paper. 'You left the children alone?' he almost shouted. I just sat there and cried, while he called around, trying to find a way to get me back to Zante."

"Well, you can imagine our surprise when, just then, Arturs Ullis showed up at Karlis's office to say good-bye. He said he was heading north to wait out the war in the forests of Estonia, where he was certain there would never be a front. I could almost see the wheels turning in my husband's brain when he heard this. 'Forget Estonia, go to Kurzeme, to the forests of Dundaga,' Karlis advised. Elza can go with you part way; she needs to get back to Zante. At first, Arturs was not convinced, but Karlis's powers of persuasion can be quite something, and Arturs left the office to look into it."

Elza shakes her head as she recalls her surprise. "Somehow, Arturs managed to obtain the necessary travel permit, but in exchange, had to give a ride to two women of rather loose morals."

"Prostitutes?" I ask.

"Something like that, I guess," Elza shrugs. "And so we set out quite comfortably, in a truck loaded with odd bits of furniture and some food – loaves of black bread, salt pork and a sack of sugar that came from goodness knows where – and also a wooden barrel filled with liquor and some empty bottles and jars. I climbed up and sat beside a pregnant Irma and her two-year-old Janis: the two women on the battered couch in the back. At each checkpoint Arturs got down from the truck with a bottle or two of vodka in his pockets and arranged for our passage, and so it went the whole sleepless night. Toward morning, Irma started to moan, but soon she was in agony. 'The baby's coming!' she cried. 'It's not your time yet,' Arturs almost yells, but Irma kept on insisting it was the real thing. What could I do? They headed for the nearest hospital, and I got out to walk the rest of the way to Zante. We were out in the country and the moon had set, so you can imagine how black the night. Toward morning, I managed to get a ride part way with an old man on his horse-driven cart. Then I walked the last twenty or so kilometers. A few days later, Karlis arrived from Riga with some of our winter clothing from the apartment. Not long after, he drove us, along with Omite who insisted on coming along to help, to Liepaja, where we boarded a ship to Danzig."

"That's what we did too," I tell her, and there is no need to elaborate.

"Well, Karlis returned to Riga to see to the dismantling and packing up of the presses. The newspaper, too, was being evacuated to Germany." Elza sighs, "I never did get to see our apartment one last time." In her eyes, many years later, this last bit is the really sad part of her story.

***

The next morning, I wake to find Father sitting at the kitchen table, sorting through a batch of yellowed papers. "Good morning," I say, and pour myself a cup of coffee. "What do you have there?" I ask.

"I didn't sleep much last night and then remembered I had these," he says, holding up a yellowed copy of the Camp Ohmstede newsletter that threatens to disintegrate in his hands.

My whole life has been lived within the shadow of events that are branded on my subconscious and that have forged my personality, events that happened before I was born and that I know little about. I go to my room and return with my notebook, ready for the moment when Father starts to reminisce.

***

"Our euphoria at war's end was short-lived. We had survived, but now what? We had lost everything, including our homeland, and were now stateless refugees in a country reviled by the world and destroyed by war. As we waited in a stinking, overcrowded assembly center to be processed like fish in a canning factory, I actually believed that it would be a relief to settle down somewhere for a while, even if that somewhere was a refugee camp. It didn't take long for the relief to turn into despair."

"We were assigned to Camp 224/F in Oldenburg, the British zone. Camp Ohmstede, as it came to be called, was a collection of long, low, wooden barracks lacking the most basic comforts. Originally thrown up by the Third Reich to house its slave workers from Poland and Russia, in 1945, it was turned into a displaced person's camp for Latvian refugees. In a final act of protest before they left, the now-free slave laborers had destroyed what they could and had smeared the walls with their own watery feces or a paste of dirt and urine. Some who were strong enough, had ripped apart the mattresses and scattered the straw, so that it stuck to the walls, looking like small, fuzzy animals."

"We'd been assigned to Barrack 49. The stench was unbearable, and both Omite and Mama covered their faces with their scarves and tried not to breathe. In a place like that, the future looked hopeless. Did we survive the war only to end up like this, I wondered? Like a big, rumbling avalanche, the years of war had brought everyone to the same, miserable, muddied level. Mama broke down, and for the longest time, would not be comforted."

"Each ramshackle building was a warren of rooms with board walls, some further divided by a dingy sheet or a tattered blanket. Bunk beds, a rough board table, a small wooden cupboard, and a few nails for hanging clothes were the only furnishings. Until UNRRA (United Nations Relief and Rehabilitation Administration) provided us with DDT powder, we shared the straw mattresses with other living things—fleas, bed bugs, and lice—although it was hard to tell what we brought with us, and what we inherited from the former occupants."

"The wire fencing surrounding the camp and its guarded entrance gave the appearance of a prison, but the inmates were free to come and go. Although a few brave souls, mostly men, ventured beyond the gate, they always came back. There was nowhere for them to go. Everything they now owned was here. Behind them, their escape route to the west was littered with discarded suitcases too heavy to carry. Family silver, crystal, and other keepsakes packed in haste had been abandoned by the roadside or in temporary shelters. Strangers had already moved into their abandoned houses and apartments."

"The camp sprawled uneasily on the edge of a dark pine forest, not far from a bombed-out factory. Every day during 1945, more Latvian refugees arrived at Camp Ohmstede, but few left. Some had been stuck in German-occupied Poland and others, when they realized they had unknowingly ended up in the Russian-controlled sector, immediately claimed refugee status and begged to be taken elsewhere."

"At war's end, other relatives had ended up in various parts of Germany. My brother, Juris, together with Zenija and their two daughters, Silvija and Biruta, were in Halle. Juris's son, Valters, had been working as an engineering technician in southeastern Germany and had been aboard a train on the way to a new work assignment when the war ended. The Third Reich collapsed, and the trains stopped running. Valters was stranded in Russian-controlled territory with no desire to remain there. Of course, he wanted to be reunited with his father in Halle, which was in American hands. But Halle lay hundreds of kilometers distant, and there was no public transport. Not a passenger train, bus, or car was circulating, not even a bicycle. For several days, the whole country was paralyzed, like that eerie calm right after a storm. Twenty-year-old Valters started to walk. After a few days, he was able to hop a freight train or thumb a ride on a truck, but mostly he walked. It took him one week to get to Halle. When he arrived, he found that his father was just settling his wife and daughters into the apartment that had been assigned to them by the Americans. But days later, they learned that Halle and its surroundings would be turned over to the Russians. "If I wanted to grovel under the Soviet boot, I would have stayed home in Latvia!" bellowed Juris to no one in particular. Fortunately, the Americans were understanding and offered to transport the refugees who did not want to stay in Halle to the American zone. Of course, they chose the American zone. Juris's family finally ended up living in an overcrowded apartment complex in Mannheim, south of Frankfurt."

***

Bit by bit, I am able to pull together the threads of a life that had unraveled. Visit by visit, I manage to tease out the tangled ball that makes up my story and make some sense of it. It doesn't happen all at once; neither Father nor I like to dwell solely on the past. Instead, I learn how to play *Zolite* and accompany him to his once-a-week card game, and later, replace him whenever he is not feeling well. On other days, we walk along the boardwalk to the end of the pier, to watch the fishermen. Later, back at home, I write down what I have learned.

***

Aunt Elza and Karlis Rabacs and their three children, Mara, Janis, and Maija, were reasonably lucky. They landed in a camp in Kleinkotz, in the American zone. At the end of 1944, the Latvian presses had been evacuated to Berlin, where they continued to operate. Uncle Karlis had been living and working in Berlin, while his wife and children lived in Küstrin, on the Polish-German border. With the war front only sixteen kilometers away, Uncle Karlis returned to Küstrin to evacuate his family to Berlin. The train did not run to Küstrin anymore, but my uncle found a child's sled. With the sound of shelling in the distance and night falling, he piled his three children and as many of their belongings as he could onto the sled and, together with Elza, they pulled it to the next town, where they were able to board a train to Berlin. In Berlin, the Rabacs family boarded with a German widow, and Uncle Karlis continued to work at the newspaper. Their lives were far from peaceful, as Berlin came under frequent Allied attack. During one air raid, Karlis's newspaper building took a direct hit, killing one person in the basement shelter where they were huddled. Rubble blocked the exit, and their only recourse was to clamber out through the coal chute. Karlis no longer had any work, and since it was not safe to stay in Berlin, he decided to travel south, along with a dozen other Latvian families. They ended up in Bavaria, in a small village near the Austrian border, where each farmhouse sheltered a Lativan family until the war ended.

Father's eldest sister, Edite Gutmanis, a widow, had wisely chosen to remain in Denmark with her two daughters, Rita and Milda, and they escaped most of the horror and devastation that the others experienced. Another sister Elizabete Svenne and her husband, Adolfs, and their three children managed to flee to the relative safety of the Danish countryside and meet up with Aunt Edite. Father's youngest sister, Milda Rutkis, her husband, Valentins, and their two children ended up in the British zone. They had been refugees in Danzig in December 1944 when Aunt Milda went into labour. With the scream of air raid sirens and exploding bombs drowning out her cries of pain, Milda gave birth to Irene. They, too, spent several years—the lost years, Aunt Milda called them—in DP camps in Germany, before they were granted visas and passage to England.

While my extended family and the other refugees marked time and despaired about their futures, world leaders set to work restoring order out of the chaos of war. The hastily formed UNRRA was charged with caring for hundreds of thousands of sick, hungry, frightened, depressed, stateless people. It was a monumental task. One official declared, "It was the greatest humanitarian project ever undertaken, and it was set up almost overnight."

Initially, the lack of planning and the accompanying urgency made the task seem hopeless. The UNRRA had few employees, and no guidelines or precedents existed for dealing with such diverse peoples in such great numbers. The refugees and officials spoke no common language and could not even understand each other. At first, the refugees distrusted the UNRRA officials; they could not believe that anyone would actually help them. The officials saw the refugees as dirty and scheming and unwilling to help themselves. In truth, the displaced persons were like wells run dry; they had exhausted their physical and mental reserves. This situation was made worse by the fact that even though camp personnel were now civilians, nearly all had fought in the war, and the UNRRA allowed them to continue to wear their military uniforms. The sight of so many "soldiers" was upsetting to the refugees.

In Ohmstede, the camp director, Mr. Delafontaine, proudly wore his Canadian Battle Dress. This provided him with some extra authority, but he and other camp officials still had to deal with the frightened, wary camp inmates who at first refused to cooperate. It was an unavoidable impasse; their respective goals clashed. The UNRRA's prime directive was to repatriate the displaced persons as quickly as possible, and although some wanted to return home, most Latvians did not. The Latvian DPs flatly rejected the UNRRA's offers of repatriation; they preferred to resettle in the west.

Latvia, which had bounced back and forth between the Soviets and the Germans, had once again landed in Soviet hands, and this time the Soviets had no intention of letting go. For years, the Soviets had coveted the Baltic coast and its jewels, the Gulf of Riga and the ice-free year-round, western ports of Ventspils and Liepaja. Now they possessed them. Latvians had not forgotten the Soviet atrocities, especially The Horror Year, and they now feared the negative consequences of returning to their communist-controlled homeland. Imprisonment, deportation, and possible execution awaited many of them if they returned. They knew how easy it was for someone to disappear forever in the vast Siberian taiga, never to be heard from again. It had happened to President Kārlis Ulmanis, who had been deported in July 1940 by the Soviet authorities. At best, and it was not a happy thought, returning Latvians would be forced to live as second-class citizens, become russified, slowly turning red like lobsters in hot water.

At war's end, the USSR claimed the Latvians and other East Europeans as Soviet citizens. "They must return," they exhorted. "They are our people."

The Latvians thought otherwise. They were Balts, not Slavs or Russians, and so they resisted repatriation. They felt betrayed when, according to a Yalta agreement, the British and Americans pledged to separate the supposed Soviet citizens and arrange for their expeditious repatriation. But in a fortunate turn of events, despite the fact that Latvia was not a member of the United Nations, the Western Allies and the UNRRA treated Latvian nationals as though they did enjoy UN status.

Even so, rumours constantly circulated throughout the drafty shacks of Camp Ohmstede. These were hard to dispel, since the camp officials did not speak Latvian, and only a few DPs spoke English or understood its nuances. As well, the DPs complained to each other that the British officials looked down on them and thought them ignorant, although many were well-educated professionals: doctors, scientists, engineers, ministers, and lawyers. Now, in the relative safety of Camp Ohmstede, they refused to cooperate. In an attempt to create order, UNRRA officials handed out leaflets outlining camp regulations and timetables. The camp inmates could not read them, but found the leaflets handy for stuffing into worn-out shoes or clothes. The fear of being forcibly repatriated sent some men into hiding in the nearby woods, but cold and hunger soon forced them to return to camp. Others threatened suicide. On occasion, women responded to talks of repatriation by becoming hysterical. Several violent clashes took place between groups of Latvians and the military police. The UNRRA officials finally relented when it became clear that British and US troops might refuse to carry out certain repatriation orders.

It took several weeks before some level of trust was established, and the camp ran more smoothly. But there were few comforts. There was a shortage of nearly everything—soap, shoes, clothes, bedding, fruit, and meat—except DDT. It was sprinkled liberally onto beds and into clothing, until clouds of the fine powder stuck to skin and hair and entered the lungs.

The refugees had to deal not only with lice and bedbugs, but also with other, more serious afflictions, and children were especially vulnerable. When Peter became ill with diphtheria, Mother feared the worst. Years ago, her baby brother had succumbed to this dreaded illness. "Your boy is very ill and must go to the infirmary," the doctor advised. It sounded like a death sentence. Both Omite and Father tried to comfort Mother, but she could not be consoled until Peter's crisis had passed, and he was back with us in the barracks.

"Mama," Father said one evening, "I'm already planning the words in my head, so that when I get some letter paper from the Red Cross, I'll write immediately to my former director in Sweden. He might be able to help." He had lost weight, and his usually round face looked long and thin. Worry lines were now etched across his broad forehead, and dark circles shadowed his eyes.

Mother nodded, but didn't give Father's plan much hope. Still, she allowed herself to admit that if it were impossible to return to Latvia, she could think of no better place than Sweden. Their first happy years as a married couple had been spent in Göteborg. Her husband brooded too much, she felt, so she tried a cheerful note. "Today, we were promised some seeds to start a garden. Do you think we'll be here long enough to harvest anything?" In those days Mother did not smile often, and if she did, only her mouth smiled, not her eyes. She sighed often, and her sighs were sadder than words could ever be. Her hair, still thick and brown, had lost its lustre, and was shot through with white strands; her skin was still smooth and soft, but ghostly pale. Mother's eyes were a startling blue, the colour of the sky on a clear day. Even in the camp, tired and ill and dressed in donated clothing, she remained beautiful.

"Good. Fresh air and sunshine will help you. You see, Mama, things are already looking up." He expressed an optimism he didn't feel. "So you must get stronger, eat more. We're all counting on you."

Mother dutifully planted and tended a small patch of earth behind the barracks. But, as she worked, she could not help but hope that the harvest would be left to others, that she and her family would be back in Latvia by then, or second best, in Sweden. Even now, she thought, tasting gall in her mouth, the Bolsheviks in Bene must be growing fat on the potatoes she had worked so hard to sow and had to leave behind.

As soon as the camp inmates reconciled themselves to the fact that they would not be removed against their will, they focused on other, immediate concerns. It was too early to think about the future, which many believed would not come anyway. My parents both believed they would not last long and worried about their children.

Food was always on everyone's mind. In a defeated Germany, food was scarce and only obtainable with ration coupons, but the camp inmates did not receive any such coupons. Those with money in their pockets found it nearly useless; there was nothing to buy. Once the camp was running more smoothly, some of the DPs were hired as drivers, cooks, or teachers. They received payment in kind; the most desirable and valuable payments were cigarettes and coffee, for which the local farmers could be persuaded to part with meat, fruit, or eggs.

Except for vague promises, the refugees had little information, and they had long since stopped believing in promises. Months had passed, and they were still stuck in Camp Ohmstede. They worried that the United Nations was growing tired, that it was running out of money, even that it was being duped by the more cunning Soviets. They feared that outside help could be as fickle as the spring sunshine that warms one moment then disappears behind a cloud. Many found it hard to be idle and searched about for something to pass the time or to better their situation.

Representatives of the International Red Cross arrived regularly, bringing with them donated clothing, magazines, books, and board games. Sometimes they distributed candy bars or cigarettes. With time, it became possible to search for relatives at other camps: From Abele and Apse, all the way to Zalite and Zeltakmens. Father located his brother, Juris, in a Mannheim DP camp and Mother's sister Elza in a camp in Lauingen, both in the American zone. Consulting the Red Cross lists, he found his sister Milda's name and those of friends and colleagues. One gloomy day was brightened by the arrival of a letter from Denmark, written by his sisters Edite and Elizabeth. "Hurrah! Hurrah! Our Hans is safe," they wrote, and the words almost leapt off the page with joy. Hans was Father's childhood name, a short form of Johannes.

The UNRRA officials' success rate dropped dramatically once they had repatriated the refugees who were willing to return to their own countries. Still under orders to empty the camps, many officials sincerely believed the DPs should return to their homelands. After all, the war had ended, and some sort of order should be restored. But the resistance put up by the Latvians in Camp Ohmstede surprised them, so they changed their tactics from bullying to persuasion. Repatriation officers spoke at assemblies, pleading in voices as smooth as butter and as sweet as honey, with their lips curled into false smiles.

"The UNRRA offers you free passage, absolutely gratis, with no cost to you whatsoever. The International Red Cross will escort you and your family safely back to Latvia. Just imagine for a moment, how it would be to smell the sweet aromas of home and hear familiar birds singing in the apple trees. The motherland longs for her most able, distinguished citizens to return to her bosom," cried one particularly eloquent speaker, as he looked out on a sea of broken humanity.

"He's a dangerous one, an agent provocateur," Father said to Mother once they were back in their room. "Did you see how his eyes shifted constantly around the room, afraid to meet anyone else's?"

"Sh, sh, Jani," admonished Mother, pressing a finger to her closed lips. The paper thin wall that separated their room from their neighbour's could not be counted on to give them privacy, and someone could be listening, ready to denounce a fellow Latvian for their own personal gain. The single, overhead bulb cast harsh shadows on Mother's face, making her look older than she was. They described to Omite what the officials had said, keeping their voices to a whisper, so as not to be overheard. Omite surprised them by saying it was something to consider.

"I know how hard it's been for all of us," Father said, "but we've got to be patient and wait for the right opportunity. It'll come. I guarantee it. Right now, it's much too dangerous to even think of going back; why, my name could be on some list made up by the red dogs."

"You've done nothing wrong. You didn't take up arms against them like Janis," Mother whispered. Her brother was constantly on her mind, and she feared for his safety. "You're just an engineer, doing what you were told." Little Peter coughed, sat up halfway, and fell back down again, still asleep. Mother got up from her chair to pull up his covers; he didn't carry any extra fat and, after his illness, became easily chilled.

"True. But those who wish me ill might take my work in the shipyards as support for the German war machine. You know it was essential for our survival." When Father removed his thick glasses to rub his eyes, Mother could see the dark circles underneath. He looked more tired than usual and often complained of shortness of breath and pain in his chest. Mother worried about him as much as she did about the children.

Not only did she love him, she relied upon him. Without her husband's cleverness and resourcefulness, they would be lost.

Omite spoke up to agree with Father. "You only did what you had to, to feed your family and give them shelter."

Father nodded and cast an appreciative glance at his mother-in-law. She had been a godsend for Erna and the children, a true angel of mercy. "Still, many seemed convinced by this *zhulik* tonight; his Latvian was better than the others'. I wonder just how many will accept his offer. Clever touch that, threatening that the UNRRA might run out of funds and not be able to offer such a generous package in the future." Father's voice grew loud with annoyance, and Mother put a finger to her lips to remind him of the thin walls.

"I've been thinking of returning home to Aleksandris," said Omite to shocked silence. "I'm tired of being passed around like a counterfeit coin nobody wants."

"I don't think we should talk about this now. It's late, and we're all tired," Father declared, and rose from his chair.

Mother didn't move. "I know how you feel," she said, "Papiņš is all alone."

"Oh, if only the soldiers hadn't destroyed our kiosk, we might still have some money coming in."

"Don't think about that now," said Mother.

Father paused at the door before making his trip to the outhouse, "Criminal, that's what it was. But to this day, I don't know if it was Erna herself who stole my heart or your delicious ice cream," Father teased, trying to lighten the mood.

The next morning, Father stirred his porridge and broached the subject again. "Marta, I've been thinking," he said, "and I do some of my best thinking at night. Maybe you should consider returning, but only under certain conditions."

Mother stared at Father, the spoon suspended halfway to her lips, then turned to look at her mother. She seemed relieved that there would be no argument between these two strong-willed people, her husband and her mother, but she was torn between wanting her mother to stay with them and the honest belief that it would be better for her to return home. "Yes, yes. Papiņš and Janis. They must be wondering what's happened to us."

"I'm old, sixty-four. It's more than a normal lifetime," said Omite. Her blue eyes had a faraway look, as if she could see all the way back to Latvia. "I want to die in my own bed. Yes, and then sleep for eternity with the light, sandy earth of home spread over me like a blanket. But before all that I want to be there to welcome Janis, God help him, when he returns."

"You know it's not good to get your hopes up too much, just leads to bigger disappointment." Father raised his arms in a gesture of helplessness and dropped them again to the table. He didn't like it when women got too emotional. Sticking to just the facts kept everything simpler.

"You can see for yourself. Hope is all we have, nothing else," Omite said.

"Well, I guess that smooth talking *zhulik* can put another notch on his belt," Father said. "For us, Mama, our hope is here, such as it is. We voted with our feet, and that's enough for the Bolsheviks to know whose side we're on."

"You're right, of course, Jani." She knew it was useless to argue with her husband, and maybe he was right. "It's just so hard to think I might never see Papiņš or my brother, ever." Mother's eyes filled with tears that ran unheeded down her sunken cheeks.

Omite lifted her hand, brown-spotted and blue-veined with age, and wiped the tears from her daughter's cheek. "Come, come, Erniņ. You'll make yourself sick and upset the little ones. We'll see each other again. Agate read my cards read yesterday, and there was no black queen."

Weeping women and fortune-tellers both made Father uncomfortable and solved nothing. He had long ago decided to strive with all his heart, if it held out, but to think with his head—no mumbo jumbo or reading of cards or tea leaves, just his brain. His gloomy early morning thoughts had also reminded him that he must tell Erna about his good suit. He had only worn it twice, once to the opera, and another time to Milda's wedding. Should his heart give out, he wanted to be laid out in it. But this was not the time to speak of such things, with Erna already so upset. Instead, he changed the subject. "Tell me, wasn't there a letter from Elza yesterday?"

"Yes, she sounded well enough, under the circumstances. Marite's happy with her school, and Karlis has started printing some sort of a camp newsletter."

"Lucky devil, that one, to have something to do. All he needs is a pencil and paper, and he's all set. I've made some plans myself, even ordered a few pieces of machinery for the workshop, but they've yet to arrive."

"Come, Peterit and Ilzite, your Auntie Elza sent more than just a letter." Omite spilled the contents of a tightly wrapped paper cone into her saucer. "Candies, for you." Red, green, orange, and yellow, the candies looked like small, round buttons. Peter popped several into his mouth, but Ilze held on to hers for a while until they melted, leaving spots of colour on her skin.

"There's something I'd like to do before I return. Jani, maybe you could help me with it," began Omite somewhat hesitantly. For a few weeks, the idea had been quietly germinating in her fertile mind, and now it was beginning to grow roots. "I'd so like to see Elza and the children one more time…it may be the last time—"

"Out of the question," interrupted Father. "Why, it's hundreds of kilometers and train schedules, when they exist, are good for only one thing," he said. It was preposterous; this idea of his mother-in-law's to travel alone, from one end of Germany to another, through a war-ravaged countryside.

But Omite's wish was not to be denied, and even Father's brain-driven logic could not dissuade her. Father and Omite argued only once more before Omite left for good. "It's blood money, I tell you. They'll want something in return, names or whereabouts," Father insisted, like the voice of doom. Suspicious by nature as well as through experience, he did not readily trust others. In his dealings with the UNRRA, his replies were always truthful but concise, and he offered them no gratuitous information.

"Rest assured, I won't tell them anything, and I'm not worried about myself, either. What more can they do to an old woman whose heart's already heavy with so much suffering?" Omite was able to stand up to anyone, even Father, who ruled his family with the authority that comes only from the conviction of being right.

Nine

A few weeks later, on a sunny day in early autumn, when the leaves on the poplar trees were turning golden and twirled in the breeze like gypsy bangles, Omite set out. In a large coat and with a wool scarf covering her white hair, she looked smaller than ever. It had rained during the night, leaving a rich farmyard smell that reminded her of Jaungulbene, and she walked with care along the wooden planks that were slick with rain and mud, then picked her way carefully around the puddles that lay in her path. She waited at the camp gate for the ride she had been promised, a ride on one of the supply trucks, which would take her to the station. After that, she would be on her own.

Omite's departure left a silence that was not easily filled. She had a habit of humming softly or singing a tune under her breath as she went about her tasks. As often as not, her songs were plaintive, filled with longing for the landscapes she had left behind. Sometimes they were sad songs of loss about fallen soldiers and motherless children or separated sweethearts. When Mother joined in, it seemed as if the whole camp were enveloped in a gloomy fog that would never lift. Then, all of a sudden, Omite would stop what she was doing, sniff sharply, shake her head, straighten up, and smile, and break into a happier folk song. But those times were rare.

After she had been gone a week, my mother waited anxiously for news that Omite had arrived safely at Elza's. The letter took almost a month. As Omite tells it, crossing from the British zone into the American zone had required all the stubbornness and guile she possessed. "I handed over my documents to a red-cheeked, baby-faced boy in uniform, who spoke to me first in English and then in broken German," Omite wrote. 'Where are you going?' he asked, and I replied, 'To the Latvian Camp in Kleinkotz.' The boy grinned at me, showing uneven, white teeth, and tipped his hat back, while regarding me with amusement. 'Kleinkotz,' he repeated in a strange accent. 'No can do,' and pushed my papers back toward me. 'That's all the way south in Bavaria,' he said, as if telling me something I didn't already know. I refused to accept them and gave the papers a little shove in his direction. 'Please, my daughter needs me, is waiting for me,' I pleaded. Exasperated now at the blank look on the face of the boy soldier, I turned to his companion for help. 'One daughter Oldenberg, one daughter Kleinkotz, *ja*?' I said, and pointed in what I hoped was the right direction. Since I lacked the English words, I had to speak with my eyes and age. I must have looked pitiful enough, as they let me through."

"She's something, all right," said Father, "using her age like a battering ram."

Elza, who had been notified that Omite was on the way, breathed more easily when her mother finally showed up. The three grandchildren rushed to throw their arms around her, and when the excitement died down, Mara showed off her new exercise book, and Maija presented her Omite with a drawing. "*Nu*, *nu*, that's really a fine picture but first, let your Omite rest a bit." Omite could see right away that living conditions were better here in the American zone than they had been back in Camp Ohmstede, in the British zone. She soon realized that she was not needed here as much as she was at home, making her resolve to return to Latvia all the stronger.

With rest and care, the blisters on Omite's feet healed up, but her back continued to ache. She moved slowly, painfully, and there were days when she could barely rise from her cot. "Rheumatism," she announced. "I hate to return home like this, almost a cripple. I'd only be a burden."

"Maybe the camp doctor has something to ease the pain," suggested Elza.

"What does he know about the suffering of the old? His aspirins are like candies; they lift the spirits for a moment. I need something that really works, a permanent cure."

One sunny morning, when the air was dry and crisp, Omite felt a bit better, so she commandeered a wheelbarrow and a spade from the garden shed and sweet-talked the kitchen supervisor into giving her an empty burlap sack. "Mara, Janis, come with me. I need your help," she said, and with her two older grandchildren, she hobbled toward the pinewoods across the road from the camp. The thick foliage blocked the sunlight, and the only sound was the snapping of twigs underfoot, as the three of them followed a well-worn path into the woods.

"Are we picking mushrooms, Omite?" Mara asked. She liked finding the tiny, new button mushrooms that hid under the wet leaves and pine needles.

"No, no, Marite. That's better done after a rain. Today we must find the place where the trees have fallen all in a tangle and collect some ants!"

"Ants?"

"Just so, ants. Your Omite's back is very sore, and the ants will help it get better."

Mara held her brother's hand in a tight grip as they followed Omite and the wheelbarrow. She stopped in a clearing where the fallen trees had opened up a patch of sky. "Ah, I think the ants are hiding in here," she said, kicking at a rotting log with her boot. A few large, red ants emerged, then scurried away. "Quick, Mara, the shovel."

Omite worked diligently, alternately banging the logs with her shovel and scooping the ants into the sack that she had propped open with a stick. The ants did not readily accept their fate and tried to escape, crawling everywhere, even up the shovel until they reached Omite's hands. Mara and Janis could not stand still and jumped around in an attempt to rid themselves of the ants. In the end, Omite decided it was faster to stuff the decomposing pieces of wood into the sack, than to try to scoop out the ants. Soon the sack was full of rotting wood, and Omite tied it securely with a length of twine. "There. That's that." She straightened slowly, one hand supporting her sore back. "Let me see now, I hope you children didn't get bitten."

"Just one or two Oma," Janis said, giving his leg a scratch.

"I've something back at camp that will stop the itch," Omite promised, which made Mara worry that it would be another of her smelly homemade remedies.

Elza had a large kettle of water on the boil by the time her mother and the children returned. While Omite undressed, Elza emptied the kettle into the water already in the tin bathtub. Then Omite untied the sack, extracted some of the bigger pieces of rotting wood and whacked them on the side of the tub. Red ants rained into the water, shuddered, and then pirouetted briefly before they lay still. She shook the bag to make sure it was empty, then lowered her white bulk into the murky soup. Dead ants, grubs, leaves, and scraps of wood floated around her like the remains of a shipwreck. Omite hugged her knees and sat still, only moving now and then to crush a wayward ant. She remained like that until the water cooled. When she finally stood up, she looked dirtier than before her bath. Bits and pieces of ant, as well as whole ants, pine needles, and other debris stuck to her body, but Omite seemed not to notice.

The following morning, Omite pronounced herself cured. "No more aching bones. I'm fit enough to go now." Elza contained her surprise, but was left to wonder if it was the ants or her mother's strong will that did the trick.

Although Mother had stopped singing after Omite left us and went to Elza's, there was other music in Camp Ohmstede. Our neighbour on the other side of the partition joined a choir, and we could hear her practicing at all hours. It drove Father crazy. Camp inmates dusted off the musical instruments they had managed to lug this far, tuned them, and played familiar, lilting melodies. Folk dancing was popular, too, especially among the teenagers, as it gave them a rare opportunity to socialize. They hopped and skipped and waltzed in circles, and they never seemed to tire.

As life in the camp became routine, and the threat of forced repatriation melted away, the UNRRA officials began to worry about boredom and the unrest it could bring. They pinned notices to the bulletin board, encouraging the Latvians to organize activities and to help run the camp. Soon, Boy Scout and Girl Guide troops formed, and the YMCA and YWCA offered a variety of activities such as after-school basketball and volleyball. English classes and university lectures became available for the older students. Those whose university education had been interrupted by the war made plans to attend the newly founded DP Hamburg College. Hope was beginning to take root in the wasteland of broken lives.

Father had always boasted of his knowledge of English, but he was among the first to sign up for formal lessons. After the first class, he returned to our barracks duly chastened, shaking his head in disbelief. The teacher's spoken English bore little resemblance to the English he pronounced in his head, when he perused a written page. All the Latvians, including Father, had difficulty pronouncing the simple word *the* correctly. He stuck his tongue between his teeth and tried, but the sound always came out like *zuh*. He pressed his tongue against the inside of his front teeth and pursed his lips at the same time, causing his children to giggle, but did no better. It's not the King's English, it's the devil's." Used to a language in which every letter is sounded out, he couldn't fathom the mysteries of silent letters or swallowed consonants.

Still, Father practiced diligently, and soon he tried his hand at writing. With the help of a German-English dictionary, he composed letters in formal, stilted English. "I am Mr. Janis Zalite, am graduated from the University of Latvia as mechanical engineer and have much related experience in naval architecture," he wrote. "I am available for work in your company immediately. I require only visa to your country."

Slowly, Father's English improved, but his mood did not. Short-tempered and exacting by nature, he became ever more irritable. He was not used to being idle or spending his days with women and children. "I need to use my brain and hands," he told Mother over and over, "just as much as I need sleep or food." "Work makes the man" was Talavija's motto, and Father subscribed to it wholeheartedly.

During the long days with nothing to do, Father often thought back to his first summer in Latvia, the long-ago summer of 1918. His father had brought him, his mother, and his two siblings, along with the three cousins who had been living with them in Moscow, across the border to safety in Latvia. They left behind the chaos, starvation, and brutality of the Bolshevik Revolution and settled temporarily on the Zalite homestead in Vidzeme. He was eleven, and in order to help feed the family, he worked as a shepherd boy, watching over the grazing cows and sheep of a nearby farmer. At the start of the summer, he had received a pair of *pastalas*, shapeless leather moccasins, that protected his feet from the morning dew and the rough stalks of the pastures. In the fall after the harvest, with his *pastalas* worn to shreds, he was given a small share of the harvest, which he proudly presented to his mother.

On those evenings when he did not have English class, Father sat at the rickety table and read *Venta*, the camp bulletin. If he was lucky enough to have a cigarette, he would light it and after smoking half, he would hand the rest to Mother. Sometimes they would share a glass of clandestinely distilled spirits that burned their throats on the way down. Gaunt and balding, he looked and felt far older than his thirty-eight years. During stressful moments, his heart fluttered like a caged bird trying to escape, and at other times, he complained to Mother that someone must have stretched a rubber band around his chest, it felt that tight. When that happened, he would stretch out on his cot, fully clothed, and with trembling fingers, undo the buttons of his shirt in an attempt to relieve the pressure. He lay as still as death. Mother warned us not to make a sound before shooing us outside. On days when his heart was behaving, Father bounced me on his knee, slowly at first, then faster and faster and faster, until I was in full gallop and giggling with glee. Then it was Peter's turn. Father crossed his legs at the knee and held Peter's hands as he balanced on Father's foot and rode up and down, laughing.

The months passed and the Latvians in the camp began to wonder whether they would ever see their homeland again. The more gullible believed the false rumours of an impending Soviet withdrawal from the Baltics, and some even declared that they would be back in their own beds in Riga within six months. They repeated the mantra over and over: "the Allies have not recognized the USSR's annexation of the three Baltic Republics". The more realistic refugees like Father did not listen to or participate in talk of returning to Latvia. Spirits rose and sank daily, but they plummeted to new depths when excerpts from Churchill's speech appeared in the Latvian newspaper, *Tevzeme*. His words, "From Stettin in the Baltic to Trieste in the Adriatic, an iron curtain has descended on the Continent," sent a chill down everyone's spine. There would be no returning to the homeland for a very long time.

As they realized that the diplomas they had so carefully preserved during the flight were now as useless as the paper money in their pockets, the men in the camp began to think about their lives in a new light. Father renewed his letter writing efforts, while at the same time, he drew up plans for a woodworking and metalworking shop, where he could instruct select individuals in a useful trade. "Think about it," he told Mother. "They can learn and maybe even earn something, and later when they're resettled, their skills will be in demand."

Mother agreed, but added a mild warning, "Just don't get your hopes up too much." Privately, she worried that his approach, which could be as abrasive as sandpaper, might bring him unwanted attention, and only serve to anger camp officials. Still, anything was better than seeing her husband so forlorn and irritable.

But nothing could stop Father once he was convinced he was right. Together with another engineer, Karlis Samtiņš, Father approached the camp director for a suitable space to build a workshop and credit to buy the necessary tools.

"Jani, these things take time. Please be patient," she beseeched, when Father grumbled about the delay. She worried that Father might somehow annoy camp officials with his insistence and jeopardize their safety.

"You only think like a woman—of survival and a soft bed. Men respect determination and action."

Mother fell silent, but the bitter words she swallowed gnawed at her insides.

"That's the basic difference between us," Father continued, unaware of her pain. "A man can't live without work. What kind of an example is it for the children to see their fathers slouching around all day, playing cards, and drinking homemade whiskey to make them forget? Don't worry. I know what I'm doing."

"Of course, Jani, of course," Mother agreed. She had learned early in their relationship that it was better to agree than argue with Janis. Since their marriage, she had yet to win an argument with her husband. Still, she worried.

Father knew that the UNRRA urgently needed drivers and mechanics, and that both were in short supply, but he was looking toward the future. " My plan is to equip a workshop and train skilled craftsmen to produce basic manufactured articles that are needed by both the camp's inhabitants and its administration," he wrote. "The camp families long for the simplest things, such as wooden clogs to keep their feet out of the mud and wooden pegs to secure freshly laundered clothes to the line."

In actual fact, Father's plans were more grandiose. He would start small, but eventually, if he could obtain sufficient raw materials, he would meet not only the needs of Camp Ohmstede, but also the needs of the other nearby Latvian camps, Tervete and Mezotne. With hard work and God's help, the Zalite Workshop might even expand to supply the occupying armies with simple manufactured goods.

Father was relieved when he finally received limited approval from the camp committee. The spotty success of the UNNRA's repatriation program opened up some empty space in Barracks 52, and he gleefully claimed it for his workshop. When the tools—hammers, saws, drills and various sized drill bits, a lathe, some soldering equipment—he had ordered from a supplier in Hamburg finally arrived, he could begin to train the thirty men he had selected and start production. That night, Father, Samtiņš, and a few others celebrated. Several of the chemical engineers had found a better use for their weekly ration of tasteless, ashen macaroni. By adding water and sugar to the unpalatable noodles and allowing the mixture to ferment, they obtained a foaming grey mass, which could then be distilled into a clear, head-splitting, gut-rotting, alcoholic brew.

Busy now, Father felt almost happy, but dared not let it show. He knew that happiness and success bring only envy, especially in the camp, and jealous, capricious gods might snatch away this small success without even blinking a godly eye. In the evening, as he related the events of the day to Mother, his voice was subdued, and the corners of his full lips barely lifted, but his hazel eyes shone with satisfaction. Mother understood Father's superstitious nature and curbed her enthusiasm as well. Instead of rejoicing, Father hummed softly to himself as he bent over his plans, worked out production schedules, and calculated costs, income, and payment schemes. He, himself, would draw no salary at first, but he would instead endeavor to pay a small stipend to his apprentices.

As the mud dried up and summer approached, the pounding of hammers and the whine of drills filled the air, drowning out the birdsong, and Father was satisfied that his life was back on track. Work made the man, and he was, once again, starting to feel like a man. "For you, Mama," he said, and handed her a paper-wrapped bundle. "One dozen wooden clothes pins to keep your washed clothes on the line, no matter how strong the wind blows."

"Thank you, but you work too hard," Mother replied, though she was glad of the offering. Just yesterday, she had had to rewash some clothes, after a gust of wind had lifted them from the line and dropped them in the mud.

"Soon," Father promised, "I'll bring you some clogs, so you can work in the garden plot and save your shoes from the mud."

Some days, electricity was rationed, and other days, a shortage of raw materials halted production, but still the Zalite Workshop began to sell practical household items that included wooden shoes, clothes pegs, and a few benches. Next, Father planned to make wooden suitcases. He figured they would be in demand, since life in the camp could not go on forever, and what better symbol of its transitory nature than a suitcase standing ready in a corner, visible proof that the possibility of leaving was only a signature away? With a suitcase in your hand, you could leave the bundles behind, and step out into world with your head held high. He didn't say as much, but the children believed that Father dreamed of being carried away from the camp by big, strong Oldenburg horses with a well-crafted suitcase at his feet.

Father easily transferred his ideas for a suitcase onto paper. A graduate of the University of Latvia in mechanical engineering, specializing in naval architecture, he had envisioned a future for himself in designing sleek, unsinkable, ocean-going ships, not rectangular, wooden boxes. Using a straight edge and his mechanical pencil, he drew several views, open and closed. Two sturdy hinges joined the matching halves of each suitcase. On the outside, he penciled round clasps that locked firmly, and a thick, smooth metal handle that would be comfortable to hold. He planned to protect the vulnerable corners with rounded metal discs, shaped to fit. When Father's prototype was ready, he painted it a dark burgundy, the only colour available. "Look, Mama, I've painted my first suitcase with my own blood and sweat." Mother shook her head at his exaggeration, but even so, she looked in admiration at her husband's accomplishment.

News of the Zalite Workshop spread, and Father could soon select only the ablest applicants. Even so, some of the men, used to working with their brains and not their hands, did not know the proper way to swing a hammer or wield a saw. Father proved to be an able teacher, but he often lacked patience; for him, there was only one right way to do something—his way. "Dummkopf," he shouted, when one of the apprentices broke a valuable and irreplaceable drill bit. At times, Father's mature, educated pupils resented being reminded of their lowly student status, but they did not complain when their skills improved and the workshop prospered. Along with woodworking, Father taught metalworking. He hoped to manufacture bicycles and baby carriages, two items that were sorely needed in the camp.

To ease the crowded living conditions and to make room for new arrivals, during the summer of 1945, Latvian refugees built two new camps, Camp Tervete and Camp Mezotne, only four kilometers from Camp Ohmstede. Camp Ohmstede remained the largest, with over eight hundred displaced persons. When word spread to the new camps that clogs, clothes pegs, and even baby carriages were being produced in the Zalite Workshop, buyers rushed over to purchase these items. Even after the new camps had set up workshops of their own, speculators arrived daily to snatch up the good quality, reasonably priced goods made under Father's guidance. Then they returned to their own camps and sold the goods at a profit.

Just before Christmas, an announcement appeared in the camp newsletter:

"December 23, the Zalite Workshop will hold a display of the wooden toys made by the fathers of Camp Ohmstede for the children of Camp Ohmstede. Afterward, the owners may take their toys home."

Christmas 1944 had been dismal for many, but especially for those like us who had been in Swinemünde, a target of heavy Allied bombing. By comparison, Christmas 1945 in the DP camp was almost luxurious. As the families of Camp Ohmstede gathered together on Christmas Eve in a room fragrant with the scent of pine and burning candles, they celebrated their own survival, as well as Jesus's birth. Some young men had ventured into the nearby forest and chopped down a tall, bushy evergreen; laughing and singing, they dragged it past surprised officials and into the camp. They set up the tree, and the women decorated its boughs with paper garlands, colourful ornaments fashioned from yarn, and candles set securely in metal holders. Beside the tree, a full pail of water stood ready if needed. That evening, when the children were allowed to enter, they were awed by the splendour and excited by the presents piled under the Christmas tree. Painted wooden toys, rag dolls with yellow braids, button eyes and red, embroidered mouths, and stiff wooden soldiers waited patiently for children to claim them.

Babies stared round-eyed, and toddlers gaped openmouthed at the wondrous sight before them, but the older children clapped and skipped in joyful anticipation. Families squeezed together on the wooden benches and listened as the minister read the familiar Christmas story. They sang well-known Christmas carols like "Lo How a Rose is Blooming" and

"Silent Night", and they prayed silently, fervently, and sincerely that this splendour was a sign from God that their lives would soon return to normal; they could not bear to live under such crowded, disheartening, and unhealthy conditions much longer.

When the last notes of "God Bless Latvia" faded away, and the women had wiped away their tears, it was finally the children's turn. One by one, skinny boys and girls, dressed in their best clothes, stood in front of the tree to recite the verse each had committed to memory, a verse that spoke of the magic of Christmas—the star, softly falling snow, or sleigh bells.

"Come, little Peter, now don't forget to bow," Father reminded my three-year-old brother. Father guided Peter to the front of the hall so that he could recite the four short lines he had committed to memory. For his effort, Peter received the gift of a cutout plywood horse on a wooden platform that bumped along on wooden wheels. When the presents had all been handed out, women poured muddy looking coffee made from chicory, and everyone helped themselves to plates of open-faced sandwiches and spicy pepper cookies that, while not quite as good as the ones back home, tasted a lot like Christmas.

The New Year came and went, and the wet winter stayed on like an unwelcome guest who doesn't know when it's time to leave. The Zalite Workshop continued to function under its provisional license, but without formal approval, it was always in danger of being shut down. Hopeful yet fearful, Father continued to seek the permanence that he so desired for his undertaking. While Mother worried about jealous gods and other spirits, Father feared that an envious colleague or overzealous official might jeopardize his success.

When the letter from the camp director arrived, it was almost as if he had been expecting it. "It has come to my attention that the prices being charged for goods produced in the Zalite Workshop are too high. Speculation should not be tolerated, as it can only lead to inequalities and jealousies," Delafontaine wrote.

Father could not contain his anger, and Mother was unable to calm him down. "What does that soldier turned inexperienced bureaucrat know about running a workshop anyway? Can you believe that someone has sent in an anonymous complaint, and they write me this without even bothering to hear my side?"

These were questions without answers, and Mother knew it was better not to say anything.

"The devil take him! The Zalite name is my pledge of honesty and decency." Father paced the small room like a caged lion and swore like a sailor, while Mother tried to get him to sit down. She was always worried about his heart, and such a display could do no good, not to his heart and certainly not to his cause. Would they ever be able to lead a normal life again outside the camp? In secret, she wondered if it wouldn't be best to return home after all. Red Cross representatives, armed with glowing reports of conditions at home, continued to canvas for candidates to repatriate. Recently, one official who had just returned from a fact-finding visit to Latvia had said, "There is little to criticize and much to applaud." Father said he was not to be believed.

Father fought to clear his name, presenting proof that he did not speculate, but that the men who came from other camps to buy his manufactured goods at favorable cost only to resell them later at inflated prices, were the speculators. The workshop continued to operate even while he proceeded to seek formal approval from the camp committee. More than once, he approached different members of the committee and asked to be allowed to present his case personally at their next meeting. Without the official stamp of approval, he could not enlarge the workshop, nor could he risk buying more equipment. As an UNRRA sanctioned activity, it would be easier to obtain the much-needed raw materials and increase output.

On September 2, 1946, after been denied permission to attend their meeting, Father wrote a letter to the Military Government 816, through UNRRA Team 146 and the Ohmstede camp commander, asking for a written license to operate the Zalite Workshop on behalf of the displaced persons.

"I presume that you know the Zalite Workshop," he wrote, "and I make the perhaps not quite modest assertion that through my past activities, I have proved to be able to satisfactorily meet the demands made on the management of the workshop. I would like to continue, expand and broaden activities and increase output. One of many urgently required articles is suitcases, and I could produce these in large quantities and sell them at a manufacturing price approved by you. I, on my part, would take care of the work with still greater energy and extend it in the interest of all the DPs, who on the one hand would find employment, and on the other would be provided with urgently required articles. Also, utility articles such as wooden suitcases and trunks for the troops of the occupation armies could be provided. I have tried to maintain prices as low as possible. The Camp Committee itself must take responsibility upon itself for the pricing as it did not help provide the necessary raw materials."

Mother looked at Father in horror when he had read the letter to her. "Do you want to end up in jail?"

"Of all people, I thought you'd be on my side."

"*Nu, nu,*" she soothed. "You know I am. It's just that sometimes, sometimes your words can be very strong. Couldn't you soften them a bit?"

"Facts remain facts," Father insisted, undeterred. "Listen, there's more."

"If the DPs can't afford the shoes, the blame rests on the Committee's shoulders. Along with a shortage of raw materials, without the Committee's help, tools are expensive and difficult to obtain. Today enough oak wood to produce two wooden candlesticks costs 200 grams of dried peas. Can we deny our families their nourishment?"

By this time, Mother's face was as grey as the blankets. "Dear Lord, help us."

"Is that all you can say? Nothing supportive?" Father continued to read:

"To add to the costs, which must be recuperated in the sale of the goods, I pay as high wages as possible to my workers. For the first two months I have taken no pay myself. We have to pay for electricity to the Camp Committee even though the camp doesn't pay for it. As well, my workshop has produced certain items for UNRRA and the camp for which they have yet to pay the RM 272 for raw materials. And with the future so uncertain it is impossible to obtain even short-term loans...."

"Please, Jani, don't talk about defaulting on loans. That's like waving a red flag at a bull." She looked at her sleeping children, so in need of vitamins and proper, nourishing food. She felt continually exhausted and sometimes failed to keep the food down—it was not easy to swallow—but she didn't want to add to her husband's worries. Her high cheekbones stood out in the harsh light of the overhead bulb, and her long, straight nose looked paper thin. The shapeless dress she wore, a gift from the Red Cross, hung from her bony shoulders.

"You talk like a woman or a child who's just peed his pants. I know what I'm doing," said Father, and he proceeded to sign the letter and seal the envelope.

In the end, Father lost his battle to keep the workshop open, but by that time, it no longer mattered. He had been offered a job. The family could leave the camp. Gotaverken, the Swedish shipyards where he had worked for two years right after his marriage, wanted him! The letter, dated September 20th, 1946 was addressed to Shipbuilding Engineer Janis Zalite, Camp 224/F – 224 DP Assembly Centre, D..A.O.R. (via Great Britain), OLDENBURG (Oldbg). Germany. British Zone.

"According to copy of letter from Statens Utlannings-kommission your visum by now must be ready in Hamburg. We hope to see you here as soon as possible. Yours sincerely, AKTIEBOLAGET GOTAVERKEN."

The news made Father feel light-headed, and he sat down to reread the letter. This was more than he had hoped for, but he was not at all surprised that Gotaverken wanted him back. He knew his profession, and he was good at it. Hundreds of ships were waiting to be built to profit from the certain post-war boom. In a rare, tender show of affection, Father took Mother's hand, kissed it, and pressed it to his heart. "Feel how steady. And just think, Mama, we're among the first to have real work and the chance to start over. Of course," he checked himself, "I still have to secure those visas."

"It's such wonderful news," Mother said, and kissed Father's cheek. "Thank goodness we don't have to go to faraway Brazil."

The good news spread quickly through the camp, renewing hopes and spurring on more letter writing. Mother held back her tears of relief until the required important papers were signed and embellished with a bouquet of colourful stamps.

"See how your Shaksi looks after you and the little ones," he murmured into Mother's hair, as he folded her into his arms. His own eyes unexpectedly misted over behind his wire-rimmed glasses. "We'll leave as soon as the Red Cross can arrange for our passages to Sweden, maybe even before Christmas."

"Thank you, for taking such good care of us." Mother held on tight and did not want to let go.

"It'll be a relief to leave this place and all the pencil-pushers that only stand in the way of man's dreams," he added softly, as he stroked Mother's once-dark hair, now streaked with white.

The good news did not stop with the job offer in Sweden. Omite wrote that Janis had been granted permission to return home to Latvia from exile in Siberia. At the happy news about her brother, Mother's blue eyes filled with tears, tears that sent the words floating across the page.

"I plan to travel to Riga as soon as possible," wrote Omite from Camp Kleinkotz. "Your brother, Janis, will be disappointed if I am not there to greet him. Of course, Papiņš has been alone all this time and needs me. Here, the children are reasonably well, but Elza once again suffers from a sore throat. The Americans here are a queer bunch, God help us. Because of them, our bellies are groaning from all the meat we have eaten. A few of our neighbours could be heard moaning in their beds all night. No peace for us. You're probably wondering, so I'll explain. Some of us, the more enterprising, had managed to barter for piglets from a local farmer, and these were happily growing on slops from the kitchen until our American hosts declared the whole pig business unsanitary. Yes, unsanitary! Imagine. The food is good enough for us, but bad for our pigs! The Americans are well known for their constant washing; only their flag is held in higher regard than cleanliness. Did they think that we would sleep with the pigs in our beds? Karlis wrote about the ruckus in the paper, and we had a good laugh. Even the fact that the piglets were corralled in the nearby woods could not convince the soldiers to let us keep them. I think they imagined the germs flying through the air and into their open mouths as they snored. Well, Daughter, nothing to be done except make sausages. Of course, this caused another hullabaloo. More germs, I guess. We all ate our fill of meat so tender you could cut it with a fork. Except for mine. I thought no, I would not obey such a silly order. What could the Americans do to me anyway, an old woman?"

Mother's face crumpled as if she were about to cry, but she changed her mind and laughed instead. Father had a surprised look of disbelief on his face. "Marta needs to learn to respect authority and—"

"Wait, Jani, there's more." Mother put her hand gently on his arm.

"Well, when they found out that I still had my pig, they took it from me and threw me in jail. I guess they thought I was crazy, too, since they stripped the laces from my boots and gave me only a spoon to eat with. What did they think?"

"I really believe it's for the best that Marta return home as soon as possible," Father said, as serious as a minister chiding his flock. Still, a hint of a smile played around the corners of his mouth.

When, at last, the day arrived for us to leave Camp Ohmstede, we were packed and ready. Father's prototype suitcase from his workshop was filled mostly with his heavy woollen suit as well as the few family heirlooms he had managed to salvage. Father fashioned a crate with some of the wood from his workshop for the rest of our belongings, including some silver cutlery, a silver fruit bowl, grandfather's silver tankard with the here's-looking-at-you glass bottom and the initials 'PZ' inscribed on the front, as well as a handful of silver five-Lat pieces. Most precious of all was the large oil portrait of his father.

On a raw wintry day, at the end of December 1946, with a promise of snow in the air, we gathered at the camp gate and waited impatiently for the International Red Cross car to arrive. Peter ran out of the gate a little way to see if the car was on its way, while I held Mother's hand and hopped on one foot, a feat in which I took great pride. Peter loved anything that moved, especially if it had a motor, and he could hardly wait for the transport to arrive. Father was still busy making sure that all our belongings were accounted for and properly labelled. At last, the small convoy of two cars and one truck arrived, and we climbed aboard. The convoy made its way slowly north toward Libeke, along roads scarred as much from the fighting as from the heavy trucks lumbering back and forth in the post-war years. Then it crossed into Denmark, and we proceeded through a grey, rain-soaked countryside dotted with farms and small villages that seemed part of another world. It was dark by the time the convoy reached the ferry terminal and much later still when we boarded the ship. At last, we were on our way to Sweden. A new year was starting, and so, too, were our lives.

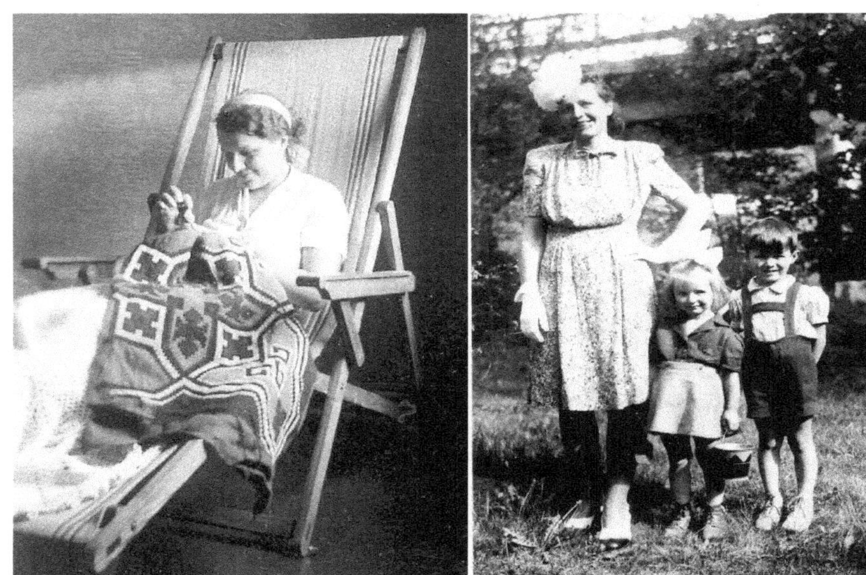

(left)1948 Mother in Sweden, relaxing with needle point. (right) 1949 Mother, Peter and Ilze in Hindas, Sweden. Mother is modeling one of the hats sent from America

Mother's 1950 passport photo with Peter, Ilze and Roland.

SWEDEN

Ten

With a blast of a whistle that brought Peter's hands to his ears, the ferry slipped from its moorings, turned its prow into the wind, and headed for Sweden. Outside, the wind whipped up whitecaps that sent foam scudding through the air like clouds before a storm, while inside, faces peered at rain-streaked windows for a glimpse into the gathering night.

"For once, we're lucky," Father said to Mother, "to be in here, safe and dry, and not out there on some leaky fishing boat, exposed to the elements as it struggles to reach the Swedish coast. I believe, in all honesty, that I made the right decision." He hoped that this move would be the last one for a long time. His wife deserved the good life he had promised her when they married, and his children, pale, skinny, and fearful, had not had a real home for years.

The wind rattled the windows, and the rain drummed a plaintive song, as Mother shifted the weight of her sleeping daughter. "Yes, this time we are fortunate, but please, Jani, come and sit down," she urged, patting the bench. "I don't know what you see out there."

It was some time before Father was able to relax enough to sit down. The excitement he felt was a mix of confidence and anxiety, much as when he had presented himself for his oral exams at the University of Latvia. He preferred to be in complete control, to be the one making plans, the one asking the questions. His years at university now seemed to belong to another, more carefree life. Had he once been a young student whose only concerns were good grades and a good time? Was it a mere ten years ago that, full of hope and brimming with confidence, he had sailed to Sweden with his new bride? When he saw his reflection in the window, the unfamiliar face surprised him. Had he really aged so much? Father forced these silly thoughts from his head; this was no time to be morbid. Real work, comfort, and safety lay just a few hundred kilometers ahead in Göteborg. But like the sea, his thoughts were agitated, and he alternated between feeling strong and feeling vulnerable. There were so many unknowns and everyone depended on him. Softly, so as not to wake her, Father stroked Ilze's hair, marveling at its silkiness. He was so much older now, almost forty-two, and he did not know how much longer he had. With God's help, he hoped to live long enough to educate his children. But nothing came easily anymore; everything seemed to require more effort, scheming, and luck, and most distressingly, the good will of others. He disliked asking for permission or for some small favour, and he certainly did not want anybody's false sympathy. All he wanted was the chance to prove himself.

"I was just thinking about our first trip to Sweden…," Mother said, but didn't finish her thought.

"Don't worry, little wife, we'll be back on our feet in no time. The government has some kind of assembly centre for immigrants. You and the little ones might have to stay there for a day or two while I find a us a place to live in Göteborg."

"Oh, no. Can't we stay all together this time?"

"I don't think its possible or practical. A hotel is no place for children," stated Father. He could feel himself getting irritated. Why this constant having to explain, when he himself lacked any explanation, having to assure others, when he himself felt unsure? Blood throbbed in his temples like a ship's engine come to life. All he had was an offer of work, nothing more. He didn't even know if he would be able to support a wife and two children on his salary. "No, Mama, it's all set. You and Peterits and Ilzite will be properly looked after."

Mother wanted to cry but had no more tears. Besides, she knew it would do no good and would only serve to upset Father. She could well imagine that in post-war Sweden, apartments were as scarce as extra kilos on a refugee, but she could not bear to relive what she went through in Germany. She should have refused to board the ship in Liepaja if Janis wouldn't agree to accompany her and the children, but then as now, it was impossible to disobey her husband or to change his mind once it had been made up. "But an assembly centre," the very words sent ripples of fear down her spine, "aren't we immigrants with visas and not refugees?"

"Of course we are. But Ernushka, it all costs money, and until I earn my first pay and find a place to live, quite impossible." All he knew was that the director at the shipyards had booked him a room in a small hotel in Göteborg. "Look, I'm certain you'll be well provided for, and just as soon as I can, I'll return for you." Father shifted his gaze; he couldn't bear to see the look in Erna's eyes. "Don't worry, it won't be anything like Germany. And Sweden's practically untouched by the war, most likely profited from it. Everything will be just fine, eh, Marija Luiza?" He hoped he sounded convincing, but so much of his former confidence and bravado had slipped between the cracks in all the rundown places he had stayed in the past three years, that he couldn't be sure.

Mother closed her eyes and drew a deep breath. "Well, if you promise it's only for a short while." She knew that her husband's refusal to change direction once plans were made was as much due to superstition as a stubborn faith in his infallible logic. And although Father was not outwardly religious, he believed that each decision, once made, was entered into God's logbook, making it part of destiny.

To Mother's immense relief, the Swedish assembly center was unlike any she had experienced in Germany. It was intact and staffed by smiling workers who knew what they were doing. Our family was ushered across an open, cobblestone courtyard and into a large, heated room, furnished with two divans and numerous chairs lined up against one wall. A sparkling chandelier hung from the high ceiling. Electricity and smiling faces—it was a good start.

After breakfast the next morning, Father bade his wife and children good-bye. "Be good children and listen to Mama. And Erna, this is the perfect opportunity for you to brush up on your Swedish. *Prata ni Svenska*! Speaking the language is like using the right tool—it makes everything so much easier. You too, little Peter," he added cheerily.

"Yes, Papa, I will," Peter answered solemnly, nodding his head.

"I'll try my best," Mother promised, "but I don't have your knack for languages. And don't forget, it's been ten years." It felt more like a lifetime ago. Janis picked up languages the way others contracted diseases, she thought, absorbing new words through the pores in his skin, and he expected her to do the same.

"For my part, I'll do my best to find an apartment as quickly as possible. The office promised to help with telephoning around during the day, and after work, I can search the newspaper advertisements."

Father was pleasantly surprised when he arrived in Göteborg. It was a much larger, more crowded and vibrant city than the one he had left nine years ago. "It is like a Hans Christian Anderson fairy tale with sparkling lights everywhere to brighten the otherwise dark winter night," he wrote Mother soon after he arrived. "Haralds and his good wife met me at the train and helped settle me into the small but comfortable Royal Hotel, where I now write this letter. They send you kind regards and look forward to meeting you again."

After Father registered and deposited his belongings in his room, he accepted Haralds's invitation to dine at his home. Haralds, who had been Father's former director in 1936 at Götaverken, pointed out the sights on the ride to his home. Father smiled and nodded and commented at the appropriate times, but his mind was otherwise occupied. He could not help worrying. How much did the hotel room cost? How long would he have to stay there, paying money he did not have, before he found a place to live? When would he be able to send for his family? The mental calculations that usually gave him some measure of comfort now eluded him; there were too many unknowns. It was amazing, he thought, how quickly things change—in the blink of an eye, really. Having lost everything and wasted two productive years of his life in a displaced persons' camp, the post-war economy was a mystery. But for a few hours, in the warmth of Haralds's candlelit apartment, partaking of a fragrant fish stew and boiled potatoes and drinking aquavit, Father's heart softened, and he allowed himself to feel a glimmer of optimism. Soon he would be back in his former life at the shipyards, bending over blueprints and discussing important, ship-related details. "*Skol*," he answered Haralds's toast. "To your health."

The following morning, Father awoke early. He had always been an early riser and fond of repeating "the morning sun holds gold in its mouth" to anyone who would listen. He shaved with care, but his reflection in the mirror both surprised and distressed him. His fine, thinning hair had receded further and had left him with a wide expanse of brow, like the Jurmala beach at low tide. His once full cheeks were sunken, and his eyes haunted him from behind his thick glasses. He sniffed and his nostrils flared. He looked as old as he felt. Father slapped his cheeks a few times to bring the colour back, but he knew it was only a temporary solution, just as when Erna pressed her lips together to redden them. Still, what could he expect? He was no longer young and had already lived most of his life. Fortunately, what mattered most, his brain, was intact. This thought comforted him slightly, and he cheered even more when the aroma of real coffee greeted him as he entered the dining room. After a hearty breakfast of bread, ham, and two kinds of cheese, washed down with several cups of strong coffee, and topped off by a cream-filled bun, Father felt ready to face his new work responsibilities.

After making sure he had a selection of coins in his coat pocket, Father boarded the tram that would take him to the shipyards. He sat on the edge of his seat, near the front door, and looked for recognizable landmarks. When he neared the harbour, he was surprised to see that the shipyards had expanded to nearly twice their former size, and a half dozen tall cranes strained to reach the low clouds that hung over the city. Off to the left, an oil refinery billowed smoke, adding to the haze. It all created an impression of progress and wealth he had not seen for a long time. Haralds was the first to greet Father, and he presented him to his former colleagues and several new, young draftsmen who flashed ready smiles. Why are they so happy to see me, when they don't know me, Father mused. On the way to Director Bergstrom's office, Father was shown the expanded design department with its soldierly rows of inclined drafting tables. The director greeted him like an old friend and pumped his arm up and down enthusiastically. Dry-mouthed and suddenly aware of the stale odour emanating from his suit, Father handed over his documents and waited. Only when the preliminaries had been dispensed with, did Father allow himself to ask the question that was uppermost in his mind, "What is my salary?"

The director, a tall, sandy-haired man with pale eyes, patted Father kindly on the shoulder, as if they were old friends. "All in good time Herr Zalite, all in good time. For certain, the pay will be sufficient for a family of four." Bergstrom meant to be reassuring, but his vague answer did little to satisfy Father's need to know the exact amount so he could make his calculations. He longed to be able to write Erna and tell her the exact amount of her food allowance. But, for that, he would need to know not only the amount of his wages, but also deductions and expenses, including rent and transportation.

Being in control, making rational, informed decisions, and planning for the future of his family made Father feel secure. Yet, here he stood, in a shabby suit and patched shoes, with his insides churning and an occasional stabbing pain in his chest, like an ignorant child at his father's knee. Apart from Bergstrom's casual assurance, he had no idea how much he would earn. The few silver lats he had salvaged were now just pretty souvenirs until Latvia was free once again.

Two days later, when Father wrote to Mother, he was despondent. He had begun to realize that the chance of finding an apartment was only a remote possibility. And while he still lived at the Royal Hotel, he hoped to move to a smaller, less expensive room as soon as one became available. "My mood barometer is falling. How are things with you? They're not throwing you out yet, I hope? Perhaps you could go see the director and ask for some hotel coupons, as mine are running out. Write to me as soon as you get this, and go immediately to the station to mail your letter."

Father's letter continued, "I can eat well once a day at work for 40 ore. Today, we had sausage and potatoes, the sausage is a fixed amount by coupon, but the potatoes with gravy can be eaten without limit (I made good use of that). As well, I can drink as much milk as I like, also bread and butter. Sometimes, I buy oranges for the evening—seventy ore a kilogram, in which there are eight, so each one costs ten ore. I have not yet been to the movies. Besides I have a bad cough, even without smoking.... But start writing me about yourself, I know nothing. Write me your telephone number, and I will try to phone you between three-thirty and four on Saturday. Mail it at the station, but be careful crossing the street—observe that the cars come from the opposite direction as they did before. Greetings for Peteritis and Ilzinka from their father, and greetings for yourself from your Janis. (Learn Swedish!)"

Documenting expenditures and saving money was a lifetime habit Father had acquired early from his own father. It afforded him a sense of control over the present, and allowed him to project into the future. Income must always exceed expenditures. That was the best assurance that his life was moving forward, on the right track.

In the days that followed, Father searched in vain for an apartment, and even frequented several building sites. Finally, he found two rooms for rent in a large house in Hindås, a popular resort town about thirty-five kilometres from the city. During the brief Nordic summer Hindås teemed with holidaying workers and their families, who stripped off winter stockings and long pants and bared legs that looked like the stems of plants left to over-winter in a dark corner of the cellar. But now, in the dark, cold winter of 1947, the resort was empty and quiet, a suitable place for his family to rest and recover.

"The Villa Hagalund, as the house is called, sits on the edge of a pine forest, only a ten-minute walk from the local hotel, where we can eat for the first few days. Close by is a lake that the landlady, Fröcken Olsen, assures me slopes gently, and where little Peter could learn to swim. Get busy and crochet for yourself a swimsuit! The villa has electricity and central heating, a plus, but no running water or indoor toilet (big minus)."

Father wrote his letter describing the villa and its surroundings the very same night he found it, at nine-thirty at night in the Göteborg train station. He was exhausted, having spent the day house hunting, and he tried to sound positive, in spite of not being overly enthusiastic. So far from work and with only an outdoor toilet, the villa was far from ideal, but he had no choice. He would have to rise early and pay extra for travel. "But in thinking of you and the children, it might be best to live in Hindås until the fall—the air is clean and the town is quiet. Probably too quiet, as there are no movies, but Fröcken Olsen offered to look after the children if you someday wished to go into the city. Meanwhile, apartment complexes are being built all over, and I'll try to find one that will be ready for us in the autumn. Then, Ernushka, I'll buy you the golden chair I have long promised you—a chair to rest in after the day's work is done. Hindås will be ten times better than Bene, and I will be home every night. The situation provides some measure of comfort—central heating and electric cooking. And the children will have fresh air and can spend all day in the garden, where Fröcken Olsen has strawberries, raspberries, and perhaps currants. But I don't want to talk you into it. Think about it, and I will telephone tomorrow, that is Thursday, February 6 at 6:30 p.m., right after your dinner. I have to reply by tomorrow evening. We could move in on Saturday, February 15. I would have enough time to buy the children beds. Think about it (also about the outhouse)." Father concludes his letter with a small drawing of a train, and adds, "The train is bringing the letter to Mama. The picture is for Pecinkam. Greetings to Ilzuliti."

The mood of Father's letter and his desperate arguments convinced Mother that Hindås was their best, and likely only, option. But when Father's next letter advised her what trains to take and where to change trains to get to Göteborg, she felt betrayed. Her husband had promised to come for them. Probably sensing her anguish, Ilzite was crying again, and Peter clung to her in a way that was hardly normal for a boy of his age. How could she possibly make such a trip on her own, changing trains and hurrying from one platform to the other to make the proper connection? The situation was too reminiscent of the recent war years, with refugees so desperate to save themselves and their own families, that a woman alone with two babies, failed to evoke any help or even sympathy. Mother felt her stomach churn and a knot of worry form.

Mother read the letter again, carefully; she would have to commit the trip to memory, since there would be no time to study it in the rush from one platform to another. "Your train arrives about half an hour before I can be there. I will be a bit delayed, as I need to retrieve my salary, and you know, it is blessedly necessary at this time. Wait inside the station where it is warm until your Janis comes with the pay envelope."

Father instructed Mother to send their belongings directly to Hindås the Thursday before, so they would be there upon the family's arrival. "I don't have money to send you for the expenses so you must squeeze it out of the establishment. Impress upon them the need for the following: 1) Money for rent; 2) Food coupons for the four of us for two weeks (we can eat at the nearby Hindås Turisthotel); 3) Train tickets to Hindås; 4) Pocket money (also for me); 4a) Food coupons for three days; 5) What is my situation for work clothes? 6) Money for sending our goods." The wish list was impossibly long, and Mother despaired of filling it. She could only hope that the up-to-now benevolent authorities would realize her plight and provide the necessary coupons and money.

Even with temporary housing assured, Father was no more relaxed than before, and the continued stress and worry were telling on his health. On weekends, he visited building sites and filled out applications for apartments and villas, but he was not optimistic. He knew that false hope eroded the spirit, making the letdown more painful when it came. But neither was he a pessimist; the numbers spoke for themselves. He calculated that he had only a fifteen percent chance that his efforts would be successful.

One day, right after work, Father hurried to the store to buy beds for his children. Then he arranged for the beds to be delivered directly to the Villa Hagalund in Hindås. He was satisfied with his purchase, but the effort left him dead tired. "Mama, once you are here," he wrote, "I won't have to run around so much. You must help me, or I won't live as long as is necessary to see the children grow up. My heart hurts, also. Erna, you have to learn Swedish so you can help organize things, but I won't teach you, as I don't have the nerves needed for that.... Forgive me that the letter is not as happy as I would like. Your Janis."

Father's rheumatic fever-damaged heart began to send out warnings that it was being overtaxed. Stabbing pains accompanied him on his rounds of work, shopping, and house hunting. He felt unwell, even in the morning, and spent the day feeling dull and cranky. But he could not allow his personal tribulations to affect his work. Once again, Father's worst fear—that of not being in control of his life—was being realized. He stared at his ragged fingernails; they needed cutting, and he had no nail scissors. To add to his already full plate of troubles, a Siberian cold spell immobilized Göteborg, including the ferry that took him to and from work. Now the same trip by tram took longer, affording him less time to get everything done.

In his next letter to Mother, Father's words were bitter and dispirited. Father's pride had been hurt when he learned that the social services would provide coupons for food and other necessities, but not cash. "Maybe such a procedure is necessary for other unconscionable elements who would drink it away and then beg for more. Since you won't be receiving any cash, I am sending you 15 krona so you can proudly show the movers which bundles to carry and tip them accordingly. Don't strain yourself; it is unnecessary. Your Janis will earn more.... You must, however, promise me one thing. Don't bring any little crawling house pests with you. If you must, ask for some of that powder, but discreetly, so they don't detain you."

Perhaps it was due to the cold and the shortage of daylight, but Father found the Swedes more rigid this time around, or perhaps, after all he had been through, he himself was less resilient, less able to adapt. He worried about everything, even his table manners, which due to bad food and dismal surroundings, had deteriorated in the DP camps. During his noonday meal at the shipyards, Father carefully observed the delicate, and to his mind, overly finicky eating habits of his fellow employees, and copied them. He had disgraced himself the very first day by dribbling gravy on the tablecloth, leaving spots that continued to reproach him the rest of the meal. “I am learning to eat with an upturned fork in my left hand,” he wrote. “You see, Mama, how we have to keep learning, even in our older days. But today I fared quite well. The trick is to spear some larger, hard piece of meat on the end of the upturned fork, then with the knife, to carefully place some mashed potatoes on top, all the while calculating, very carefully, how much to put on, to avoid the whole thing collapsing. I will demonstrate to you when we meet. I would have been happy to receive a letter from you today, but there was none. Please greet the little ones, and apologize to them that I have not drawn a picture. Thank Pecinkam for his drawing. (We have already spent 750 krona since arriving in Sweden!) Your Janis.”

Eleven

The move to Hindås was undertaken with great anxiety, but achieved without incident. As Father had described, the house was cheery and its rooms spacious. It smelled of floor wax and flowers; the landlady, Fröcken Olsen, liked her floors spotless and the air perfumed. The Zalite family occupied two downstairs rooms and shared the front room; it was an unheard of and luxurious amount of space. Two small cots awaited the children in the smaller room. The front room opened onto a glassed-in, but unheated veranda that could be used as soon as the sun strengthened.

Mother and Fröcken Olsen, a spinster, dry and flat as *knäckebröd*, soon became friends. The only drawback was that Mother worried about her little ones misbehaving in Fröcken Olsen's presence, since she had never married and was not used to children. Her fiancé had perished in the Great War, and heartbroken, she would not give her heart to another. But Father claimed that she remained alone, because she never really grew up. She was small, with a girlish body and blonde hair held in place with a large, silver barrette. When Mother's coupons ran out, and she once again had to cook meals, she shared the large kitchen with Fröcken Olsen and Fru Svenson, a middle-aged woman from a nearby resort, who came weekly to help.

Shortly after the family had settled in, true to Swedish hospitality, Fröcken Olsen invited Mother for afternoon coffee. This sent Mother into a flurry of activity that included wetting down Peter's cowlick and scrubbing the dirt from Ilze's knees. Expertly, Mother tied a white satin ribbon around a handful of her daughter's silken hair, a ribbon that threatened to slide out any moment. Atop Ilze's head, the giant bow crouched like a small animal, ready to spring. "Try to keep still, so it doesn't slide out," Mother warned her a few minutes before it actually happened. She ran a comb through her own dark, shoulder-length hair, now streaked with white, and pinned it up into a roll at the base of her neck. Around her neck, Mother fastened a necklace of amber beads, round as eggs yolks and smooth as polished stone. A final inspection revealed the need to spit into her handkerchief to give her daughter's face a polish, and they were ready.

The children's eyes grew round, but Mother's face fell when they saw Fröcken Olsen's pretty table. Each place was set with a gold-rimmed, flower-strewn plate, a matching doll-sized cup, a shiny knife and fork, and a tiny spoon that looked as if it were meant for a doll's tea party. Scattered over the white linen cloth were plates of sandwiches, jam-filled tarts, and lacy cookies. The children couldn't take their eyes off a crystal bowl filled with candies that sat in the centre of the table. Mother exchanged her worried look for a stern glare meant to warn the children to not to touch anything. "The table's lovely, but you should not have gone to so much trouble," she said in formal, singsong Swedish, the result of earlier rehearsing. She was genuinely embarrassed as there was no way she could reciprocate. With one hand, she held on to her daughter's wrist, and with the other, moved the sugar bowl out of reach.

Peter's eyes looked bigger than the plate in front of him, and he let his storybook slip to the floor. "Is it a party?" he whispered to Mother.

"Oh, it's nothing at all," replied Fröcken Olsen, belittling her efforts in the proper Swedish way. "Just a little coffee for us, and some fresh milk for the children." She filled the adults' cups with strong, black coffee and offered around the bowl piled high with cubes of sugar. Using silver tongs, Mother helped herself, and then placed one cube onto each of her children's plates, while Fröcken Olsen prudently removed the delicate cups and saucers from in front of the children and exchanged them for mugs of warm, sweet milk.

"You are very kind. Everyone has been most helpful and generous," said Mother, all the while keeping a wary eye on her children. She gasped when she saw Peter spear a large chunk of herring with his fork and stuff it into his mouth, whole. Out of stock phrases and too shy to try her broken Swedish, Mother resorted to nodding and smiling, and the one-sided conversation soon lagged. But, in time, warmed by the coffee and her hostess's genuine kindness, Mother's reluctance slowly melted away.

"*Ja*," Mother agreed, "Here is like my Latvia. Same Baltic, but Latvia's not so rocky, but sandy and flat, like an offering...." Mother stopped, and her face grew red when she realized her words might be misinterpreted. "I mean flat like pancake." She ended with a short, dismissing laugh that made her look young again and very pretty.

The old Swedish woman's blueberry eyes darkened to blackberries. "So many Balts have risked their lives trying to reach Sweden; I wish we could have done more," she said sympathetically. "It must be so painful to no longer have a country." At the same time, she rose to deposit an almond tart on everyone's plate.

"*Ja*, only twenty short years of independence between the wars."

"War has destroyed so much happiness," Fröcken Olsen admitted, and allowed only the briefest shadow to cross her face. Then, she continued in a sprightly tone, "Why, just last week, a fishing trawler full of refugees limped to safety into Gotland." With a delicate motion, she picked up a cube of sugar, placed it on her tongue, and sucked her coffee through it, as if trying to sweeten a sad situation.

For a while, the conversation stopped, as each woman privately weighed the extent of her loss. In the ensuing silence, Peter tugged at Mother's arm, hoping for another sandwich. It would have been easier if she could have talked about what she had been through, but she held back, certain that no one else could understand. Sweden shared the Baltic Sea with Latvia, but as for suffering, it might as well have been on the other side of the world. In hope of restoring a light mood, Mother continued, "Look at us now, so fortunate here in your lovely villa, where it's so warm and cozy, eating cakes and drinking coffee. Don't misunderstand, but we hope to be able to return soon to Latvia," said Mother, not really believing her own words.

"Our government must do more to help the displaced—build more apartments, give them work," said Fröcken Olsen. "It's not as if we haven't benefited enormously from our so-called neutrality." Her eyes searched out Mother's in an attempt to send her a kind and reassuring look. "Perhaps, Fru Zalite, there are some things you need," she suggested. "You might leave the little ones with me one day next week and get to know the city, perhaps shop?" Her small mouth curved into a smile, showing small, even teeth, and tiny wrinkles appeared at her eyes.

"*Oh, Tak sa mycket*, thank you, but I really cannot. You already help so much, and the children are very naughty," Mother replied graciously and somewhat untruthfully. Peter looked at Mother with hope in his eyes; he was certain that the kind old lady would ply him with goodies in Mother's absence.

At supper that evening, Mother described to Father the elegant table that Fröcken Olsen had set and her offer to look after the children. "It's not as if I'm not trying to give you a good life, Erna."

"I didn't mean that…."

"Think about her offer. You could buy yourself something pretty." Father then rose from the table, and pulled open the drawer of a nearby desk to retrieve a well-thumbed notebook. "I'm saving all I possibly can, so we can get properly settled, but maybe there's a krona or two I could spare.

"I can make do with what I have, but Ilzite needs new shoes, and Peter, why he's growing like a weed, no doubt making up for lost time."

"Please, Erniņa, it's been so long since you had something new. But you're right; we've got to be careful, and money doesn't just grow on trees. I'm worried about the political situation in Europe, especially Stalin's expansionist policies."

"Don't talk about that, I beg you. It does no good and only gives the children more bad dreams."

"They've no idea what I'm talking about. That Stalin, he's like an octopus reaching out with all eight tentacles, in every direction, to grab what he can," Father couldn't help adding, before falling silent.

Slowly, day by day, winter lost its grip, and the days grew longer. The sun lost its white metallic brilliance and warmed to a more cheery yellow, allowing the children to spend more time outside, before their cold feet and numb hands brought them back indoors. Fresh air, sunshine, and cod liver oil was Father's recipe for restoring health, and it worked. Cheeks filled out, skin colour deepened, and spirits rose, including Father's. Even Mother admitted to gaining a half-kilo.

The Saturday before Easter, just as Mother finished dyeing eggs using the dried, outer skins of onions that she had saved, Fru Svenson appeared in the kitchen, her eyes red and her face as long as a Swedish saga. "I'll come back when you're done," she murmured, and turned on her heel to go.

"No, it's all right. I'm almost done here." The bacon fat Mother used to make the mottled eggs shine like polished marble had made her hands greasy, so she washed them, then dried them on her apron. "What's wrong? Are you unwell?" Then she scooped up Ilze, and sent her off to play with her brother.

Fru Svenson collapsed heavily into a chair, her hands between her knees. "I thought this time it would really happen—but no, no. Eric will be so disappointed, and I don't know how to tell him."

"Astrid—may I call you Astrid?" Mother went over, and put her arms around the distraught woman's hunched shoulders. Her voice was low and soothing, "Try not to worry. It doesn't help one bit. And you're still young. Why, look at me—thirty-seven years old with two little rascals that make me feel fifty!" Mother pulled her chair close, and continued in a low voice, "You know, it took me six years of mud baths, sulfur springs, and vile concoctions—we tried everything." Mother's cheeks turn pink. "Then, out of the blue sky, Peteris arrived, and not two years later, Ilzite."

Astrid seemed not overly convinced, but she straightened and nodded. "Thank you for understanding."

"We can talk again later if you like, but I'm sure everything will be fine." With the arrival of spring and warmer weather, Father thought it would save him time if he cycled to the train station, so he bought a secondhand bicycle at a reasonable price. On the first day, he left in good spirits but, unused to such strenuous activity, he arrived home red-faced and out of breath. The children had been waiting by the road and begged Father for a ride, but he waved them off, and they walked to the house together.

When Mother saw the state he was in, she helped Father off with his jacket, and urged him to sit and rest, while she hurried to get a glass of water. "It's easier in the morning, mostly downhill, and I just push off and coast. Coming back's harder." Between breaths, Father took small sips of water. "I just don't know how much longer I'm going to be around."

"Please don't talk like that, only rest a bit. Supper's ready, but it can wait." Peter and Ilze stood in the doorway, impatient for dinner to be over, so they could ride on Father's new bicycle. "It's still a long day for you, getting up early to catch the train and working so much overtime, and then on the weekend, trying to find an apartment."

"Yes, but what choice do I have? If your Swedish were better, you could help me." His words hurt. Mother had been trying so hard to improve.

Over dinner, Father made a deal with his children. Upon his return the next day, if they said the magic words in Swedish and without a mistake, "Papa, let me ride the bicycle with you,“ Father would lift, first one and then the other, onto the metal seat and walk the bicycle to the house. It wasn't long before they both learned to speak the language properly and could have all the rides they wanted.

With the arrival of the summer solstice, the small resort town of Hindås took on a new life. Much as Latvians celebrated their John's Day, the Swedes celebrated June 23 with all night merrymaking and the lighting of giant bonfires that banished the shadows and sent sparks up into the sky. From then until the end of summer, the hotel and surrounding villas filled with loud city people. The adults spent their time playing croquet on the grass or lounging on wooden chairs. They exposed bare arms and legs and, like flowers, turned their pale faces to the sun to slowly rid themselves of winter's unhealthy pallor. With their arms linked, girls in pretty summer dresses promenaded down the main road, hoping to be noticed, while the boys feigned indifference. The Zalites, too, revelled in the warmer weather and spent more time outdoors. Fresh air, wholesome food, and a daily spoonful of cod liver oil were doing wonders; the children grew, and their angles softened.

One summer day, Father returned from the station with a large cardboard box balanced on his handlebars. "Peter, run and tell Mama to come and see," Father said, and setting the box down on a wooden table, reached into his pocket for his penknife. "It's from America! The Abeltiņš!" he called to Mother, when she appeared at the door, still wearing her apron.

"Really? The Abeltiņš from New York City?"

"Just so," said Father as he cut the string and handed it to Mother.

"Do you remember when she visited Latvia with her sons, the year before we were married? Here, Ilzite." Mother handed the string to Ilze, to roll into a ball.

"They were a well-fed bunch, but the boys spoke only a few words of Latvian." Carefully, so as not to damage the stamps or return address, Father removed the brown paper wrapping and folded it.

"What is it Papa?" asked Ilze.

"Elza must have given them our address," said Mother, "but how strange she would send us a parcel now, months before Christmas."

Father wiped his forehead with his handkerchief, then spread it out on top of his head. "I suppose the Americans don't know what to do with their money." He opened the flaps and looked inside. "Hats, Mama! The box is full of hats!" Father couldn't believe his eyes, as he lifted out one curious shape after another. There were seven hats in all. "One for each day of the week, it looks like."

"Is there a letter?"

"Coffee," said Father and pressed the bag of beans to his nose, "candy bars, and yes, a letter." Father suggested Mother try on a hat and handed her a dark green velvet hat with a small veil.

Mother patted her hair. "I wasn't expecting this," she said, running her fingers over the smooth velvet. But Father insisted, and after tucking in a few stray hairs, Mother set the hat gingerly on her head and pulled the veil down over her eyes. "How do I look?" she asked, cocking her head to one side.

"Just like Marlene Dietrich," said Father, as the children clapped.

When the water in the lake had warmed up, Father decided that Peter should learn how to swim. Standing waist-deep in the water, he cupped one hand under Peter's chin, and with the other under Peter's belly, told him to sweep his arms in a wide circle and, at the same time, to kick his legs out like a frog. Mother, who did not enjoy swimming, sat on a blanket and observed, as Peter splashed about and swallowed water, and Ilze dug in the sand. Mother had dutifully crocheted herself a bathing suit over the winter months, and she wore it now to please her husband. The suit, which fit rather nicely when dry, soon became wet and stretched and sagged around her knees like winter woollens hung out to dry. Mother never wore it again.

The summer drew to a close, the vacationers withdrew to their city lives, and Father continued his search for a place to live. One day, he arrived home with good news, his face flushed from pedaling as fast as he could. He took Mother by the waist and whirled her around, "Hurrah, I've just signed the lease to an apartment!"

"Jani, be careful, these aren't mine," cried Mother, clutching four plates.

Father unbuckled the straps on his briefcase and showed Mother the papers. "Lagerstromplatsen number two, Göteborg. Sounds grand, eh? A brand new apartment complex that's just being finished, Mama, and it's modern, with running water and a real toilet!"

Mother could hardly believe that their three years of homelessness were almost over. "It's too good to be true," she said with tears filling her eyes.

"Come now, no use to cry now, after everything."

Mother wiped her eyes with a clean corner of her apron. "This'll be our first real home in a long time, since leaving our Tomsona iela flat. If I'd known then what lay ahead, I don't think I would ever have left."

"Careful now, you don't want to upset the children." Father had not expected such a reaction, so he just patted his wife's shoulder. "There, there, it could've been worse. At least we're not under the Russian boot. Just be thankful we're alive and together."

"I am. Really, I am. I just couldn't help it for a moment," Mother said and, rising slowly, went to the stove.

"You should try to be more pragmatic, like me. We've got to make plans now," Father said.

Before the Zalite family left Hindås for their new apartment in Göteborg, their landlady invited the family to celebrate the crayfish festival with her. "I do hope you like crayfish," she said.

"I adore them," Mother answered without hesitation.

"It'll be late, since we normally feast on crayfish in the evening, by the light of a full moon and a few lanterns, so it's a good idea if the children have a nap in the afternoon," Fröcken Olsen explained. "And it's a messy business, so we'll eat in the garden."

On the evening of the crayfish feast, a light breeze set the paper lanterns swaying and lifted the edges of the brightly coloured cloth. Pink and purple asters from the garden adorned the table, and two large bowls, one at each end, held crimson mounds of boiled crayfish, their antennas quivering in the air, making them appear alive.

Since the hour was late, and to make sure they would not appear too hungry, Mother heeded Father's warning and fed Peter and Ilze one slice of buttered bread each. "They must behave properly," Father had said. He took care to arrive at the appointed time, not a moment earlier or later.

"It is so kind of you to invite us," Father said. "My Erna tells me you've become good friends."

"Yes, indeed," replied Fröcken Olsen. "I've enjoyed watching the children blossom." She lifted a large bowl in her two small hands and passed it to Mother.

"Yes, the fresh air and sunshine have been like a tonic. My, these look wonderful," Mother said and helped herself to one.

The conversation lagged as crayfish legs were ripped off and the claws cracked open. Beady, black eyes stared out, unseeing, from severed heads, as the remains piled up in another bowl. Peter sucked the sweet flesh from one leg and chewed as he cracked another for his sister. As the one bowl emptied and the other filled, the hour grew late, and it became time to go inside. Father took the children by the hand and went inside, while Mother helped their hostess bring in the dishes. "Perhaps you could return next summer at vacation time, so I can see how the children have grown."

"We'll certainly try," Mother promised.

One week later, the family left for Göteborg. "*Tack sa mycket*, thank you very much," said Mother to Fröcken Olsen, as she hugged her good-bye. Mother was genuinely sorry to be leaving; she had grown fond of Fröcken Olsen, and from her, had learned what Swedish she knew. "You have been so very kind to me and the children," she added. From the open car window, they all waved to Fröcken Olsen, who looked smaller than ever, standing and waving from her wide front porch.

Mother fell back against the seat, her cheeks flushed, and her eyes shining with excitement. A small straw hat from America perched on one side of her head like a helmet knocked askew by an unseen assailant. The only thing that kept it from falling off was wishful thinking and a long, pearl-headed pin. At last, she would be in her own home again.

Twelve

Our new home in Göteborg was an apartment on the fourth floor of a five-story, brick building that spanned an entire city block. Father made us commit the address—Lagerstromplatsen number two—to memory, so that we would always be able to find the right entryway and not get lost. In the middle of the buildings was a vast expanse of green divided into three sections by rows of fast-growing poplars. Children ran about on the grass below. "For now, you must not go beyond that first row of trees," said Father.

All of us, especially Mother, took special delight in the hot and cold water that appeared like magic with a turn of the lever. I snuggled into my own, familiar bed, brought along from the Villa Hagalund, but I could only sleep after Mother sang the nursery rhyme "Aija šu šu" several times and left the door slightly ajar. At breakfast the next morning, when Mother asked us how we had slept, I told her great, but Father said he had never slept better. "It was like sleeping in God's own ear."

While Mother prepared breakfast, Peter and I watched at the window, as adults lined up in neat rows on the grass below and started to bend and stretch and wave their arms about in great big circles. In the afternoon, school children appeared, skipping and running, chasing each other around, or kicking at rubber balls. We wanted to join them, but Mother told us to be patient, she had unpacking to do. The next day, instead of playing in the park, Mother took us shopping for winter coats. I winced at the screech of metal on metal as our tramway turned a corner and covered my ears at the shrill of a factory whistle or boat in the harbour. But what frightened my brother and me most of all was the unmistakable drone of an approaching airplane. In the middle of the vast expanse of Gustav II Adolf Square, we both doubled over and tucked our heads between our legs. “Please get up,” Mother begged, but until the sound faded, no amount of tugging could straighten us.

My parents never talked about the war years, at least not to us, and for many years, I had no idea why I was so afraid, or even what it was I feared. But neither scorn nor assurances worked, and the night terrors continued for many years. I would awaken with my heart pounding and seek Mother’s comforting warmth. For many years, it was even too painful to remember the good times back in Latvia, so the first years of my life were erased and unspoken; they became the lost years of my childhood.

Sometimes Father alluded to difficulties and setbacks, saying, “Our lives have been derailed, but we are now back on track,” but I didn’t know what he meant, and he did not explain. For him, what constituted getting back on track was forgetting the past and moving on. For Mother, it meant accepting the present situation and making sure her children received proper care. Since our parents had been through a lot of hardship, Peter and I were required to be good-natured and obedient at all times, and we were never allowed to complain. A child’s complaint was a red flag to Father, who equated discontent with ingratitude and ignorance, and he would not tolerate either, especially not after what he and Mother had been through. Even my bad dreams were seen as a kind of reproach, silly and immature.

Soon after we moved into our flat, Father bought Mother the golden chair he had promised her, and when most of our belongings were in place, Father unrolled the canvas portrait of his father and inspected it. Flat on the table, Opaps looked up at us from behind his oval, wire-framed glasses, serene and unaware of what he had been through. He had a broad expanse of forehead with a rather prominent nose, but a long, snow white beard and generous moustache hid his mouth and chin. It seemed to me that all the hair that should have been on his head had somehow slipped down his face. Everything, except for grandfather’s face, beard, and hands was black—black and shiny, as if it had been oiled. I tried to differentiate between his black suit and the black background, but it was not possible.

Father ran his fingers along grandfather’s hands, which were uncharacteristically still. “I’m relieved to see that Opaps came through in one piece," he said. Grandfather Peteris Zalite regarded us with a deceptively benign expression; he had been a demanding pedagogue, a strict disciplinarian, and an exacting father and husband. The image was so lifelike, I half expected Opaps to chide me for my uncombed hair.

With great care, Father measured the length and width of the canvas with a jointed wooden ruler that he unfolded as necessary, then he jotted the numbers on a small piece of paper he carried in his pocket. "Come, Peter. We need to find a proper frame for Opaps."

When Opaps returned a week later, gazing out of an ornate, gilded frame, I thought he looked pleased. Father hung the portrait in the living room, above the divan, giving grandfather a good view of the goings on, even through the open arch and into the dining room. Opaps saw everything, and his gaze never wavered. When I stared at him, he stared back. If I stepped to one side and peered at him from an angle, his eyes followed me, and he peered back. Father was pleased to see his father accorded the respect he deserved, especially since it pained him that he was unable to visit his grave.

With time, I learned more about Opaps and about my own past. Unlike his portrait with folded hands, in life, Opaps' hands had never been still. In whatever spare time he had, he carved designs on small wooden boxes that he presented as gifts to his daughters and daughters-in-law. He showed his love, not by physical affection, but by passing on his knowledge. One summer, he taught his granddaughter Rita, who was living in Denmark and had come to Jurmala for the summer, proper Latvian grammar. He loved the theatre and opera, especially *La Traviata*, and as he walked, he sang favorite arias to himself. He was hardworking, studious, ambitious, an astute organizer, and an unflagging committee member. Although he was a man possessing many admirable qualities, tact and compromise were not among them. He said what was on his mind and often repeated the phrase 'facts are facts'. For him, the truth was absolute and, like his portrait, had no shades of grey. This caused him to be harsh with his pupils, and sometimes with his wife and family, but he never lost their respect. In an independent Latvia, he had worked for the Department of Education, but his extreme, unyielding Latvian nationalism caused those in power to turn against him, and eventually, his position in the Department of Education was eliminated. Still, he remained an educator and for the rest of his life he continued to offer private lessons and to write learned articles; he worked tirelessly to improve the quality of education. In recognition of this, Peteris Zalite had been decorated with the Three Star Medal (Fourth Class) for his work helping Latvian refugees in Moscow and the Cross of Appreciation (Third Class) for his accomplishments in fostering education in his native Latvia. I was sorry that the painting did not portray the medals pinned to his chest; they would have brightened up his portrait.

Peter and I had few toys, and those we did have were simple ones, made of paper, yarn, or wood. Sometimes, after he and Mother had finished with the newspaper, Father taught us to fold the large sheets into hats, boats, or airplanes.

Mother rarely went out, except to buy food, and hardly ever by herself. But one morning she came to us with an unusually stern expression on her face and told us that she had an important appointment and couldn't take us along. "I know I can count on you to be good children," she said, "and when I return, which will be very, very soon, I'll bring you a lovely surprise." Then she brought out some sheets of newspaper, several old journals with photographs, scissors, and coloured pencils and left, locking the door behind her.

For a while, Peter and I were busy and happy. I coloured a picture, and Peter folded a whole squadron of airplanes, large and small, even using some pages torn from the magazines. When he sent them around the room, I dropped my pencil and ran after them. However, they crashed into walls and furniture, and Peter decided that the kitchen was too confining for his efforts, so he pushed a chair over to the window, and after a brief struggle, succeeded in opening it. I nudged my chair in beside his. One after the other, Peter's airplanes soared free, and we both leaned out to follow their flight. To our delight, we soon had an audience on the grass below, all waving and shouting something we could not understand. Spurred on by the unexpected response, Peter quickly folded more paper into airplanes while I tore up pages of the magazine into smaller pieces and threw them out. I laughed and clapped as they danced and swirled about in the air currents. Suddenly, a loud knock on the door startled us.

"We're not allowed to open it," said Peter.

"Maybe it's Mama."

"It's not. She has a key."

"Maybe it's the Russian bear that's been following us everywhere," I whispered, as a shiver raced down my spine.

Just then, a key grated in the lock, the door flew open, and a man and woman burst into the room. "Get away from the window," they shouted. I recognized the man as the building superintendent, and the woman was the same one who had been waving to us from down below.

"Where's your mother?" she demanded.

"Out," Peter answered, "but it's all right, I'm five and a half." He held up his hand to show five fingers. "I'm looking after my sister."

When Mother returned, she was surprised to see a strange woman in the apartment. After turning pale, she reddened, as the woman explained what had happened. After that day, if Mother had to go out alone, she brought us over to stay with a neighbour.

Finally, for the first time in three long years, our family was properly settled. Peter and I began to make friends in our building and in the park. Father contacted several fraternity brothers from Talavija, and occasionally, our families met. Letters were exchanged with family members. The feast of Santa Lucia, then Christmas and New Years came and went. Sometime in late January, an airmail letter arrived from the United States. "It's from Juris, in America," Father said, after examining the envelope. He slit open the flimsy letter, scanned it, and then read it aloud:

"Aboard the troop carrier *S.S. Marine Tiger*, we steamed past the magnificent Statue of Liberty and slid into New York harbour on Christmas Day," wrote Uncle Juris. "It was the best present anyone could wish for—a new country unspoiled by war. Zenny and the girls were relieved to be on dry land again. I must admit I was also; I don't have the sea legs that you have. Somehow our ship's arrival was news and a photographer from the *Daily Mirror* snapped a photo of Zenny and the girls that ended up in the paper the next day. You see, your brother is already famous in America and he hasn't built any roads or bridges yet! The Catholic Relief Organization had rented us a small room at the Hotel Chelsea in Manhattan and provided a few kopecs for living expenses.... If you are worried by recent events in Germany or the attitude of the Swedes, I strongly advise you to consider coming to America."

"What does he mean by 'recent events in Germany'?" asked Mother.

"It seems that the Bolsheviks have once again duped the gullible Americans and grabbed a large chunk of Germany for themselves. But see, your Janis got you out of the DP camps a whole year before Juris did."

One Sunday, a few months later, we attended a gloomy church service during which many tears were shed. Afterward, the congregation gathered over coffee as usual, but instead of happy greetings and hearty handshakes, there were somber faces and hushed conferences. No one talked of anything but the fact that the Swedish Government had caved in to Soviet demands and had begun returning home the Latvian Legionnaires who had made it to Sweden. Everyone knew that for the Legionnaires, it meant certain death. Sweden tried to defend itself by claiming it was the price to be paid for neutrality, but the Latvians were outraged at this betrayal. Rather than return to Soviet hands, some of the men had attempted to take their own lives. One, a friend of Father's, was in the hospital, barely clinging to life. He had slashed his belly open with a shard of broken glass to avoid being shipped back across the Baltic. Another Latvian had died, but several others, whom the Swedes judged fit enough to travel, had been carried aboard on stretchers.

At home, Father remained silent all through dinner. Finally he spoke, "It's a risky business to open the gut. That's what desperation does to a man."

I wondered if the Soviet bear had gotten to him, but dared not ask.

"Children, run along and play. Your Mama and I have to talk."

"Will this madness never end?" Mother asked.

"Apparently not. This action of the Swedish government is unconscionable. Can't they see the Soviets for what they are? Every day, Latvians are risking their lives to get here. Do we have to keep running, too?"

"Please, Jani, I can't, not with the baby coming."

Each morning before breakfast and in the evening after supper, Father listened to the news on a Grundig short wave radio that squealed like Omite's pig whenever he twisted the dial. The news did not make him happy, only more worried. It was becoming obvious that inept diplomacy and Soviet double-dealing were already endangering the post-war peace.

But Father kept most of the bad news to himself; he didn't want to upset Mother.

On a fine morning in June, when the whole city was decorated with blue and yellow Swedish flags, Mother was whisked away, and a neighbour came to stay with us. When I cried for my mother, the neighbour told me it was a day to be happy—the king's birthday—but her words failed to console me.

Several days later, Mother returned with a big smile on her face and a bundle in her arms. "Have you been good little children?" she asked. "If you have, I've a wonderful surprise." She sat down in her golden chair and folded back the blanket to reveal a round, pink, doll's face. "See? The stork brought you a baby brother."

It had been less than a year since we moved into Lagerstromplatsen number two, and I wondered how the stork knew where we lived. "It must have been a Swedish stork," I declared, "a Latvian stork could not fly this far."

Mother pushed back a stray lock of hair and said, "No, storks have great big wings that make them very strong fliers."

"A brother? What's his name?" Peter wondered.

"Rolands." At the mention of his name, the baby squirmed, opened his tiny pink mouth, and yawned, but his eyes remained shut.

"He's our lucky baby, born on King Gustav's birthday. Did you see all the flags? They were for Rolands, too."

"Now, now, Ernuška. You're exaggerating, and will only confuse the children. The city was decorated for the king's ninetieth birthday!" But despite his best efforts, Father could not conceal his own happiness with his new son.

Mother's smile told me she knew better, and ever so gently, she placed Rolands on the divan. "Ilzite, will you watch him for me while I get something ready for supper?" Although she was tired, her step was light; she was thirty-eight years old, and had delivered a healthy baby. Rolands would grow up strong and healthy and unafraid; for him, there would be no fleeing or hunger or homelessness. Mother even had real diapers, not rags, and a tub in which to wash them. What she wanted now was to spoil this last baby.

"I know what you're thinking, Mama," Father's voice interrupted her thoughts, "we've got to be careful not to spoil this one, though I'll admit, he does look like a little prince in the carriage the government provided. And what's more, we can save his baby allowance for the future."

Mother removed one tortoise shell comb from her chestnut hair, smoothed back some wayward strands with it, and jammed it firmly in place again before answering. "Can't we just use the money to buy a few things we've done without for so long? A toy or some treats?"

Rolands continued to sleep, stirring now and again, unaware of the controversy taking shape around him. I couldn't resist giving his chin a little poke to see what he could do, but he didn't do much. He only screwed up his face and rooted around for my finger.

In the excitement, I almost forgot my fears, but when it was time to sleep, I worried that if the Latvian stork could find us, so could the Russian bear. I begged to be allowed to keep the light on, but as usual, Father would not allow it. He disapproved of what he called silliness, and even more of wasting electricity. "There's nothing to be afraid of," he said and flicked off the light. His one concession was to leave the door open a crack. I found the slit of yellow light and the murmur of voices comforting. "She's old enough now to put all that behind her," I heard Father say, before drifting off to sleep. Like many other Latvian parents of that time, mine believed that if the horrors and difficulties of the war years went unmentioned, they would be more quickly forgotten. Father seemed to forget that, in thirty years, he had not been able to forget the horror he had witnessed, in 1917, when he was a ten-year-old boy in Moscow. The Bolshevik Revolution had left its mark on his psyche.

The months passed quickly, and Rolands, who was beginning to crawl around, kept Mother busy. But the news that Father heard nightly on his short wave radio continued to worry him, and the letters from Latvia were distressing. At the beginning of the summer, a letter arrived from Marija Freimanis, Father's sister. "Thirteen-year-old Janis was at school and witnessed the soldiers rounding up the children of those who had already been arrested. That night, we didn't sleep as the heavy trucks rumbled past our house taking away our neighbors, friends, and colleagues. It was awful. They were singing the familiar farewell song: *Projam jaiet, projam jaiet.* I cry even now, as I write this to you."

It was through the Latvian Association that we learned the details. During the last week of March 1949, about fifty thousand Latvians who had resisted the collectivization of their farms were rounded up and forcibly deported to the Soviet Union. The Soviets' criminal action led to more Latvians taking refuge in Sweden, and the Latvian Refugee Committee in Stockholm had its hands full trying to help them. The plundering by the Berlin Blockade and the Red Army, and the rape of civilians in Soviet-controlled Germany gave Father many nights of troubled sleep. He worried about the worsening of relations between the east and the west, and he wondered if it was advisable to remain in a country that seemed to lack the necessary backbone to stand up to the Soviet Union. He felt that he could not count on the Swedish government to protect the many Baltic families who had settled or sought refuge here. Perhaps he should take his brother's advice after all—something he was loath to do—and move far away, to America.

It was a difficult decision, but once again, Father began to write letters to consulates, enquiring about visas and work possibilities. "Mama, how'd you like to live in Argentina?" Father asked one day, out of the blue. Mother paled and looked at Father with a strange expression on her face that I had not seen before. "They need shipbuilding engineers, and they've offered us free passage and a good salary."

"Argentina?" Mother dropped her sewing in her lap. "Isn't that in South America?"

"Yes, but of course, nothing's been decided yet. I'm just testing the water, seeing what are the possibilities." He himself wasn't so keen to move to a country where the seasons were all backwards—summer was winter and winter, summer. If he didn't plan properly, they might end up suffering through two winters!

Mother could not bear the thought of moving again, of starting over in a country she had barely heard of, or of learning another language. "I don't think…," she rocked back and forth, ever so slightly, "is it Spanish or Portuguese…what…?"

The subject of Argentina was not raised again, but Father continued to write letters and to save money in earnest. One night, as I lay in bed awake with the door open a slit, I heard Father tell Mother, "There, now we've a safe place to hide our extra krona." He had taken down Grandfather's painting, and with the same pungent glue he used to repair our shoes, had pasted a sturdy envelope to the back of the frame. With increased emphasis on saving, there was never enough to cover all our needs. Mother's feeble offers of help were dismissed; she already had her hands full.

"Believe me, Erna, I'm doing all I can." Father's voice had a sharp edge to it. "I already work as much overtime as I possibly can." They had not planned to have a third child, and he felt stretched to the limit, about to snap. He could hardly believe the cost of passage to New York for a family of five.

"I know you are. I just thought I could do something too."

Mother was silent for a long time, not sewing or moving, until Father finally asked, "What are you thinking, Mama?"

"*I am thinking deep thoughts…*" Mother replied. It was a standard answer, the first line of her grandmother's favorite song.

Father's baritone joined in with the next few lines, "*Why does good fortune elude me? Why does my foot falter at every step*?" Somehow, inexplicably, the plaintive but familiar melody and words made them both feel better, and the subject was dropped.

In August, Peter turned seven, and soon after, he started first grade. He came home from school one day, proud as a rooster in his school uniform. On his head, perched a cap emblazoned with the school crest. I missed him terribly, and Rolands seemed to take up more and more of Mother's time. It was no better when Peter came home from school. Mother fussed over him as if he had been gone a week, and in the evening, Father asked him what he had learned and helped him to cover his schoolbooks with brown paper. No one paid any attention to me unless I did something naughty, such as pinching Rolands and making him cry. To make matters worse, my January birthday meant I would have to wait two more years to start first grade, even though I was only a year and a half younger than Peter. I begged to be allowed to go to school sooner, and Father agreed to look into the possibility. He was told that schools were overcrowded with immigrant children, and the teachers did not have time to help each child individually, but if I learned to read on my own at home, I could be admitted a year earlier.

Some weeks later, a letter arrived from Karlis Rabacs, informing us that the family had finally left Camp Kleinkotz in Bavaria, and they were on their way to a new life in America. Uncle Karlis, who had the keen eyes of a journalist and the heart of a poet, had also somehow managed to hold on to his sense of humour. But it was obvious from his letter that he still worried about the Soviets, even aboard the *SS Marine Jumper*, an American troop carrier. In the camp newspaper, *Latvija*, as well as in other publications, he had taken a strong stand against the illegal annexation of Latvia by the Soviet Union.

"I traveled incognito as *#277*," he began. "With me for our safety, twenty-seven others have joined me here at the very bottom of the ship. My first meal on board equaled the food in Riga's Hotel De Roma, only the devils did not serve alcohol.... Professor Delvigs soon revealed that he had a bottle of Hennessy.... The men are assigned various jobs and I chose the kitchen—only Negroes there. I peeled potatoes and practiced my English. My kitchen companions tried to convince me to eat up everything in the kitchen. But that was not possible, there was too much food there."

His family was also on board, but in separate quarters for women and children. "Still," he wrote, "out in the mid-Atlantic, when the *Jumper* started to rock and sway, we were all in the same boat. I have given up my breakfast to the Atlantic, and the Negroes have dumped huge amounts of uneaten food into the ocean. I soon recovered and resumed peeling potatoes and eating oranges and other round fruit. For the first time in my life, I bought a whole carton of cigarettes—spent almost half of my capital. The other half I spent for a pair of nylons for Elza and the rest on chocolate."

"On June 23rd, as we approached American coast, the winds were calm and the day sunny. It was not yet visible, but even so, maybe the good weather was due to the Statue of Liberty. I thought of Jani and how we celebrated the summer solstice back home. We received our visas and the results of our medical exam. The next day, we exchanged our visas for landing cards. Real Americans—not IRO officials—arrived on a motor launch to carry out inspection. President Truman himself did not greet us, but he sent his underlings—customs officials and stevedores.... We relinquished our carry-on baggage, and disembarked as model passengers with nothing but a toothbrush in our pockets. Driving through the city, I saw some tall buildings, possibly they were skyscrapers. Otherwise, I did not notice any America. Tasted Scotch whiskey. I guess I am not a DP any longer. So! Karlis."

My aunts and uncles and cousins popped up like corks, across the Atlantic Ocean. Uncle Juris and his family were already in New York, as was Cousin Valters, and now, Mother's sister and her family were there as well. New York was on everyone's mind. All, including Father, believed in the power of the Statue of Liberty to hold back the red menace. Other relatives immigrated to Canada: Cousin Rita and her husband Laimonis had recently arrived in Toronto, and the Stromanis family whose daughter, Margrieta, was Mother's goddaughter, had settled in a small town east of Montreal.

The day that Father's Grundig announced the start of fighting in Korea, we ate in silence. The unspeakable had happened. I scooped up meat and potatoes, but could not swallow. The silence meant that something too dreadful for words had occurred. Father's worst fears were confirmed: the Soviets would keep right on swallowing one country after another and only a miracle could save them. Latvia would never see freedom again.

A few Latvians, among them Roland's godfather, Arvids Klaviņš, who had already risked his life once by escaping to Sweden in a fishing boat, became determined to reach America. They scratched together enough money to purchase a derelict and no longer seaworthy coastal vessel, with the idea of sailing across the North Atlantic. "I prefer to take my chances at sea, than be squashed on land under the boot of a Bolshevik," Klaviņš declared, trying to convince Father to join him. Father refused. He admitted that although Arvids Klaviņš was a fine fisherman and able sailor who knew the Baltic intimately, he had no experience in the Atlantic.

"You're crazy," Father said, when he realized his friend was serious. "If you had children, you'd understand." Father watched him go, doubting he would ever see him again.

However, this time Father was wrong. Months later, news of a miracle arrived. The leaking and overcrowded ship, carrying seventy Latvians, had landed somewhere south of Boston. They had been taken into custody by the US Coast Guard and were being held on Ellis Island.

"I just hope they don't return them to the Soviets," said Mother.

"The Americans would never do that," Father replied, sounding very sure. The news of Arvids's safe arrival was a godsend, but Father continued to be worried by world events and by concerns about his own future. What had he done wrong that he was doomed to spend his whole life fleeing from country to country in search of freedom?

In his blackest moments, he wondered if there was no safe place on earth.

While all around me, the adults worried about far-off world events, I was happy at school, and did my best to please the teacher. I was Ingrid now. The school preferred to use my middle name, Ingrid, which was a common Swedish name, instead of the more Latvian Ilze. "We all have to learn to adapt," Father said. "It's part of life. Look at your Uncle Juris. His American colleagues call him George, because they couldn't pronounce the soft *j* of Juris. I'd likely become John. It's not so important what people call you, as long as you yourself know who you are."

As the possibility of going to America increased, I wondered what name my teachers would find for me there. Uncle Juris wrote to us about the Easter parade along Fifth Avenue, and I imagined my aunt and cousins marching in step to the beat of a band. He described trains so noisy that conversation was impossible while they were passing, and buildings so high they swayed in the wind. However, what intrigued Mother the most was my uncle's description of an automat machine that dropped food, ready-to-eat, right into your hands, with no dishes to wash!

With the start of the Korean War, Father began to seriously consider leaving Sweden. He wrote letters to relatives and fraternity brothers living in Canada and the United States, asking them for advice and about possible work opportunities. He did not want to abandon a profession he was good at, so his options were limited. He was relieved when Laimonis Goba offered to make the trip from Toronto to Montreal, to personally present Father's letter and credentials at the shipyards. Some weeks later, Laimonis wrote that Canadian Vickers had expressed an interest in Father. The time had come to decide. Each evening, after the children were in bed, Father laid out the pros and cons before Mother. Nothing was said to the children, but Peter and I wondered why a doctor's visit was necessary, when no one was sick. We went to school as before, and after school we played on the grass below or with our friends, but something had changed in our lives.

The festival of Santa Lucia came and went, and Christmas brought the usual excitement of *piparkukas* and *pirags* and candles on the tree. On Christmas Eve, lying under the tree like a real hibernating bear was a sheared beaver coat for Mother. As Mother ran her hands over the soft fur and examined the silk lining and clever storm cuffs meant to keep out the snow and cold, she expressed surprise that Father Christmas would be able to afford such an expensive gift. Father urged her to try it on, and when she threw the heavy coat over her shoulders and lifted the high collar against an imaginary wind, Father approved, but I thought she looked a lot like a bear. Mother's fur coat came with a matching fur hat—for me! I pulled it on over my ears and tied the wide satin ribbons in a bow under my chin. After admiring myself in the hall mirror, I removed the hat, and for the rest of the evening, it lay in my lap, as warm and soft as a kitten. "Now, Mama, you're all set for Canada," Father announced. "You also," he said, turning to me. I could not see his eyes, only the reflection of a dozen lights dancing on his glasses.

I soon discovered a new game to play with Rolands. With my fur hat pulled down over my ears, I pretended to be a big, bad bear, and on all fours, I chased my brother from room to room, scattering throw rugs every which way. The first time, Rolands was so startled he did not know whether to laugh or cry or run to Mother, but he soon warmed to the game and ran away, squealing. It felt good to wear my hat and become the Russian bear that I had worried about for so long. Often, Rolands ended up in Mother's lap, and I snuggled up beside her. Mother had no choice but to jab her stubby embroidery needle through the canvas so it wouldn't get lost, and put aside her sewing.

"*Lāčplēsis* (Bear Slayer) was a mighty hero, a giant with the body of a man, with the exception of his furry ears. And it was just those ears—the ears of a bear—that gave him his great strength, like you, Ilzite, when you put on your hat and pretend to be a bear. But *Lāčplēsis* was not pretending...," Mother paused and ruffled Rolands's hair.

I made a face at my brother to hide my embarrassment. "We were just playing." It was not too different from Father, I thought, when he claimed to be strong as a lion, because he was born in August, under the sign of Leo. Mother continued the story in a voice as smooth and sweet as honey, and by the time she finished, Rolands was asleep.

After the New Year, Peter and I returned to our separate schools, but something in the air at home was different. Father and Mother held more private conversations and brief, whispered exchanges than before. Soon I noticed other changes, too, such as books being sorted and dishes piled into boxes, instead of being stacked on the shelves. One by one, the few paintings we owned disappeared from the walls, leaving behind their pale rectangular shadows. Grandfather witnessed the upheaval in our lives, until one day, he too was gone. That was the day that Father finally told us outright that we were immigrating to Canada. "Tomorrow will be your last day at school."

"It can't be. I'm singing in the spring concert, and you're invited." Out of nowhere, angry tears stung my eyes. Father always stressed the importance of regular school attendance.

"Our class has an outing next week," said Peter.

"Your teachers have been told, and tomorrow, you can say good-bye."

"It's for the best," Mother added, but she sounded neither convincing nor convinced.

"You'd better have a good reason," Peter challenged, squaring his slim shoulders, but he quickly withered under Father's angry look.

"I think you'll like our ship, the *Gripsholm*. It's modern and fast; the crossing should take only nine or ten days." Father reached behind him for the brochure. "Look, here's where our stateroom's located," he said, as he unfolded a page, "and here's the children's playroom, full of toys and games. Your Aunt Edite and Cousin Milda arrive tomorrow from Copenhagen. We'll be traveling together."

Peter could not help showing his interest. "How big is the boat?"

"Ship, not boat," Father corrected, "Fifty thousand tonnes."

"Wow!" Peter examined the diagram more closely.

"But Papa, I really like my school, and I'm already way too big for a playroom." I stamped my foot, and turned to Mother for help. "I want to stay right here." In desperation I added, "My teacher doesn't want me to go. She says I'm one of her best pupils."

As usual, I failed to impress Father. "No theatrics. You go where your parents take you. Tomorrow, you can say good-bye to your teacher and to your friends. I think Mama has some cookies for you to share with your classmates."

Peter was still busy looking at the brochure. "How can such a tiny propeller push such a big ship across the ocean?"

It was just the kind of question Father relished, and he praised Peter for asking it. "Physics makes it possible, and at a reasonable speed, too. Naval engineers like me made all the necessary calculations, when they designed the ship. You must study hard so that someday, you too can be an engineer." Then, he turned to Mother, "This time, Mama, we travel in style. There's even a ballroom."

"Wonderful. Remember, Edite wrote us that she's sewing Milda two new ball gowns?"

Father slapped the brochure against his open palm. "Eighteen-year old Milda has her gowns and you, Mama, have your new set of stainless steel cooking pots, the best that money can buy. So far, everything's going according to plan. Now you see how all the krona we've saved are being put to good use."

I stared at the empty wall where Grandfather's portrait used to hang. How was he taking all the changes, I wondered? I was sure he didn't enjoy being ripped from his golden frame, rolled up, and packed away in some dark box, any more than I liked having to leave my school and classmates. We thought alike, but neither one of us had any say in what was going on.

"Papa, please show me the ballroom." My only remaining hope was that I would be allowed to stay up and watch the grown-ups dance.

"It's here, an extension of the dining room, but don't get any false hopes. Children eat their meals in the playroom. Don't worry, though, I'm sure you'll have a lovely time." Father's broad shoulders drooped. He had to assure everyone, but who was giving him the support he craved? He had resigned from Gotaverken and there was no turning back. Passports, visas, police clearance, medical reports, and tickets had all been obtained, and they were safely tucked away in his briefcase. His own fate, and that of his family, had already been entered in God's great ledger book; they were in His hands now.

The next day, while Peter and I said our good-byes at school, all the beds and our heavy, dark furniture vanished from the apartment, bought by new immigrants. To Mother's horror and our shame, the removal of the sofa had revealed our hiding place for uneaten bread. Bits of bread and ugly grease stains, that no amount of scrubbing could erase, remained on the wall. Since bread was almost sacred and could never be thrown away, Peter and I, and even Roland once he caught on, had opted for the lesser transgression of parking our unwanted crusts out of sight. My voice echoed in the empty rooms and my steps resounded on the bare parquet floor, as I ran from room to room. Roland climbed onto one of the steamer trunks, which sat in the hall, waiting alongside the suitcases, including Father's wooden suitcase from Camp Ohmstede. Mother assured me that inside the trunk were my clothes and toys and our blankets and pillows. "The ones you made?" I asked.

"Yes," Mother replied, "all my cushions, cross-stitched with ancient symbols—Māra and Laima, sun and moon and morning star—they're coming with us."

(left)1956. Father and Mother at our summer cabin.

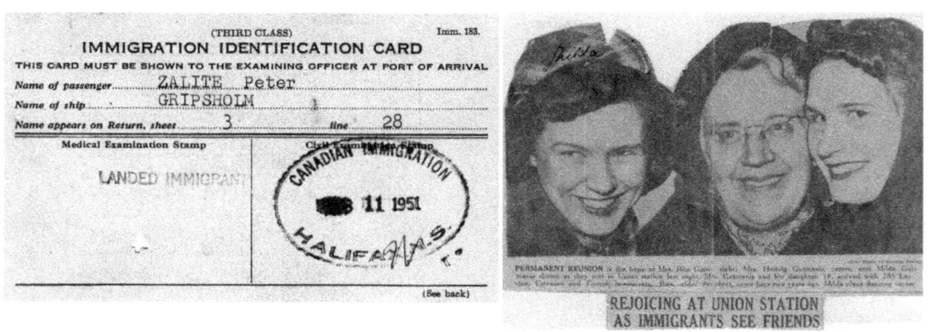

(THIRD CLASS) Imm. 183.

IMMIGRATION IDENTIFICATION CARD

THIS CARD MUST BE SHOWN TO THE EXAMINING OFFICER AT PORT OF ARRIVAL

Name of passenger ZALITE Peter

Name of ship GRIPSHOLM

Name appears on Return, sheet 3 line 28

Medical Examination Stamp

LANDED IMMIGRANT

CANADIAN IMMIGRATION

11 1951

HALIFAX N.S.

(See back)

Milda

REJOICING AT UNION STATION
AS IMMIGRANTS SEE FRIENDS

(left) Feb. 11, 1951. Peter's Landing Card from Canadian Immigration. (right) Feb 12, 1951. Toronto Star photograph of cousin Milda and Aunt Edite arriving at Union Station, met by daughter Rita.

CANADA

Thirteen

With her lacquered wood and polished brass, the *Gripsholm* was every bit the grand ocean liner that Father had promised. She—Father explained (with a rare twinkle in his eye) that ships were female because they had curves and were sometimes difficult to handle—had three chimneys called smokestacks and numerous floors that were called decks. "Yes," said Peter, who knew all about ships, "and rooms are called staterooms and beds are bunks."

We walked down several flights of stairs and along an endless, narrow corridor with a handrail along one wall. All the doors looked alike, and I wondered how I would ever find my way to the right stateroom. When the suitcases arrived, there was scarcely any space left in our stateroom to turn around. Set high up on the wall, a round porthole offered a comforting view of the sky.

A long, mournful blast of the whistle announced the ship's departure. The ship shuddered, as if it, too, dreaded the voyage ahead, but soon it was smooth sailing. Mother busied herself with two-year-old Roland, while Father took Peter and me topside to watch the city grow ever smaller, until it was compressed into the narrow space between the sea and the sky. As we stood gazing into the distance, the ship veered, and a sudden gust of wind blew salt spray onto our faces. I was glad that my new hat was securely tied under my chin, or the wind might have snatched it away. Bravely, Peter gripped the rail with both hands and looked over the side into the green, churning water below.

"Come, we'd better go inside before we're wet through," Father said, and pushed open the heavy door.

The playroom turned out to be a delightful place, with toys and games and children of all ages, and a separate room for the babies. In the playroom, several older girls organized the games and provided paper, glue, and scissors, so we could cut and paste as much as we wanted. They even made us laugh with funny puppets. Mother spent most of her days in the playroom, watching over Roland, who was too young to take part in the games, and too old to be in with the babies. She left for only short periods, to eat in the dining room with Father, Aunt Edite, and cousin Milda. Sometimes, Aunt Edite, who wore her rimless glasses perched on her nose just like Father, stopped by the playroom to keep Mother company. They perched on small chairs and talked about Canada. My aunt was considered knowledgeable about Canada, since her daughter Rita had settled in Toronto the previous year. "Everyone is on a first name basis," said Aunt Edite, "no matter how old, or if they are complete strangers."

"What about the teachers?" Mother asked and my aunt admitted she did not know. Another popular topic was food, what was available and how much it cost.

But best of all were the times that eighteen-year-old Milda stopped by the playroom to visit us on her way to dinner and dancing. With painted lips and her hair swept to one side, she looked like a princess from a fairy tale in her ball gown and high heels. I employed every trick I knew—showing her toys and books—to keep Milda in the playroom as long as possible. When she finally turned to go, her taffeta skirt swirled around her legs, shimmering blue and green, like the ocean waves. I decided right then, that when I grew up, I would have a dress just like hers.

It took me a few days to get used to the constant motion of the ship and feel more at ease as I moved around. Father said it was because I had found my sea legs. I was puzzled, and told Father that these were the same legs I'd had all along. Father rewarded my cleverness with a chuckle and a pat on the head. Unfortunately, my newfound steadiness did not last long. The next day, dark clouds hid the sun, and a steady wind threw up big waves that the *Gripsholm* had to ride, before hesitating a moment and then falling into the next chasm. I lost the ability to predict the ship's next move, and with it my confidence.

"Aha, the barometer's falling," said Father. I didn't know what that meant, but it sounded ominous. He tapped again on the glass front of the barometer, which, like his briefcase, accompanied him on all his travels. "Looks like there's a bit of stormy weather ahead, so you children better stay inside." I climbed to the top bunk and tried to look out, but the porthole was awash with water, and no sky was visible. Father did not seem bothered by the storm, but seeing that I was worried, he tried to reassure me. "Ships are built by engineers, like me," he said. "We know what we're doing. The *Gripsholm* is designed to ride out any storm." He then looked at Peter and went on to explain the principles of buoyancy and stability. I was glad that Father knew about these things, but I still wished the storm would go away.

For the next two days, gale-force winds whipped up the ocean and sent water crashing over the bow and onto the decks, and we were forbidden to step outside. It seemed as if the storm was determined to push us back to Sweden. I slept off and on during the night and woke feeling out of sorts. Neither Peter nor I got seasick, but Mother's face took on a greenish hue, and Roland was quieter than usual. Luckily, none of us was really sick, as Father would not hear of it. I was relieved when Father announced that the worst was over. "See here, the barometer's rising."

Cousin Milda danced her way across the Atlantic, even during the storm, and she never wanted for a partner. No wonder, I thought, when Aunt Edite told us with evident pride that Milda was the youngest dancing and gymnastics instructor ever to have graduated from the Academy of Dancing in Copenhagen. Each evening after dinner, Aunt Edite and Father sat at a small table behind a protective rope barrier that stretched around the dance floor to keep the couples from landing in the lap of a stranger if the boat suddenly listed. The two of them sipped black coffee and smoked, while keeping a watchful eye on Milda as she waltzed. Father usually retired early, leaving my aunt to sit alone, tapping her feet in time to the music.

On the last day, the ship buzzed with an excitement that grew with every passing hour, until at last, with the help of several snub-nosed tugboats, we arrived in Halifax Harbour at Pier 21. Just as Father had promised, the *Gripsholm* had indeed proven itself seaworthy. I wanted to run down the gangplank right away, but Father's firm hand on my shoulder held me back. "We must wait for a Canadian doctor to come on board to make sure that everyone is healthy enough to disembark."

He pulled off one glove and pressed his palm to my forehead. "Thank goodness the fever's gone," he said. Father had worried about me while I stayed in my bunk, cheeks red with fever, moaning about missing the children's good-bye party in the playroom. He busied himself checking labels on boxes and counting our belongings, while Mother made sure we had all of our hats and mittens. After what seemed an eternity, we hurried topside, where I breathed in my first lungful of cold Canadian air and immediately coughed it back out again.

We had said our good-byes to Aunt Edite and Milda earlier, as we had been issued different landing cards and had separate final destinations. They were to continue their journey to Toronto that very night, whereas Father had decided that we would spend our first night in Canada in a hotel. "Nights are meant for sleeping," he said, when I asked why we weren't taking the special train. "In the morning, after we've all had a good night's sleep in real beds, we'll board a regular, scheduled CNR (Canadian National Railway) train."

Father led the way along the gangplank, and Peter and I, holding hands, followed right behind. In her fashionable fur coat and close-fitting felt hat, Mother might have been mistaken for a film star instead of an immigrant, if only she did not have Roland in tow. "Keep close together now," commanded Father, as we stepped from the gangway and entered the top floor of the transit shed. I did as I was told; the room was cavernous, and it would have been easy to get lost. With our landing cards in hand, Father shepherded us to a long wooden bench and warned us not to move. "See those wire cages? They're for naughty children who wander away from their parents." With all the good things I'd heard about Canada, I felt certain it couldn't be true, but I wasn't taking any chances. I didn't move.

Mother shrugged her heavy fur from her shoulders and tried to make Roland sit beside her. Having left her voice somewhere on the high seas, she could not speak and was limited to hand signals and facial gestures. By the time Father returned, Roland was wailing and straining at his leather harness. Mother's silent entreaties had no effect on him, but one stern look from Father, and Roland stopped fussing. The room was crowded and noisy, and by the time our numbers were called and we faced the immigration officer, I too felt like crying. Nervous and dry-mouthed, with the blood throbbing in his head like the ship's engines,

Father answered the questions as best he could. His eyes followed every move the man's hands made, willing them to stamp the words "Landed Immigrant" on our small rectangular Immigration Identification Cards. Finally, the official was satisfied. "Welcome to Canada," he said, and stamped the cards.

He welcomed us, but in reality, we were not all that welcome. After World War II, the Canadian Government wanted to increase immigration, but at the same time maintain the British essence of the country. We were not British, but as northern Europeans, we were considered to be a shade more desirable than the peoples of southern Europe or elsewhere. On May 1, 1947, a date when we had attained the relative safety and comfort of Sweden, but many thousands of refugees still remained in the DP camps of Europe, Prime Minister Mackenzie King had declared in Parliament "...the people of Canada do not wish, as a result of mass immigration, to make a fundamental alteration in the character of our population." When Louis St. Laurent became Prime Minister in 1948, Canada's immigration laws eased slightly.

Father asked around for the name of a hotel, and we soon piled into a taxicab. The taxi's worn springs and soft upholstery offered us our first real welcome, and we sank back, grateful to have arrived safely. Father also looked pleased, until the driver pulled up to a brightly lit hotel and a uniformed doorman opened the car doors. "Good evening sir, welcome to the Hotel Nova Scotia," he said and whistled for a bellhop. The Hotel Nova Scotia, Father soon found out, was the finest and most expensive hotel in Halifax, unsuited to an immigrant's pocketbook. I knew that we did not have money to waste on luxuries and, for the first time, Father looked unsure of what to do. He pulled Mother aside to discuss his dilemma, but in the end, he decided there was no other choice but to check in. It was late, everyone was tired after a long day, and Mother's arms ached from carrying the sleeping Roland.

"It's always best to proceed as planned," Father said, giving in to his own exhaustion and accepting a situation beyond his control. But when the desk clerk advised Father that he would need to book two rooms for his family of five, Father felt a rush of anger. He managed to control his outrage and limited himself to muttering a few raw Latvian words instead.

"I'm sorry sir, but it's hotel policy—for health and safety reasons," said the black-suited desk clerk, twisting his words around his tongue like a lanyard around the rigging, so that Father had difficulty understanding him. How is it possible, wondered Father, that this wet-behind-the-ears, well-fed clerk dictates to me what is healthy or safe for my family? After all we have been through and endured, whether crowded like tinned sprats in a refugee camp, or huddled together in a shelter like animals, while Allied bombs rained down as if the end of the world was near, it comes to this?

Fortunately, Father's respect for rules and authority helped him accept hotel policy, even as his agile mind searched for a way around it. With only a moment's hesitation and barely hiding the disdain he felt toward the desk clerk, Father slapped some bills on the counter and in a loud voice, proclaimed, "All right. I take one room only, for my wife, Frau Zalite, and the two small kinder. I will sleep in another place with my oldest."

"Very good, sir," replied the clerk. "Please fill out this form. And I will need a home address."

Home address? Father thought. He had no home; if he had one, he wouldn't be in this predicament. Wisely, Father said nothing and proceeded to fill out the required form, writing down the Stromanises' address in Plessisville. He could not risk being turned away by this man. Mother did not understand what was being said, but the old fear gripped her now in the elegant lobby of the finest hotel in Halifax. She and her babies had been turned away before, in the stinking, over-crowded assembly centers of a disintegrating Third Reich. Father signed the register with a flourish, adding the word *engineer* after his name, then ushered us up to our room.

It was only in the privacy of their room that Father explained what had happened. "I won't stay here without you and Peter," said Mother. "There's room enough for all of us."

"Of course there is, but if we flaunt the rules in so obvious a manner, the hotel might call the police, and we'd all be out on the street. Don't worry, I've already figured out what to do. I'll make sure that clerk sees me leaving with Peter, then we'll come back later. There must be a side door, without a doorman."

"Why can't I stay with Mama?" Peter asked.

"Because you are my big boy," Father answered, giving Peter's hand a squeeze. "We'll get something to eat, maybe a nice bowl of hot soup."

Before leaving, Father pulled out a dresser drawer and lined it with Mother's fur coat, making a soft, warm bed for Roland. A few minutes later, angry and defiant and overcoming a desperate desire to stretch out full length on one of the beds, Father took Peter, rode the elevator to the lobby, and stepped out into the cold February night.

Several hours later, after lingering over soup and coffee, and more tired than he had thought possible, Father scratched softly on the door. Almost immediately, Mother opened it and let the two in, closing it softly behind them. "Thank God," Mother mouthed the words, "I was beginning to worry."

Father woke early and roused Peter from a deep sleep. They dressed in the dark and together they descended the back stairs, exiting by the same side door they had used the night before. A blast of arctic air greeted them. Not yet fully awake, Peter's small frame shook. "Come, the walk will warm you, and we'll be back inside in no time," Father said, and took Peter's hand. After a few blocks, they turned back, reentered the hotel's elegant lobby, and rode the elevator to our floor. Father checked out a short while later, and we headed for the train station to have our breakfast.

The CNR train stretched the length of the covered platform and into the open air, its engine exhaling puffs of smoke like an angry, snorting bull. Father led the way down the platform to our car, and I boarded with the comforting knowledge that the train would always stay on solid ground. Once we were settled in our seats, Father pulled out a map from his briefcase and spread it across his knees. Mother busied herself with Roland, and soon, Peter and I became restless. Mother was still without her voice, and her silent entreaties failed to keep us in our seats for long. Legs apart to brace ourselves against the rocking motion of the train, we walked the length of our car and back, making a detour to inspect the toilet. We changed trains in Quebec City, and after several more hours, watched as our train chugged into Plessisville station and screeched to a stop.

"Here you are at last," said Vladimirs Stromanis as he hurried toward us, both hands outstretched in welcome. He had the loudest voice I'd ever heard. "Anna and the girls are waiting at home." The plan, arranged by an urgent exchange of letters, was that Mother and the three children would stay with the Stromanis family, while Father presented himself at the shipyards in Montreal and found a place for us to live.

"It's wonderful to be here at last. That train was in no hurry to get here, stopping every few kilometres along the way."

"It's a local," Stromanis agreed. "But now you must think in *miles*, not kilometres."

"What nonsense," Father snorted, as he ushered us out into the cold February night. Clouds of smoke veiled the waiting cars, making them look like ghosts. "Children, keep your mouths closed," warned Father, as Mother adjusted the scarf over Roland's mouth and nose. Our footsteps squeaked like baby mice on the hard-packed snow. Up above, stars twinkled in an inky sky.

The Stromanises, Anna and Vladimirs, were friends of my parents from the golden years in Latvia. These were the prosperous, progressive, and independent years that spanned the two world wars. I knew all about those years, for although the adults never discussed the war years when children were present, they spoke often and with nostalgia about the golden years. The Stromanises' elder daughter, Ieva, was Peter's age, and Margrieta, the younger daughter, was my age, seven. I could not wait to meet them.

The ride from the train station took us along narrow streets piled high with snow on either side, which made it impossible for another vehicle to pass. Icicles, some as thick as my arm, hung from the roofs and glistened prettily in the lamplight. Everyone we saw was bundled up, with only a circle of face showing, like a pale, full moon in a night sky.

Vladimirs Stromanis stopped in front of a two-story, wooden house. "Well, here we are at our castle." Unlike Father, he was always joking.

"Brrr," Vladimir neighed, and his moustache quivered. "Just be glad there's no wind. How was the crossing, Jani?"

"Heavy seas, but that's to be expected this time of year. But it's good to see you, old friend, and to know we're nearing the end of our journey." Father gave Stromanis a friendly pat on the shoulder. "It's really too bad Erna's lost her voice. She is so looking forward to seeing Anna again."

Stromanis laughed heartily, "Not to worry, Anna's so excited she'll talk for the two of them."

Father did not join in the merriment. "Ilzite suffered a fever, but seems better now. Of course, I myself can't afford the luxury of being sick." He made it sound like an enviable condition, and I wanted to remind him I'd missed the children's party.

"That's how it is when we have to earn our daily bread," Stromanis agreed, lifting a suitcase.

Just as we reached the front door, Anna Stromanis threw it wide open, mindless of the heat escaping into the night. She took sleeping Roland from Mother's arms and exclaimed, "Uppah! My, he's grown, heavy as a sack of potatoes." I took to her right away, with her kind face and friendly smile. "The girls are sleeping. School tomorrow and the nuns don't tolerate lateness or inattentiveness. But we can have some tea and cake if you're hungry." The promise of cake, along with the pungent smell of floor wax, suddenly reminded me of Fröcken Olsen and her shiny floors in Villa Hagalund. Homesick for Sweden, I started to cry.

"She's just tired," said Father, but Anna fussed over me, and I was grateful for the attention.

When I awoke the next morning, Father was already on his way to Montreal. I could see that the house was not a castle, as Vladimirs had said, but it was warm and cozy. Potted plants were everywhere, from windowsills to small tables and even on the stair landing. Scattered about on the shiny floor, ready to trip up the unsuspecting visitor, were colourful rugs, hand-woven by Anna herself. Cross-stitched pillows, much like the ones Mother embroidered, decorated the sofa and chairs. I hesitated a moment in the doorway to the kitchen, too shy to enter, and smiled at Margrieta and Ieva. I had never seen a child dressed the way they were dressed, all in black, head to toe, except for dazzling white cuffs and collars. With their shiny, white faces, and their hair pulled back into two tight braids, they reminded me of birds. I didn't envy them their school uniforms, but I did secretly wish that my parents had thought to name me after a flower, like theirs had, and that my father joked and laughed and hugged me like theirs did. I sat down and aimlessly stirred my porridge. Peter sat down beside me and, in Swedish, asked Ieva a question about school, causing her to giggle. She replied in Latvian.

"Don't your girls speak Swedish?" Mother asked Anna after the girls were gone, her voice barely above a whisper. She looked very pretty with a flowered scarf wrapped around her neck.

"Not much anymore. They speak French now. It's a Catholic school, run by nuns."

"Goodness," was all Mother could manage. Having to learn English was bad enough, but French too? Mother looked at me and then at Peter, and I could see that she was worried.

"It's the only school nearby," Anna explained, setting down a teapot. "You're lucky, you'll be in Montreal with English schools and plenty of Latvians for company. We're the only Latvian family here. With all the adjustments the girls have made this past year, we can't expect them to keep up their Swedish as well."

Mother stirred honey into her tea and sighed, "True, it's amazing how fast the young learn, not like us." She took a sip and grimaced with pain as she swallowed the scalding brew. "But goodness me, all that religious hocus-pocus on top of a new language. Janis is pretty annoyed with me; he doesn't believe I tried hard enough. I was getting somewhere with my Swedish, and now I have to start all over with English." Mother attempted a laugh and sounded more like a seal barking.

"Please, Ernin, drink up while the tea's hot, and save your voice. We've the whole week to talk. My dear, dear friend, you can't imagine how overjoyed I am to see you and to speak in our own language," said Anna, giving Mother's shoulders a hug. Anna set down a plate of buttered toast and a jar of homemade jam. "You'll be able to buy decent bread, too, instead of this white foam."

Despite her sore throat and sense of dislocation, Mother was happy to be sitting in Anna's spotless kitchen, drinking tea, and speaking Latvian. It was as if they had never been apart.

"Lucky you, Roland is such a fine boy." Anna attempted a smile, but her eyes betrayed her sadness; her firstborn, a boy, had drowned some years ago, before the war.

"Thank God little Roland was born after the war and didn't have to go through what the rest of us did." Mother's eyes filled with tears that she quickly blinked away.

Mother and Anna sat for a moment in silent acknowledgement of each other's suffering. Then Anna brightened. "Just think, Janis must be halfway to Montreal by now."

"I do hope it goes well for him. It hasn't been easy," Mother said.

I imagined Father riding the express bus to Montreal, his leather briefcase balanced on his knees, mentally rehearsing answers to imagined questions, and now and again, looking up a word in his dictionary. He wanted to make a good impression tomorrow when he presented himself at Canadian Vickers, but he worried that he might use the wrong word or phrase. Experience had taught him that it was always best to be prepared.

While the girls were away at school, I spent the morning drawing and colouring, while Peter looked at Ieva's books. Roland was content to play with one of Margrieta's dolls. Mother helped Anna tear rags into narrow strips that she would later weave into a rug on her loom. "I'm shocked," Anna said, "when I see how wasteful Canadians are. They toss perfectly good things away."

Mother examined a rectangle of fabric before making a small cut in the selvage. "I guess it's understandable. They've not seen hardship the way we have."

"True. Why just last summer, I talked a fisherman into giving me the eel he'd caught, instead of tossing it back."

"Mmm, smoked eel," said Mother. "It's been a while since I've tasted that delicacy."

"Here, they even fish in winter, through a hole in the ice."

Peter looked up from his book, "Aren't they afraid of falling in the hole?"

"No," Anna laughed, "By January, the ice is so thick, they drive their trucks right onto the lake."

"Can I try it?" Peter asked, looking from Anna to Mother.

After school, Ieva showed Peter her French reader and notebooks—she called them *les cahiers*—but he was dismayed that he could not make out the strange words. "It's French, silly," Ieva said, taking back her book. "I can do my homework later. Why don't we play cards, instead?"

Before bed, Ieva and Margrieta undid their braids and brushed their hair one hundred times until it shone golden-brown in the soft light. Then their mother fashioned loose braids to keep their fine hair from getting tangled while they slept. The braids were also meant to prevent Ieva from twisting her hair around her finger as she slept and yanking it out, leaving small, coin-sized bald spots.

Later, Anna confessed to Mother, "I just don't know what to do. I've tried everything, and Ieva herself has promised to stop pulling out her hair, but when she's asleep, it seems her nerves get the better of her good intentions."

"It's a pity really, but I'm sure time will help," said Mother. "Ilzite still suffers from bad dreams, and have you noticed how she chews her nails until they bleed?" Mother shook her head in dismay. "It doesn't help that Janis is so strict with the children." Immediately, she regretted her disloyalty to her husband, and added, "He means well."

Over the next few days, with the help of Anna's hot, sweet, lemony tea, Mother's sore throat eased, and she regained her normal speaking voice. Mornings passed quickly, spent cooking and cleaning an already spotless house. Like a magician, Anna was able to find dust that barely had time to settle on the furniture, and with a stroke of her cloth, swish it away. In the afternoon, Mother sat in a comfortable chair by the big picture window where the light was better, surrounded by greenery, while Anna worked at her loom. To keep the edges from fraying, Mother hemmed a fresh canvas with quick, even strokes, and then consulted a small pattern booklet. I leaned on her arm, excited to see what new design she planned to sew, but drew back, disappointed. Here were the same old designs, nothing that spoke of this new country and its frozen, white landscape. Mother narrowed her eyes to thread the needle with green yarn and then counted the squares in the pattern. Up and down went the needle, leaving a trail of evenly spaced, slanted stitches that looked like grass bent by the wind; then back again, to complete the crosses. I interrupted Mother's soft humming to ask her what she was making this time, and she looked at me in surprise. "Why, it's a pillow, for our new home." I realized right then what Father had been trying to teach us all along: we can't escape who we are, and Mother knew it better than any of us. I snuggled closer against Mother's arm, closed my eyes, and breathed in her familiar, comforting scent.

The next day, the cold snap eased, and we were able to go outside. Peter and I kicked at clumps of snow as we walked along, ahead of the rest. Many of the store windows were decorated with red paper hearts and fat babies shooting arrows. We wondered aloud what they meant.

"Today is Valentines Day," Anna explained with a smile.

"Valentins' day," repeated Peter, and looking at Mother, he asked, "We have Uncle Valentins and Cousin Valentins, don't we? Is it their Name Day?"

"No. Uncle Valentins and Aunt Milda live in England," said Mother. "And I've heard he now prefers to be called Valentine."

“The hearts mean you can send a card to someone you like. When we get home, I have some red paper, and you and Ilze can make your very own valentines.”

“Can I send one to Daddy in Montreal?” I asked.

“No, sweetie. Papa will be back in a few days, and you can give it to him then.”

On Saturday afternoon, when Father returned from Montreal, we forgot all about the cards we had made. Father called to us from the entryway to put on our coats and boots and come outside. On the street, barely visible behind a snow bank, sat a brand new car.

“It’s called a Vanguard,” Father said, in the same proud voice he had used when naming a ship that he had helped to design. The maroon coloured car resembled a giant ladybug, but without the spots. It was squat and round, with windscreen wipers in place of antennae, and black wheels instead of legs. “Made in England,” Father added with pride, making his new car even more special. He opened the doors and trunk, and the beetle looked poised to take flight into the wintry sky. In a flash, before Father could stop him, Peter jumped into the driver’s seat, gripped the steering wheel, and pretended to drive. Mother poked her head inside, breathed in the smell of the new upholstery, and ran a gloved hand over the smooth stitching. Father undid the latch and lifted the hood, then propped it open with a metal stick in order to demonstrate to Vladimirs the spotless engine.

“Well, well, good for you, Jani. Didn’t waste any time at all,” said Vladimirs, with obvious approval and perhaps, a hint of envy. He bent over to take a closer look, and when he straightened, declared in his loud voice, “If it’s fine enough for the queen of England, it’s good enough for me. This calls for a celebration.”

“Why not?” Father agreed. “I could use a little something to help me relax, after staring at the road for the past I don’t know how many hours. All in all, it went without incident. The Vanguard rolled down the highway like one of Mama’s spools of thread, all the way from Montreal. No problem.” Father rocked back on his heels, obvious pleased, and for a moment, the worry lines across his forehead disappeared, “Yes, indeed, just so. What do you think Mama, should we call our new jalopy ‘Little Spool of Thread’?”

“Jalopy! Goodness, gracious, Jani, don’t call it that,” Mother teased. “It might take offense.”

"It came straight from the factory," Father declared. "Right out of the box."

Vladimirs ushered everyone inside, leaving Father to lock up the car. "Let's hope he hangs on to this one," he joked. More than six years had passed since 1944, when Janis had been obliged to abandon his Opel on the Liepaja waterfront.

"Don't mind him," Anna told Mother, as she removed her scarf. She returned from the kitchen a few moments later with a tray holding several small glasses and a bottle of her homemade, plum brandy.

Peter and I begged to be taken for a ride, but Father explained that the car had been driven enough for one day and needed a rest. After the toast, Father lifted the glass to his lips and threw back his head to swallow the sweet liquid, all in one smooth motion. His eyes flew open, and he shuddered with satisfaction. "I hope the children behaved themselves," he said, looking from Mother to Anna for reassurance. "Come now, ladies, tell the truth."

Mother glanced at Anna, who had risen to refill Father's glass, and said, "Of course, they were little lambs, all of them. But much better, you tell us everything. Did you find work? Do we have a place to lay our heads?"

"So many questions. Yes. You are looking at the new Chief Draughtsman at Canadian Vickers." After being congratulated, and between puffs of his cigarette and small sips of brandy, Father told the story of finding us an apartment. "At first it seemed impossible. Mama, you saw the hundreds of people on the *Gripsholm*, all of them needing a place to live, and there are more ships landing in Halifax every day. I prayed it would not be a repeat of Göteborg. I studied the newspaper, and early Saturday morning, I went to the address in the advertisement. By the time I got there, there was already a long line. After one long hour, it was almost my turn. Can you believe that the man in front of me was offered the last apartment?" We all groaned. "Yes, that's exactly how I felt. But—bad for him and good for me—the poor fellow didn't have enough money for the deposit, and your Janis did!" Father slapped his knee, bumped the table, and almost spilled his drink. "For once, Laima smiled on me. I handed over the cash and signed the lease, without ever setting eyes on the apartment."

With Father's triumphant return, our visit with the Stromanis family came to an end. Early the next morning, we said our good-byes, and

Father, in his usual reluctance to praise anyone or anything, shook Anna's hand, saying merely, "Thank you, Anna. I see it wasn't at all bad for my family to spend the week here."

Surprised and hurt at what she mistakenly perceived to be an insult, Anna shrank back and closed her mouth, reconsidering what she had been about to say. She then turned to Mother, "Write as soon as you can. I want to hear all about your new apartment and life in Montreal, especially the Latvians you meet."

"It was wonderful, Annina. A hundred times thanks for your hospitality." Mother embraced her friend and kissed her cheek, wishing all the while that her husband could be more diplomatic, less direct.

Preoccupied with the long drive ahead of him, Father was unaware that he had offended anyone. However, had he known, he still would not have given the incident much importance—he valued mental toughness and a thick skin; in his mind, both were necessary for survival in a harsh world.

Mother settled into the middle of the rear seat with Roland on one side and me on the other. A strange, new car smell greeted us, not unlike a pair of new boots. Mother looked pleased, "Well done, Shaksi. You accomplished so much in a short week: the car, an apartment, a new job."

Father nodded his acknowledgement into the rearview mirror, then pulled out the choke, and pumped the gas pedal several times before turning the key in the ignition. Beside him in the front, Peter studied his every move. The engine sputtered once, before settling down to a steady pace. "You see, Mama, if we hadn't salted away all those krona behind Opaps, we'd be out on the street, sleeping in a snow bank—no car, no home, nothing."

Mother shivered at the thought, and I snuggled deeper into her fur. "Of course, you did the right thing," she allowed. "The best possible for all of us." I learned something about Father that day that Mother already knew: although Father himself was not lavish with praise, he craved it as much as anyone.

Fourteen

We moved into our third-floor apartment in a brand new brick building on Barclay Street, in Côte-des-Neiges, a west end neighbourhood. The apartment smelled of fresh paint and consisted of a living room, a kitchen, two bedrooms, and a white tiled bathroom. A space heater in the hall provided much-needed warmth. In the kitchen, a back door opened onto a small, metal platform and a narrow, scary, metal staircase that led to the ground.

Mother had her Swedish stainless steel pots and pale green dishes decorated with pinecones, but we had no furniture. Father quickly solved that problem by answering advertisements in the "for sale" section of *The Montreal Star*. Not all of his purchases met with Mother's approval, but there was nothing she could do. When Father's latest acquisition, a large, ugly sofa, was carried up the stairs and deposited in the living room, she threw up her hands and looked at her husband in disbelief. "What is that?" she gasped. The overstuffed, high-backed sofa, balanced on thick, stubby legs, looked like the hippopotamus I had once seen in a picture book. Mother sat down, and I hopped up beside her, but the scratchy, worn cover did not feel comfortable on my bare legs.

"A few of your nice cushions, and you won't even notice the colour," Father suggested, but Mother's lips were set in a narrow line, and she did not answer. More furniture arrived, some of it acceptable to Mother, including a bed with a rusted metal frame for me. A coat of bright pink paint, and my bed looked as good as new, although nothing could be done about the squeaky springs.

We lived far from Father's shipyards, so each weekday morning, he rose early, dressed, and downed a bowl of oatmeal, while Mother prepared a bag lunch. He then hurried to catch the first of three buses to transport him across the city, from Montreal's northwest to the southeast. The third bus finally disgorged Father, along with a noisy crowd of blue collar workers, at the gates of Canadian Vickers. Soon after arriving, he had been promoted to Steel Section Leader, and like his bosses, he wore white, long-sleeved shirts with starched collars. He complained that Mother's ironing was not good enough, so every Saturday he left three shirts at the laundry. The bus ride home at the end of the day was more arduous, and Father arrived home hungry and irritable, having stood most of the way. As soon as she heard his heavy steps on the stairs, Mother first unlocked the door, and then hurried to the kitchen to put dinner on the table. Much, but not all of Father's bad mood could be attributed to the long bus ride, some of it arose from the fact that, at forty-three, he was now working in his fifth language, English, and it was not his strongest. German, Russian, Latvian, Swedish—he spoke these all with ease, but despite diligent study, he found English grammar and pronunciation daunting.

Peter and I parachuted mid-year into separate classrooms at the local elementary school, expected to understand and speak English and master the lessons without any extra help from the teachers or our parents. For a time, I found it frustrating, but since I had no choice and wanted to fit in, I learned quickly. It was not always easy, as I found myself wedged between two different worlds, one at home and another at school. Our home life remained the same as in Sweden, centered on Mother and the Latvian language and traditions that she cherished. Beyond our front door, a wider world beckoned that I wanted to be part of, but did not yet understand. What made matters worse was the fact that post-war immigrants like us were often blamed for overcrowding in the schools and for Canada's emerging identity problems. I had enough of an identity problem of my own. In the first seven years of my life, my family had fled an occupied Latvia, survived Allied bombings in a war-ravaged Germany, settled in a Sweden bursting with refugees from all parts of Europe, and finally, immigrated to Canada, a young country still clinging to its British roots.

Not long after we settled into our new apartment with its collection of mismatched, second-hand furniture, a letter arrived from Aunt Edite. She and Milda had boarded one of three special CNR trains organized by the government to bring the three hundred eighty-five Scandinavian and Baltic immigrants arriving in Halifax aboard the *Gripsholm* to Montreal and Toronto. They now lived in Toronto with Rita and Laimonis.

"We did not have a chance to say a proper goodbye upon our arrival in Halifax, for you disembarked before us," Aunt Edite wrote. "Our identification cards put us in Group 13, and we were among the last to go through immigration. When we finally boarded the train it was after two in the morning and we didn't get rolling until well past three. You can imagine how exhausted we were."

Father stopped reading aloud and patted Mother's hand. "You see, Mama, even though it cost some dollars, at least you got a decent night's sleep in an elegant hotel."

"The train was hot and stuffy, crowded with people and baggage," Aunt Edite continued. "By the time Milda and I finally got on board, we could not find two seats together. Luckily, it was a short night. In the morning, we both felt sick; I with a headache that squeezed my temples in its vise-like grip, and Milda felt seasick, and no pill could help. The next night was better, and we rolled into Montreal in the early morning, but were kept waiting on a siding before we were allowed to disembark. Around our necks hung cards with our train numbers to be sure we made the right connection. I felt like some sort of prisoner. In Montreal, I was finally able to send Rita a telegram so she could meet us.

"At 5:25 p.m., we pulled in to Toronto Union Station. No sooner did we emerge on ground level and embrace Rita, than a reporter interviewed us and a photographer took our picture. The next day, February 14, Milda, Rita, and I were pictured almost life-sized on the front page of the *Toronto Daily Star!* So you don't think I am making this up, I include the newspaper article. See how famous your sister is! I guess Canadians don't have enough news to fill their papers, and are happy that our arrival gave them something to write about."

Father unfolded the newspaper clipping to show us the smiling faces of my aunt and cousins. "Funny coincidence, isn't it? Zenny and her two daughters, Biruta and Silvija, were also pictured in a New York newspaper upon their arrival Christmas Day."

"Your sister's quite a celebrity," said Mother.

"Let me see," I cried and crowded closer. "Is Milda in her ball gown?"

My question was ignored, and Father continued reading. "Toronto is bigger than Copenhagen, and at first sight and at least in the winter, it is grey and dingy due to the factories. Rita assures me it will be prettier in the spring when it is green. Laimonis works from five in the afternoon until midnight; Rita is not working now, as she is expecting next month. Soon, we will start to look for work for Milda, then later for me… With warm greetings, Ede."

Father put down the letter, took out two cigarettes from the package on the table and handed one to Mother. He first lit his, and I watched in fascination as blue smoke escaped from his mouth and wrapped itself around his nose until, with one strong breath, he blew it up toward the ceiling. Then he leaned over and lit Mother's cigarette. "How lucky they are to have four breadwinners in one family," he said, shaking the match to put it out.

"Jani…"

"It's okay, I know. You have your hands full already." Father's brusque reply did not make Mother feel any happier, just more determined than ever to help by squeezing as much as she possibly could out of every penny she spent.

As the weeks and months went by, my English improved, as did Peter's, and we started speaking English to each other at home. Mother did not mind too much, but Father did not approve and always reminded us to speak Latvian. "*Runajiet Latviski,*" he ordered, over and over, until we grew tired of hearing the words. I never gave a thought as to whether Father grew tired of having to remind us, and sometimes, I even challenged Father by daring to ask him, in Latvian, "Why?" If I was near enough, Mother placed a hand on my arm or shoulder in an effort to restrain me, but if I happened to be farther away, she had to make do with a silent warning. Once, I even dared to add, "We're in Canada now," under my breath, before scurrying from the room.

"Because I say so," was Father's standard reply. He did not feel it necessary to provide an explanation to his children. Like a ship's captain, he expected to be obeyed without a murmur or question. "And don't glare at me that way," he would add, if he didn't like my defiant look.

Just how quickly I was adapting became evident one unseasonably warm March day, when the teacher asked me to explain to Sven, newly-arrived from Sweden and speaking not a word of English, that the class would be going on a field trip and he needed to bring back the signed permission slip, along with a dime to cover the expenses. All eyes turned to stare at me, as my mouth and mind went as dry and empty as a desert.

"Go ahead, Ilsa," the teacher prompted, her arms folded across her chest, "we're all waiting."

If I had thought my legs would support me, I would have run from the room, but instead, I just sat at my desk, dumbstruck. I took a deep breath and lifted my head to meet Sven's steady blue-eyed gaze, and groped about for the proper Swedish words: *field trip* and *permission slip* were nowhere to be found. And how, I wondered, do I translate *dime*? There were no dimes in Sweden, only krona and ore. I squirmed in my seat and shrugged my shoulders. A few children tittered, while others exchanged knowing looks.

"Did you not hear me?" The teacher was at my side, hands on her poky hips. I could smell her now, a mixture of perspiration and lily of the valley. The fluorescent lights hissed and brightened momentarily, and I willed the bell to ring, although I knew it wasn't yet time for recess.

"*Ja*, Miss Bindman. I mean, yes, but I cannot speak the *Svenska*," I replied softly, trying to keep my voice flat as a Canadian prairie, without a hint of its Swedish lilt.

"Nonsense, Ilsa. Don't keep the rest of the class waiting."

I wanted to obey, but at that moment, I could not speak one word of Swedish. I wanted to tell her to ask Father whether or not I could still speak Swedish. At the dinner table, Father would sometimes attempt to converse with us in Swedish, just so we would not forget. He saw the value in knowing many languages, but neither Peter nor I saw the point of such an exercise, and Mother's Swedish had remained rudimentary, so he soon gave up, but not before reminding us that at forty-four, he still spoke the German and Russian from his childhood.

The class relished this little drama that delayed the promised math quiz. The teacher straightened and drew in a breath through her nose, "Well then, take Sven with you into the cloakroom and do not come out until you have relayed to him my simple message."

On legs that had turned to strands of liquorice, I walked the few steps to Sven, grabbed his hand and pulled him with me through the open doorway. Tears stung my eyes. The cloakroom smelled of wet wool, egg sandwiches, garlic, and sour milk. Soon, a bright anger directed at Sven replaced my humiliation. We stood in the dim light looking at each other, both embarrassed, until Sven uttered few words. To my surprise, I could understand him and my Swedish came flooding back. With difficulty, I managed to convey the message.

I could hardly wait to get home and complain about my teacher's meanness. I needed sympathy and hoped that my parents would be as outraged as I was. "She was so unfair," I finished, lamely.

Mother had understood earlier, offering me an extra cookie, but at dinner, Father sided with my teacher. "You must always listen to the teacher, instead of creating such a fuss."

"But she wanted me to speak in Swedish, in front of the whole class," I whined and slouched down in my chair.

Father raised his eyes from his plate and glared at me. "*Sitz grade*, Ilze," he commanded in German. "Sit up straight."

I sat up and tried again. "It was so awful. Everyone was staring at me. Imagine having to speak Swedish in front of the whole class."

"Silly girl. There's nothing shameful about speaking Swedish or any other language. Next time, do what the teacher says, and you'll be spared embarrassment." Father resumed eating. For him, the discussion was over.

It wasn't over for me, and when Mother shot me a warning look, I ignored it. "But Dad…."

"No buts. The teacher knows best. That's why she's the teacher."

"But she's mean. She made me feel like an immigrant, in front of everyone," I moaned.

Father set down his knife and fork. "Ilze, we *are* immigrants. It's nothing to be ashamed of. We don't owe anyone anything—not the government, not our sponsor, no one. I, myself, paid for our passages on the *Gripsholm* out of my own pocket. Now finish your food."

While Mother set out small bowls of red jelly studded with fruit cocktail, Father continued, "Mama, it's a complete mystery to me how the children can forget a language so quickly."

"But they learn just as quickly. Don't be too hard on Ilzite, she's just trying to fit in," Mother said, providing me a small measure of comfort.

"It doesn't help to make excuses. Life just doesn't work like that. And in the classroom, the teacher rules, like a…like a lesser god. Period." Father chased the last of his jelly around his bowl, thanked Mother for the meal, and retired to his room to listen to the news.

Next to his bed, on top of a low table, sat Father's shortwave radio that was so special no one, not even Mother, was allowed to touch it. Each evening after supper, when Father switched it on, the radio hummed as the tubes inside warmed up, and a display panel lit up to reveal an impressive array of lines and numbers. When he turned the knob in search of the right station, a slender vertical bar flew across the face of the radio, causing the bypassed announcers, singers, and actors inside the box to squeak and burp in protest. Father seldom listened to music, preferring instead to keep abreast of world events. The Korean War and Stalin's expansionist policy, made evident by the discovery of a Soviet submarine lurking in the Bay of Fundy, worried him now.

My brothers and I left the worrying about world events to Father. On Saturday mornings, Father turned on his radio for us, and my brothers and I sprawled on the floor in front of the wooden cabinet, listening to *Big Jon and Sparkie*, *Cisco Kid*, and *Hopalong Cassidy*. We sang along to "Teddy Bears' Picnic" and laughed at the witticisms of *Our Miss Brooks*. A few years later, when Father brought home an RCA Victor television set, we no longer listened to radio in our Montreal apartment, but for many years, the sound of the Lone Ranger's pounding hooves and his cry of "Hi-ho, Silver" continued to echo around our small summer cabin.

Children's radio proved to be a great teacher, and I quickly learned to speak English. Peter excelled at school, especially in mathematics, and was moved from his grade two class into a grade four classroom without much thought for his social adjustment. Schoolwork was never a problem, but as I made friends, I began to realize there was a big difference between my experiences and home life than those of my Canadian friends. Language, food, history, and expectations were all different. I was leading two distinct lives: an English Canadian life at school, and a Latvian one at home and in the Latvian community. Like my classmates, I ate baloney or Cheez Whiz sandwiches on white Wonder Bread, but my sandwiches were left whole and without lettuce. Mother did not cut them into dainty triangles, nor did she slice off the crusts. I was expected to bring home any part of my lunch that I did not eat, as well as the lunch bag, to be reused the following day. It horrified me to see apples, with only a bite or two missing, end up in the trash bin. Other children noticed the differences between us as well, and once, I was called a DP.

"What's a DP?" I asked Peter after school. He was at his desk, cutting out small shapes of paper-thin balsa wood for a model airplane he was making.

"Displaced Person," he replied. I picked up an oval wafer he had just separated from a larger piece, and he quickly added, "Hands off."

I dropped the piece. "But it's not true. We're not displaced anymore."

"You and I both know we're landed immigrants, so don't pay any attention. Some kids just like being mean. Now go play with Roland; I'm trying to build something here."

I was glad I had not told my parents about being called a DP at school. As it was, Father worried too much. At forty-four, he was concerned that his heart, damaged by rheumatic fever, and at times beating erratically, would give out before his children were grown and properly educated. Mother suffered from stomach problems and severe headaches that would not go away. When she stood in one spot for too long or carried heavy grocery bags home from the Dominion store, the veins in her legs puffed up into painful, angry purple knots. After a particularly trying day or some unexpected setback, and thinking the children could not hear them, they argued about who would die first. "I don't have much longer, Erna," Father might say. "You must learn English, so you'll be able to manage without me."

"Don't talk like that, Jani. I, myself, will be gone long before you." Mother could not imagine life without her husband, any more than I could imagine our lives without Father. "Why don't you call the doctor in the morning and have your heart looked at?" Mother pleaded.

"You know there's nothing to be done for my heart," replied Father, stretched out on the chesterfield, rubbing his chest. "What I really need is some rest." Money was tight, and he did not want to spend money on a doctor, unless he was certain the doctor could help him or until it became absolutely necessary.

Father had other concerns, and like the state of his health, he did not share them with his children. He excelled at what he did, but as an immigrant, he was denied the responsibility, status, and compensation that his education and experience warranted. Since Canadian Vickers was a subsidiary of a British company, new supervisors were brought over directly from England, making it difficult for Father and others to advance. They spoke the King's English as if their mouths were filled with marbles, and they proudly sported their school ties, something Father was unable to do. The discrimination sliced through Father's professional pride, leaving raw edges that would not heal. He had worked in numerous shipyards in many countries, employing four different languages, without any problems.

In an unguarded moment, Father confessed his disappointment to his brother in New York. Juris wrote back immediately and urged Father to come to America. "America is a true melting pot and everyone has an equal chance," he wrote, but Father dismissed the idea; neither he nor Mother could face another upheaval in their lives. Instead, he worked harder and longer hours to prove his worth to the company. In his scant spare time, he enrolled in a real estate course with the idea of someday owning his own home. If he did not live long enough to see his children grow up, at least his family would have a roof over its head. At long last, he hoped to put down roots.

Two of Father's sisters, along with their families, still remained in Europe. However, both aunts, Elizabeth in Denmark and Milda in England, were eager to immigrate to Canada as soon as possible. They each wrote to Father to ask his help in finding jobs for their husbands.

In her letter, Aunt Milda sounded especially desperate. Her husband, Uncle Valentine, having run away to sea at the rebellious age of fourteen, was an able seaman. "If all goes well for you in Canada, do not forget us and Valentine," she wrote. "I have heard that there are good jobs to be had on the inland lakes. Try to get Valentine a job on the lakes, so he could also come home. Remember that a stranger who was without money, influence, or even related to you, helped you, so I think that as a brother and a person of stature it will be easier for you, if you only want to help and make the effort. I hope my heart will get better, so we can also start our new life."

Soon after, he received another long letter from Milda. In it, she described her difficult life in England in greater detail. "In spite of the happiness all around, at the opening of the Festival of Britain by King George VI, don't believe that life is easy here. Food is still rationed—sugar, butter, eggs, meat—and I am often at a loss as to what to prepare for dinner. At present, since his ship is being refitted as a cargo vessel, Valentine is working in Southampton and he is able to come home every night. He was offered a good job with good pay on a ship sailing to New York, but since I was sick, he turned it down.

"Valentine is really in need of a home life, and I am sick of going around to meet him in different places and always with the problem of where to leave the children. Fortunately, small Valentine and Irene are happy children, who want only to talk in English. I, too, am only prepared to go to an English-speaking country such as America or Canada, where I don't have to learn a new language. I said as much to Mr. Marshall in the Transport Ministry when he offered Valentine Venezuela. Of course, England is too crowded and there is no future here for the children. If Valentine could get a job on a ship on the lakes and be home as well, we would both be happy, but if he has to be gone on a long trip, there is no use for us to leave, as we can do the same thing here. I am too old to dig ditches or to work on a farm. We are not after so much money, since we don't have so long left to live, nor can we just throw away a few years, as we had to do in the German camps. Life in the camps, I would just like to erase from my memory for those are the truly lost years."

But what could he do, thought Father, as a newly arrived immigrant himself? Milda's letter only added to his woes, but he could not disappoint his sister. As soon as he was able, he inquired about work possibilities for his brother-in-law in the Montreal harbour.

My parents limited their interest in my school life to a quick perusal of my report card, including the number of absences and times I was late. Good grades and regular attendance were of the utmost importance; the rest seemed not to matter. Once a year, on Parents' Night, my Mother and Father perched on small chairs, looked through my desk, and nodded and smiled as they listened to the teacher's observations. The visit satisfied Father's academic concerns, but afterward, he still wondered about the family backgrounds of the children with whom I spent my days. He measured a man's worth by his education and chosen work, both clues as to the values he would instil in his children. Not knowing something so fundamental bothered Father; little wonder then that all of my family's social and cultural life took place within the growing Latvian community in Montreal.

The Latvians in exile had lost so much—their country, families, houses, and land—that they were determined to hold on to the intangibles that remained: their language and traditions. Many among them still believed that life in Canada was temporary, and they would someday be able to return to their homeland. Not content to merely sit around and wait, they busied themselves founding their own social, cultural, and political organizations, patterned on those they had left behind. These provided support and a sense of belonging, momentarily banishing the loneliness and isolation that comes with unfamiliar surroundings. It was more than simply speaking their own language or hearing their names correctly pronounced. It was an affirmation that they were important and deserved respect, and what better way to do that than among those sharing a common history? However, this did not mean they all shared the same political views, or social ideals, so the number and variety of organizations multiplied.

The members of Talavija, Father's fraternity, soon found each other and held regular meetings; their wives and children became lifelong friends. Our family joined the Trinity Latvian Lutheran Church, attending services sporadically throughout the year, but faithfully on Christmas Eve and Easter morning. Most Latvians chose to settle in Montreal's English-speaking west end, where we too started out, but Father's job at the shipyards in Maisonneuve dictated that, as soon as possible, we move to the predominantly French-speaking east. This meant that we lived too far away to easily attend Saturday morning Latvian school, and we were spared the formal study. As a result, whenever I wrote the obligatory thank-you letter to an aunt or uncle or godparent, I had to turn to Mother for help. Even then, my letters rarely pleased me, and as I grew older, they remained stilted and childlike.

For weeks after Mother received the letter with the news that her father had passed away, she carried on as always, preparing meals, washing clothes, mending, and sewing. But she was more distant, lost in her memories of the past. Finally, when she had written the necessary letters, and was ready to put aside her grieving, she wanted to share those memories.

One Saturday, when Mother and I were home alone, baking bread—Father attending a meeting of the Latvian Association, Peter at Boy Scouts, and Roland outside playing with friends—she confided in me.

"Oh Ilzite, I feel so bad that I carried on with everything for nearly three weeks, not knowing that Papiņš was gone. I should've been aware something had changed, don't you think?" It was not a question I could answer, so I said nothing, and Mother stroked my arm absentmindedly and continued. "Omite's your only living grandparent now, and you really should know more about her." I guessed she was not yet ready to talk about Opaps.

"Your Omite, Marta, was not afraid of anything, not hard work or loneliness or the Bolsheviks." I stood by the stove waiting for the milk to boil, watching intently as the first tiny bubbles broke the surface. If I looked away, even for a moment, the milk would erupt like a dormant volcano awakening and spew droplets everywhere. I removed the pot from the element and threw in a large glob of butter that I pushed around with the spoon and watched grow smaller and smaller until nothing was left but an oily, yellow film on top of the once-white milk.

"Bolsheviks. That term's no longer used," I said in a condescending tone. I had little interest in the Bolsheviks; they were about as real to me as the marauding Mongols centuries earlier. Along with intelligentsia, nomenclature, and proletariat, the word sounded so old-fashioned, just like the people that used it. I suspected I was being too hard on Mother, and said no more, as I feared she might stop telling me her story. To be fair, Mother only rarely used such words; they fell more often from my father's lips. I stirred the milk and butter mixture around and around, willing it to cool, so I could add the yeast.

"All right then, Soviets, Reds, if you don't like the word Bolsheviks, but that's what we called them." Mother tested the temperature of the milk with the tip of her finger before adding the yeast. "I wish you'd just listen sometimes. It's important to know these things. Something could happen to me, just like that, and you'd never know. Like that!" Mother clapped her hands together, sending a white cloud of flour into the air. I was surprised at Mother's actions and almost laughed, but stopped when I saw her blinking back tears. She turned her back and dabbed at them with a corner of her apron, then went on. "Like you, I helped my mother bake bread, but we never had such fine, white flour as this. This is like the sand at Jurmala, sand so fine that it stuck to wet skin like glue, impossible to rub off." Mother shook her head at the memory. "Wheat flour was only for *pīragi* and sweet cakes; otherwise, we used a coarse, grey, rye flour to make dark brown bread." Without bothering to measure, Mother scooped flour into the bowl of liquid. When the flour was moistened, she beat the mixture with a wooden spoon for a full minute, reddening with the effort. "Here, now it's your turn," she said, handing me the spoon.

I could only manage to stir, not beat the stiff dough.

"You may not remember her, but Omite knew you from the moment you were born, a well-padded baby. Oh, you were big, thank God; the extra fat saved your life."

I suddenly felt like crying too; my eyes stung and I squeezed them shut, so I would not cry.

Lost in her own thoughts and busy greasing the pan, Mother did not notice my sudden distress. She drew in a long, deep breath that raised her chest and shoulders before expelling the air. She turned to me and her eyes had never looked so blue. "Sometimes I wonder what would have happened if your Omite had not gone looking for Papiņš, not found him. I might not have been born into so much suffering."

Mother's words shocked me. I had never heard her talk like that before. I figured I had stirred enough and turned the bowl over, dumping the living, breathing mass onto the counter. Then I gathered it up with both hands, folded it over, and started to knead. "How can you say that? What about me and Peter or Roland, huh? Don't we make you happy sometimes?"

"Of course you do, all three." But Mother's dark mood was not so easily dispelled. Although she did not sing the words, I recognized the song she was humming as the one about orphaned children.

I punched and folded and slapped the dough, and begged her to stop. "Why don't we sing something a bit more cheerful? *Kur tu teci, kur tu teci* …huh.?" That was the happiest song I knew; it was about a rooster going courting.

Mother stopped humming and fell silent. Angry and confused, I gave the dough one last punch, as if it were somehow responsible for all the pain Mother felt. My parents were right after all: the past is much better left alone.

"I think it's ready," Mother said softly, as she gathered up the ball of dough and dropped it into a greased bowl. I covered it with a clean linen towel. "Now, we must wait for it to rise," she added. "Come and sit with me," her soft voice pleaded, and reluctantly, I followed.

"I'll talk about happy times, I promise. My parents lived in Vidzeme, in the very heart of Latvia. It's a beautiful place of farmlands and meadows and small, shallow lakes. But there were bogs, too, peat bogs that could swallow you up in one gulp, and we always had to be mindful of where we went. Although they weren't farmers, they kept several cows, so we had milk and cream and cheese. There's nothing more wonderful than warm, rich milk, right out of the udder."

I thought otherwise, but did not want to interrupt Mother. I was not especially fond of the cream that floated at the top of the milk bottle and was glad when Mother poured it off to use for coffee. "Did you have other animals?"

"Oh, yes. When I was little, we had a horse, and usually, some pigs, so we had meat and bacon." Mother picked up her needlework and began to stitch; it was impossible for her to sit with her hands folded. "When my parents began their married life together in a small, brick house that clung to the very edge of a baron's vast estate, the new century was full of promise." One row completed, Mother started on the next.

"I wish we could have a pet. Did you ride the horse?"

"The horse was Baltiņš, since she was mostly white." Mother held up her work to examine her progress before switching to another colour of thread. "Like most men, my father was conscripted into the Imperial Russian army—you know Latvia formed the western part of its vast empire—and my mother was left to run things on her own. Oh, but she was a hard worker and optimistic about the future in the way that young people are."

"Wasn't she awfully lonely?"

"I suppose so. Life in the countryside can be lonely and harsh, but if that's all you know.... Your Omite had her hands full with the animals and garden. She knew from a young age that life was not a rose garden. She groomed the horse and with her singing, she coaxed milk from the cow and made cheese. Her rounds of cheese were like yellow moons fallen from the sky. Sometimes the cheese was smooth and other times it was dotted with caraway seeds that she had collected along the roadside. Anything extra, she sold to her neighbours and passers-by at a roadside stand. She fattened the greedy pigs with whatever scraps she could spare. She ground hemp seeds leftover from fibre-making into a spread to eat on dark, coarse bread."

I made a face and turned away, but Mother did not notice. "We didn't have peanut butter or that Wonder Bread you like so much. Our bread was black and solid, like a brick, something to really chew on. Anyway, Omite's reputation grew and so did her stand, from a few hastily nailed-together boards, to a small country store." Mother seemed to forget that I was beside her. Her words had taken her back to her childhood in Vidzeme.

"When I was a little girl, I had to help in the store. We sold what we grew or made, but also purchased goods from the city. From the time we could see over the counter, Elza and I helped out after school. Year-round, Baltiņš clip-clopped to the train station, pulling a wagon in summer and a sleigh in winter, and returned with bottles and cloth, and at Christmas and Easter, the finest chocolates from Riga's Laima factory. Look here," Mother said and reached under the coffee table to bring out a photo album, grey with dust. She wiped the brown leather cover with her sleeve and opened it to a page filled with small, square, black and white photographs with frilly edges. One of the photos showed a young woman, smiling and hatless, striking a pose beside the Laima clock. "That's me," Mother said. "That was a popular meeting place, and your father, Janis, and I often met there for dates."

At that moment, as Mother patted her hair and adjusted the two small tortoise shell combs that smoothed her dark hair back from her face, I was struck by the sudden realization that my mother had once been young and in love. The war years had robbed her of her spirit and youthful looks—her hair was now dyed black—but not of all of her girlish mannerisms. "You see your father made sure I had no excuse for being late."

Mother left me to look at the other photographs while she checked to see if the dough had risen sufficiently. When she returned, she took up her sewing once more and continued to tell me about Omite. "My sister Elza was the oldest, born in 1905, a year of revolution and peasant unrest. She was a delicate, serious baby and must have sensed that something unusual was going on. As she grew, she developed the strong will of her mother."

I was still fascinated by the thought of owning a horse. "Mom, did you ever get to ride Baltiņš?"

"No, she was a work horse. In winter, from a distance it looked like a ghost horse was pulling a sleigh across the sky. After Baltiņš was gone, I sometimes imagined I saw her in the clouds." Mother put down her needle and held my hand in hers for the longest time, until I finally pulled it away. "I did miss her. Papiņš complained that Baltiņš was overly sociable. On nice days, when many people were on the road, it took him forever to get to the railway station. He had purchased her from a peddler who sold dry goods all through Vidzeme, so whenever they met anyone on the road, the horse would neigh a greeting, halt, and wait patiently while the latest news and gossip were exchanged. We were not allowed to ride her, but sometimes she would lie down in the straw, stretch out her long, bony legs, and we would snuggle up against her great big chest to feel her heart beating." Mother's face broke into a rare smile that showed her small teeth. "Now, isn't that a lovely memory?"

I was not sure whether to believe this part of the story at first, but Mother's delight convinced me it must be true. She smoothed the hair back from my forehead and continued.

"But let me get back to Elza. The year my sister was born, the peasants' rumblings of discontent, which could at first be disregarded like distant thunder, became louder and louder, until they exploded into violence. After a hundred years of oppression, the peasants were ready to break free from the Russian Empire. That was a terrible year, many peasants lost their lives, and the baronial mansions of sympathizers were torched in the most brutal reprisals. I don't know where it was worse, in the countryside or in the towns. But trying to stop history from unfolding was as futile as spitting into the wind."

"Did Omite's store burn down?" I asked.

"No, luckily, your Opaps didn't have the time to take part in secret meetings and protests, so they were spared. Soon after Elza turned two, a baby brother arrived, little Ervins." Mother's voice cracked with emotion. "It didn't take long before the diphtheria smothered him. So far from the city, there wasn't much anyone could do, even though Father tried. He hitched Baltiņš to the sleigh and took his sick baby in search of a doctor, but by the time he found one, it was too late." Mother sighed, "Those were hard, hard times, Ilzite." Mother blew her nose and tucked her handkerchief back up her sleeve. Omite was left to mourn her loss alone, because soon after, Opaps was conscripted to the Russian Imperial Army, to fight for the czar."

"It's not fair," I blurted out. "Why did he have to go away at a time like that?" I didn't like the fact that almost no one in Mother's stories could act of his or her own free will. War, disease, the czar, even the weather dictated every aspect of their lives.

"He had no choice. About a year later, as my mother was returning from milking, her arms hard as tree limbs from the full pails she carried, she saw an omen. A stork flew overhead, and on her neck, she could feel the draft caused by the beating of its strong wings. The large black and white bird landed on the roof of the school across the road and looked right at her. Omite set down her pails without spilling a drop, and hugged her arms to her chest. Her arms ached to hold a baby again. Little Elza, dark and quick as a gypsy, but much too quiet, needed a companion. And Papiņš's last letter, two months on the way, had not said one word about returning home."

"For the rest of the morning, Omite went about her chores, quietly thinking. Like many of us, her best ideas came to her while she worked. That evening she shared her newly hatched plan with her mother, your great grandmother. 'Why, it's unthinkable,' said Oma, 'too dangerous. You're just a woman, and you've the girl to think about.' But once her mind was made up, my mother could not be dissuaded, and my grandmother finally agreed to care for Elza and mind the store in Mother's absence. There was another omen, too, even more important. Not long before, the law requiring anyone who traveled more than fifteen kilometers from home to carry a passport had been abolished. Omite was free to go. Determined to find her husband and bring him home, my mother sold two pigs and stitched the rubles into the lining of her wool coat. By midsummer, she was ready. Then, with a basket of provisions on her arm, she set out."

"Walking?" I asked, incredulous.

"Yes, but a neighbour saw her and took her to the train station in his droshky."

Finally, I thought, someone was doing something, instead of just accepting whatever came his or her way. I was too young to realize that merely surviving during those hazardous times required courage and endurance. I looked at my mother's face, hoping to see a similar spark of courage or defiance, but all I saw there was resignation.

"My goodness, where's the time gone?" Mother turned and glanced at the clock. "We've got baking to finish. The rest will have to wait, okay?" *Okay* was one of the first English expressions our family adopted.

Much as I tried, I could not bring the image of Omite's face readily to mind, nor could I remember the gentle touch of her work-worn hand on my cheek. Did she smile at me when she saw me emerge, fat and bawling, into a troubled world that snowy afternoon in Aboliņ Clinic or was her greeting tinged with sadness for a world at war? In photographs, she gives nothing away.

I poked my finger into the swollen belly of dough that threatened to spill over the sides of the bowl. "Needs a bellybutton," I joked.

"It's risen beautifully," Mother said, as she punched it down. She divided the exhaling mass in three, and gave me one piece that I proceeded to roll between my hands into a long skinny loaf.

Mother sat down at the kitchen table. Her thoughts were still back in Vidzeme, with her mother. "We know little about what happened during the search for my father, she never talked about it, but I'm the living proof that she found him and got him back home to Jaungulbene!" Mother blushed prettily and rubbed some sticky dough from her fingers. "What I do know is that it took three dangerous and difficult months in Russia before Omite finally found Opaps in an infirmary, outside of Moscow. Omite spoke a passable Russian from grade school and managed to convince or bribe the commanding officer into letting her take her husband home as soon as he was well enough to travel.

Mother's clear blue eyes seemed to be straining to see something only she could see. "You know, I've so often wished I had her courage." I knew she was thinking of her mother and her brother, both a half continent and an ocean away, trapped behind an iron curtain that was more impenetrable than the brick walls of our house. Expertly, with one hand, Mother cracked an egg on the edge of a small glass bowl and let the gooey contents spill out.

"How did they get home?" I asked, as I beat the egg with a fork until yellow foam sloshed over the edges of the bowl.

"My father couldn't travel right away, since the fever had robbed him of his strength, but Omite gathered herbs and used whatever she could find or buy to boil up into soups. When he was strong enough, they made the long trip home. It was on the train that Omite first saw Irma."

"Aunt Irma?"

"Yes, Irma was a little girl, traveling on the train with her mother, who was very sick and slept most of the way, as did my father. But the little girl—Irma—was lively and pretty and reminded Omite of her own little Elza back home. Well, Omite befriended Irma and her mother—I don't recall her name—and by the time they rolled into Riga, Omite had promised to take Irma if anything happened to the girl's mother. You see the mother worried that she might not live much longer, and she had no relatives who could help."

"That's so sad. Wasn't there a doctor on the train, or someone to help her get better?"

Mother hesitates before answering. "No, Ilzite, there wasn't, not in those days. Sadly, the mother didn't recover and some months later, Irma came to live with us." Mother sighs as she squeezes my hand, "I suppose, in a way, it helped ease Omite's sadness at the loss of her baby."

"And Elza had a playmate," I said, hoping to cheer Mother up.

"Yes, and the next year, in the spring, I was born." Mother added softly.

"I'm so glad," I said and hugged Mother for a long time. When at last I lifted my head from her bosom, we were both smiling.

"And that's how my Omite and Opaps got their three little girls. We'd better attend to the bread now. It must be ready for the oven."

I gave the egg mixture one last whirl, then brushed it over the tops of the loaves. Then I sprinkled caraway seeds on top and watched, fascinated, as they landed and stuck, mysterious hieroglyphs of a long-forgotten language.

Mother slid the pan into the oven. "Now, all we do is wait."

"And then eat!" I added, licking my lips.

Fifteen

Some months went by before we had any more news from relatives. Then one evening, when we were finishing up a tasty dinner of pork chops smothered in an onion and sour cream sauce, Father broke the news that his sister Elizabete Svenne, Adolfs, and their three children were coming to Canada. "I tell you, that Adolfs is full of surprises," Father told Mother, and my brothers and I stopped talking and became all ears. Father retrieved the letter from his pocket and began reading. "I am going to seek my immigrant visa as a Danish farmer, as I hear Danish farmers are highly regarded in Canada. I have been inquiring about suitable farm properties," Adolfs wrote.

"Crazy man," Father said, as he put down the letter to accept a cup of coffee. "Adolfs knows as much about farming as I do about flying an airplane—zilch."

"Well, after all, he was a judge in Latvia, and he is pretty clever. Maybe he's learned something, living in the Danish countryside," said Mother.

"Pshaw. Adolfs wouldn't know which end of a cow to milk. Still, he can be quite persuasive, I'll give him that much." Father found his place and continued reading.

"Fate has decided our future," wrote Adolfs. "Latvians here doubt that, barring some miracle, Latvia will be free any time soon. Even so, it has been a difficult decision. It is not easy to leave the Baltic coast and its proximity to Latvia, but Elly and I have to think of the children's future. I don't think life in Canada will be any better, but it will be safer. Our children want to grow up, and they want to live. I have held on in Europe the longest, and you know I always said you shouldn't run from terror when there is no terror to run from. The good thing is we now have four wage earners—me, Elizabeth, Valda, and Dita. Only Juris is still in school."

Father sat back and rubbed his cheek. "They'll be on their feet in no time, with so many family members contributing," he said, without looking at Mother. Then, he went on. "In your last letter you are a bit down, since you feel you are at the bottom of the pecking order—a British one at that—but I believe all is going to be well with you. You are working in your field, you have an apartment and a car, and your children are in school. You are one of the luckiest Latvians. I am happy for you and congratulate you with all my heart. I hope you will someday become a director or something much like it."

Mother seized the opportunity to add her praise. "He's right, you know. Maybe you could relax a bit now. You're a true lion." Father, born in August under the sign of Leo, always welcomed being compared to a lion, the king of beasts.

As the sun's rays grew stronger and winter lost its icy grip, the snow began to melt, revealing the debris left behind by the builders. Barclay Street became a sea of mud, difficult to navigate. We tracked mud into our building and up the stairs until finally, a city crew arrived and poured cement for the sidewalks. Mother was pleased, but no one was as happy as Roland, who was given a red tricycle for his third birthday and never tired of pedaling up and down the street.

The lilacs were in bloom when we received another letter from Uncle Adolfs, this one mailed from Brevenhaven in Germany. "We are sailing to Canada aboard the 12,000 T. *Anna Salen*," Adolfs wrote. "Of course, it is no *Gripsholm*, except there are lots of Swedes and Danes on board. It is the first day of June, and the weather is beautiful. With the help of a gramophone, Elizabeth has started giving English classes. She has ten students, Latvians and Estonians. Classes are held every day from eleven until three or four. She is a good teacher."

The Svenne family arrived in Canada, and went straight to the Tobe farm in Niagara-on-the-Lake, where they had a work contract. We next heard from Adolfs when he was settled in his new home. "We live in a hut with 'antique' furniture, so our start in Canada is not brilliant, but we must honour our contract. We have to stay until the fall, then we are free to look for work elsewhere. We all want to go to Toronto. My first job is to clean up the garden. I work ten hours a day for four dollars a day. We look forward to your planned visit in August, when you have holidays. There is a waterfall nearby that is a wonder to see, and maybe by that time, some of the fruit will be ripe."

"Yipee!" I cried. "Let's go visit right away."

Father told me to calm down. A lot could happen between now and August.

In spite of being a modern builder, an engineer who dealt only with fact and cold numbers, Father did have his softer side. He did not have great faith in people, but he believed in the restorative properties of fresh air and sunshine. Most Sundays, he brought out the Vanguard, wiped the dust from its hood, checked the oil, and took us out of the city and into the countryside. Peter always sat in the front, beside Father, and the rest of us, picnic basket at our feet, occupied the rear. Father drove off the island, mostly to the north or west, exploring the side roads, hoping to find a place to picnic and swim. Once, Father drove south across the Jacques Cartier Bridge to Caughnawaga to see the Indians who looked fierce in their paint and feathers, dancing to the beat of a drum. Mother marvelled at the fine beadwork on their clothes and moccasins, but the rest of us were more interested in their bows and arrows and tomahawks. Another time, we crossed the ferry to Oka, and Father bought stinky cheese that he and Mother thought very delicious, but which I refused to taste. My favourite direction was north, to where the Canadian Shield protrudes from the earth. It felt so good to lie stretched out on the sun-warmed rock, eyes squeezed shut, with my face upturned to the sun. I could not think of any other place I'd rather be. If a wind were blowing, I could imagine the sound of waves splashing against a rocky, Swedish coast, bringing back a memory so faint it seemed part of a fleeting dream that cannot be recalled upon waking.

For many weeks, we rode in comfort, but when the Beikmanis family, friends from Latvia, arrived in Montreal, Father invited them along on one of our outings. Father's Vanguard groaned and sank low under the weight of so many bodies. Father and Juris sat up front with Peter between them. In the rear, sat Mother with Roland on her lap, Arija, Anitra, and me, all jostling for a bit of space. Father drove more slowly, trying to avoid bumps and holes in the road, not wanting to damage the suspension. It was hot in the back seat, but Father would not allow us to roll down the back windows, and we had only his little triangle side window to cool us.

Sometimes, if we couldn't find a suitable public place to stop, we made do with the roadside for our picnic. The adults stretched their legs and we children ran around beating down the tall grass with our feet, laughing as the grasshoppers scattered. Mother extended the blanket and held down the corners with her basket and other supplies. Father and Juris returned from their explorations, puffing on cigarettes, in an effort to keep the mosquitoes at bay. Peter searched the ditches, in hopes of catching a frog, while Anitra and I gathered daisies and buttercups. Roland, who liked to copy whatever we did, plucked dandelions by their yellow heads, and with white, sticky, milk running down his arm, presented them to Mother. Mother accepted them as graciously as if she had just been handed a bouquet of long-stemmed roses. After a lunch of hardboiled eggs, radishes, pickles, and salami sandwiches on rye, Father and Juris fortified themselves with sips from a flask that Juris carried in his pocket. Arija lay back and closed her eyes, sighing with pleasure while Mother stayed sitting, with one eye on Roland, who had a tendency to wander. When it was time to go, we piled back into the car, our skin red and tender from too much sun, and the occasional scratch or mosquito bite, but tired and happy after a good day.

In early August 1951, Father took a holiday from work, and we made the drive to Toronto and Niagara-on-the-Lake and back, our longest trip since arriving in Canada. "This will be a real test of endurance, both for me and the car," said Father, but we never doubted his ability or the car's. With the flat of his palm, he ironed out the folds in a map of Ontario and pointed to Toronto, over three hundred miles to the west. "Spool of Thread has never rolled so far from home." I hardly slept that night, and I woke early, to the smell of frying bacon. I threw on my clothes and went to help Mother wrap the sandwiches she had already prepared. Before getting into the car, Father told us to hop right up onto the seat—something he never allowed us to do—and to slide along. I soon saw why; the floor was carpeted in brown grocery bags filled with food for the journey, enough for lunch, dinner, and breakfast the next day—cookies and Ritz crackers, tins of sprats smothered in oil and sardines slathered in tomato sauce, a wheel of cheese triangles, hard-boiled eggs, cold potatoes, a jar of pickles, tomatoes, cucumbers, and a basket of purple plums. Another basket cradled a thermos of coffee and bottles of pink cream soda that never satisfied anyone's thirst.

The streets were deserted, and even rue Décarie yawned wide and empty as we headed north. When we approached Dorval Airport, Peter begged Father to stop so he could watch the airplanes land and take off.

"No, no," Father replied, concentrating on the merging traffic, "we've a long drive ahead of us."

We stopped at a roadside table on the Quebec-Ontario border, and Peter and I straddled the imaginary line that separates the two provinces. Mother poured us all a drink, and then handed out her homemade apple bread, Father's favourite.

Around noon, we halted once more to answer nature's call and stretch our legs. We were parked on a rise, and below us the land dipped away to reveal a slice of blue-grey water in the distance, our first glimpse of Lake Ontario. On the outskirts of Toronto, we spent the night in a cabin, sleeping on cots. In the morning, we dressed in our best clothes, ate a cold breakfast, then headed to the Latvian Church and the christening of Rita and Laimonis's baby, Normunds.

"This is quite an occasion," said Father, straightening his tie and smoothing down his hair. "Normunds is the first Canadian in our family."

"When will we be Canadian?" asked Peter, as he tucked his shirt into his pants.

"Not 'til February 1956. We must wait five years."

Quickly, Peter calculated, "I'll be thirteen."

During the celebration that followed, Normunds slept off and on in his new carriage, unaware of the historic importance of this day. The baby carriage was a thank-you gift from Father for Laimonis's help in getting him his job at Canadian Vickers. Peter immediately made friends with Cousin Juris, who was several years older, and I studied Cousin Milda's every move. She was as pretty as ever, in a flowered cotton dress with a square neckline and a wide skirt. Her hair was shorter and her lips glowed a bright red. I asked her if she was still dancing. "You bet," she replied. "Next week, I start my new job at Arthur Murray Dance Studios. I'm going to teach people to dance."

"Wow," I replied, hugely impressed, although I had no idea who Arthur Murray was. Then, in a surprise move, she took one of her hands in mine, placed the other hand on my shoulder and spun me around. "How was that?" she asked. "I've just finished one hundred hours of dance instructor training. It cost me a whopping $1.75 for each hour."

"Wow, one hundred and seventy-five dollars," said Peter, who had come up behind us. He had an after-school paper route and knew the value of money.

"Sure, it's a lot of money, but it's an investment in my future. Now, I'll be able to leave my job at the Honey Dew Restaurant, where I work afternoons 'til midnight, for all of fifty cents an hour."

After the christening, the men puffed on fat cigars that Uncle Adolfs had brought from Denmark and talked about Europe. The events and politics of far-off Europe were of greater interest and far more real to them than day-to-day happenings in Canada, with the exception of statements made by Prime Minister Louis St. Laurent on the Korean War.

Cousin Valters, who was really old enough to be my uncle, had driven all the way from New York City in a 1947 Plymouth to become baby Normunds's godfather. He regaled us with stories of New York City and its marvels, the Empire State Building, television in living colour and the El, a train that rumbled high above the street one minute and the next, plunged underground, and even tunnelled under the river. I could hardly wait to visit my other cousins who lived in New York and witnessed such marvels every day.

Over coffee and yellow saffron bread, the men's talk turned more serious. "You shouldn't be too discouraged," Valters admonished. His grey eyes sought out Uncle Adolfs's as he spoke. "All new arrivals go through what you're feeling—a kind of let down. Even if you remind yourself not to have too many grand illusions, the beginning is hard, disappointing even. It can't be helped. In America, we may have our coloured television, but still, money doesn't fall from the trees, nor does it glint and beckon from between the cracks in the sidewalk. It takes time to get used to the way things are and to begin to build a life."

"Well, we're willing to work hard—all of us," Uncle Adolfs assured him. "But picking fruit? Just look at these hands." He held out his scratched, sunburnt arms with upturned palms to show his calluses. "Elizabeth's are the same. What kind of hands are those for a piano teacher? And what about my Valda, earning just $70 a month as a house-helper in a doctor's home?"

Father set down his cup, and slapped his hand on the white cloth, being careful not to upset any dishes. "Our education should count for more than it does. How do you think I feel when some Brit in short pants, the ink not yet dry on his diploma, gets promoted ahead of me for the simple reason that he speaks better English?

"*Nu, nu*, Jani, you never were very patient," said his sister Edite.

"You catch more flies with honey than vinegar," Mother added, repeating one of her favourite sayings.

"We have to swallow those slights, no matter how bitter," chimed Aunt Elizabeth in her beautiful voice, "for the sake of our children's future. After all, they're the reason why we're here."

"In the end, it all comes down to who you know, doesn't it?" said Adolfs, and for a while, everyone reflected on the truth of his words. Then Adolfs pulled out his pocket watch and announced that it was time to leave if we wanted to reach Niagara-on-the-Lake and settle in before dark.

"All right then, let's see what kind of a farmer Canada has made out of this judge," said Father, with a bitter laugh. He stood up slowly and steadied himself with one hand on the table; he was feeling the effects of too much vodka.

I couldn't wait to get to Niagara-on-the-Lake and finally see the fruit trees that red-haired Cousin Dita had described. "You're allowed to eat all you want from any tree that's already been picked," she said, causing my mouth to water. Before falling asleep, I imagined myself stripping branches of their cherries and filling my mouth with the sweet fruit. The next morning, I was not disappointed. The unripe cherries that the pickers had left behind were now fully ripe. It was hard work, but we filled a large basket and sat down at a table in the shade of a large maple to eat. Mother's blue eyes sparkled, as she wiped the dark red juice from my chin. "At last, my little ones have experienced Lejputrija," she said. Lejputrija was the place Latvians dreamed about when their bellies growled for food, an imaginary place where the bowls and plates were always full, no matter how much was consumed.

The next day, we could hear Niagara Falls long before we set eyes on the water spilling over the cliff edge in unending fury. Father bought tickets, and before I could protest, I found myself on the deck of the *Maid of the Mist*, wearing a damp, yellow slicker. The valiant little boat fought the current and bullied its way to the very foot of the thundering falls. It was too much like being back on the *Gripsholm* and riding out the storm for me to enjoy myself, but Peter and Father seemed to be having a good time. There was nothing to do but hold on and pray for deliverance. My prayers were answered; just when a wall of water was about to swamp us, the *Maid of the Mist* veered, and headed back to safety.

Our holiday ended all too soon, and it was time to say our good-byes. It was still early, not yet time for lunch, when Father slowed, pulled onto the shoulder, and turned off the engine. He got out of the car and, pale as a ghost, stretched out full-length on the grass. Cars whizzed by as Mother knelt beside him, a hand on his forehead.

Father shut his eyes against the blinding sun and took shallow breaths, trying to ease the pain. Mother loosened his tie and undid the top button of his shirt. Trying to keep the panic out of her voice, she held a flask of water to Father's lips and helped him drink. We all knew that Mother did not know how to drive. Having spent most of her time in the rear seat, keeping the peace between Roland and me, she had no idea which pedal to push or which lever to pull. At her elbow, Peter suddenly piped up, "I know how to drive. I've watched Dad."

"It's passing now," said Father, his voice weak. "Better get the children back in the car."

For a few minutes, Father slept peacefully by the roadside, as if he were home in his own bed. Birds flew overhead and settled in the nearby scrub, bees buzzed, and an orange butterfly flitted about erratically until it landed on a milkweed. Overhead, the wires sang. Mother did what she knew best, and handed out food from the almost empty bags. We were all relieved when Father rose, brushed the grass from his clothes, and squeezed in behind the wheel. No one said a word for many miles.

Back home, Mother wrote the obligatory thank-you letter, and soon after, Uncle Adolfs replied: "We were very happy with your visit and liked your children," he wrote. "They are not at all as naughty and as untidy as you fear others find them. Your sons have good qualities and will carry on the Zalite name. I am especially proud that my nine-year-old godson is earning money with such a good goal. Surely, lively, little Ilzite, with her blue eyes and quick smile will break many hearts."

"You see, Jani," Mother interjected, "there's no need to worry so about the children's behaviour. Maybe you could ease up on them a bit."

Without replying, Father continued reading: "So, you see how we live and work and save our money. We have discarded our goal of buying a farm, as it is too expensive, and everyone is feeling the pull of Toronto." Aunt Elizabeth added a line at the end, that made me wish I were back at their farm, "Right now it is peach harvest, and we eat all we can." How could they contemplate leaving such a Garden of Eden for Toronto, I wondered.

"What will Adolfs do, now that he's abandoned the dream of farming?" said Father. "He's like a fish out of water. What can a Latvian judge do in Canada? That's why real, portable skills, like mathematics and physics, are so important. Our Peter, with his good head for numbers, will be an engineer."

Sixteen

The last few weeks before school went by quickly; my brothers and I kicked a ball around in the street or hung out at a nearby playground, swinging or climbing the jungle gym. On muggy evenings, if he was not too tired, Father and I went for walks, just the two of us, walking in a companionable silence. Usually, I started out holding his hand, but soon tired of his stately pace and ran or skipped ahead. I got to know the neighbourhood at night, with its groups of girls and boys, lounging about on street corners, laughing and shoving each other playfully, and in no hurry to get anywhere in particular. They seemed to be having a good time, but I knew Father disapproved, in the same way he disapproved of the youngsters leaning over a counter at Woolworth's on Friday night, sipping sodas. By this time, the streetlights had come on, and I wondered if his criticism had more to do with the fact that he thought they should be at home, rather than any wrongdoing on their part.

Over the summer, my English had become rusty, and it took a few days to bring back the shine. I felt appropriately sorry for the newly arrived immigrants in my grade two class, but I almost laughed as they grimaced and contorted their mouths, trying to produce the right sounds. I renewed one or two friendships from the previous year, and was glad to have someone to play with during recess.

One afternoon Lily, who lived in the next building, invited me home to her apartment. I was surprised to see her remove from around her neck, a cord with a key on it, and unlock the door. "Where's your mother?" I asked.

"At work," she answered, and stepped inside her empty apartment, as if it were the most normal thing in the world. It was the strangest feeling, as not even the smell of cooking greeted us. "I'm not allowed in the living room," she said, and I had to be content with a peek through the open arch. Lily's living room did not look anything like ours. Sheer, pleated curtains hung at the window, instead of the heavy blackout drapes that Father pulled closed each night, so that not a sliver of light escaped, and no silhouette was revealed. Lily's sleek chesterfield was covered in a golden brocade fabric, with not one cushion to hug, or on which to rest a tired head. Beside the chesterfield stood a tall lamp, the lampshade still wearing its plastic cover as if no one had thought to unwrap it. A pair of dainty, elaborately dressed figurines, perched out of reach on a high shelf. We drank Kool-Aid at the kitchen table, then Lily took me to her room and showed me her dolls, lined up on the shelves of a bookcase. Some were in cardboard boxes with a cellophane front so they could be admired, but not touched.

"Are these all yours?" I gasped. I had never seen so many dolls in one place, except at Eaton's.

"Whose else would they be? I've got no sisters." She had no brothers, either, and despite all her dolls and ruffled bedspread, I was glad to have brothers and a mother who greeted me when I returned home from school. We played for a while, until it was time for me to go. Except for a birthday party, I never went to Lily's apartment again. I did not invite her to mine, either, for I had nothing as fine as her doll collection to show her.

Father worked as much overtime as he could get, but on Sundays, if he was not too tired and did not have a meeting to attend, we got to know our new city better. A favourite with all of us was Mount Royal, with its giant cross reaching to the heavens, and Beaver Lake, a real misnomer, since it was not a lake and had no beavers. But we returned time and again to feed the ducks and to explore the wooded trails that wound around the mountain like a vine around a tree. In winter, we brought our brand new toboggan, a long, flat sled with no runners that was impossible to steer. Another time, we visited St. Joseph's Oratory, founded by Brother André. The Basilica was perched high up on the hillside, with hundreds of steps to climb before the massive doors could be reached. We wandered about its cavernous, ornate interior, until we came to a small room filled with crutches, canes, and limbless plaster casts, abandoned by their owners after Brother André's prayers had healed them. Up a short flight of stairs, in an even smaller room, encased in glass and suffused in a red glow, was Brother André's heart, a truly awesome and somewhat creepy sight. Would I find the rest of him, organ by organ, somewhere else, I wondered. "No," Father assured me, "his body is properly buried somewhere behind the church."

Once, Father took us to Belmont Park, a wonderful place with a giant Ferris wheel and a clattering roller coaster too scary to ride, but with funny clowns and games of skill and hot dogs dripping with bright yellow mustard. Father was not impressed, calling Belmont Park a mere tingle-tangle; after all, he had been to the Tivoli Gardens in Copenhagen.

After several cold nights that painted the maple leaves scarlet and gold, we piled into the car and drove north to get a closer look at nature's brushwork. Latvia has nothing like this, Mother assured us, and I was glad that for once, Canada came out on top. Bright sunlight on golden autumn leaves helped to lift my parents' spirits, as they struggled to adapt to a new country and to understand its strange ways. Soon, however, the short, dark November days revealed Mother and Father's true, melancholy nature, a nature shared by most Latvians. November Eighteen, Latvia's National Day, should have been a time to celebrate, but instead, it reminded us of what we had lost. A solemn church service marked the occasion. When the congregation sang the national anthem, "God Bless Latvia", many of the adults shed bitter tears. During the silence that followed, I could hear the snapping open of purses and a faint swishing sound, as handkerchiefs were retrieved to dab at eyes and noses. I stood stiffly at attention, with my eyes fixed on the flag and tried not to cry, ashamed that my tears were not for poor, occupied Latvia, but from fear born of witnessing the grown-ups around me cry. I thought back to the last assembly at school, and how we had sung "God Save the Queen", all of us dry-eyed and fidgety, mumbling the words.

The mood changed suddenly and dramatically once the formal part of the remembrance was over, and we trooped downstairs to the church hall for coffee. Women in print dresses with strings of amber beads around their necks bustled about serving sandwiches and cake and pouring coffee; men in dark suits and sober ties, their hair carefully combed and oiled, shook hands and stood in small groups discussing the merits of different cars; little children chased about the room, while the youth, tall and awkward, gathered in a far corner. I was eight and belonged to none of the groups. At a loss, I offered to help and was immediately given a task.

"Good little helper," a pink-cheeked woman said to Mother, nodding her head approvingly in my direction.

Mother beamed, obviously proud, and I made a face. At that moment I didn't want to play the role of the dutiful daughter so that my parents could receive compliments. I deposited the dishes on the kitchen counter and stomped off by myself to sulk.

On that occasion, most of the families already knew each other, but there were a few who had only recently arrived. It did not take them long to find their way. The Latvians who had arrived in the late-1940s left the countryside as soon as their obligatory year of farm service for their sponsors ended, and moved to the cities hoping to find more suitable work. At the same time, they set up associations and societies, many of these carrying on from the camps. The Latvian Relief Society, the Montreal Latvian Society, Latvian school, sororities and fraternities, amateur theatre, as well as a Lutheran and a Catholic congregation were among the first. In the years to follow, others sprang up, including a men's choir, a dance troupe, and a children's summer camp, Tervete, as well as two groups of particular interest to Father: the Association of Latvian Engineers and the Montreal Latvian Credit Union. The Latvian Credit Union was a boon to the men discussing cars and hoping to buy one. As well, there were umbrella organizations, the LNAK, the Latvian Federation in Canada, and ALA, the Latvian American Association. In Montreal, a monthly newsletter, *Ziņotājs*, kept the Latvians informed and the community united.

Despite being from a small country, speaking the same language, and having suffered a similar ordeal, the Latvians were not a homogeneous society. They mistrusted one another and argued among themselves, and most notably, they refused to play the role of the downtrodden. My parents' friends were opinionated, outspoken, and given to boasting. Children figured prominently in their boasting; that's why good grades and exemplary behaviour were so important. If you believed the parents, no Latvian child had ever failed a test or been sent to the principal's office. At times, the only uniting issue in the Latvian community seemed to be the desire to live long enough to return to a free Latvia. Here is where Father differed from his fellow countrymen; he held out little hope of ever returning.

With our arrival in Montreal, Father had stopped running. All too aware of the erratic beating of his heart, he wanted the security of a home of his own, closer to his work. Quietly, he and Mother drew up a list of requirements for their new east end neighbourhood: a high school for Peter who would soon graduate from elementary school; a grocery store that Mother could walk to; public transportation; and safe, quiet streets. A building lot on rue Orléans in Rosemount fit Father's criteria. He was already drawing up the plans for a two-story duplex when word got out.

"What will you do when freedom comes?" a sharp-nosed Latvian asked.

"My family's future is here now," Father replied. He did not believe that Latvia would be free any time soon. The Grundig radio at his bedside never broadcasted good news.

"But Rosemount? That's down east, isn't it, full of French?" He chose to live in the west end of the city, as did most Latvians. "You'll have to *parlez-vous* and all that," he smirked, veiling his disapproval with humour, and slapping Father good-naturedly on the back.

A shadow crossed Father's face, and his mouth drew a straight line across his face. "Rosemount has everything we need."

"Maybe so, but not Latvians."

"Yes," said his wife, a sour-faced woman with bright yellow hair, who suddenly appeared at his side. "What about suitable companions for your children?"

Father sighed. These thoughts were nothing new and had concerned him, too. "Well now, it's a free country, is it not? We each live where we want." He had not expected this reaction; he had hoped to be congratulated. Few immigrants could dream of owning a home so soon; many were still without a car.

Father's worries went beyond dismissing the sometimes-envious comments of his peers. For an immigrant without a credit history, obtaining a mortgage from a proper bank was like trying to squeeze milk from a stone. He did not like debt and always paid cash, even for the Vanguard. To his mind, the banks were far too nosy, seeking personal information about salary, savings, and debts.

Many Latvians had the same problems as Father in obtaining credit. "What we really need is a credit union of our own, one where Latvians can deposit their savings, earn interest, and borrow money for worthwhile causes," he said, at the next meeting of the Montreal Latvian Society. He paused to wipe his face with his handkerchief and to let his words sink in. "You may already know, Toronto's formed a Latvian Credit Union that is proving successful." After much debate, a committee was formed to look into the feasibility and legal aspects of such a venture.

With the deed filed away and the promise of a mortgage, Father set to work studying the building code and costing out materials for a solid brick, two-family, semi-detached house with a driveway for his car. We would occupy the first floor apartment and rent the upper. When he was satisfied with his design and his calculations, he showed the results to Mother. The colour drained from her face; she looked stricken. The paper trembled slightly in Father's usually rock-steady hand, as he pointed to the figures.

"Can we afford this?" she asked.

"Oh, it's not nearly as bad as it looks," he said. "We've twenty-five years to pay it off." Neither spoke what was on their minds—they would not live that long.

In mid-November, a backhoe arrived on rue Orléans to dig the foundation, only to discover that solid rock lay beneath a thin layer of soil.

"We 'ave to blast—*kaboom*!" the contractor explained, throwing up his hands to illustrate.

"You mean dynamite?" Father stood on the sidewalk, surrounded by a gaggle of neighbourhood children, and squinted into the late afternoon sun. This was not good news. It meant delay and added cost; he would have to redo his calculations.

"*Oui, oui*. Dynamite. It's the only way."

At home that evening, Father looked to Mother for consolation. "Why does bad luck follow me wherever I go?"

"*Nu*, Jani, you know that's not so," Mother replied, the only answer possible.

"You realize, Mama, that this means more money. We'll have to count every kopek from now on."

"Of course," Mother agreed. She was already doing that, had been doing it for years.

"What can I do? All will be fine, and if it won't be fine, it will still be fine," Father said, a clenched fist on the table. "It's a fool's saying, but you know as well as I, that sometimes fools come out ahead. Okay, we'll blast away and try to make up for lost time. Every hour that machine sits idle, it eats more of my money."

Later that night as I lay awake, too excited to sleep, I thought about our new house. I liked the idea of our foundation extending down into the warm, solid, rock of the Canadian Shield.

We saw little of Father in the coming months. He worked as much overtime as Canadian Vickers would allow, and arrived home tired and irritable with hunger. Outside of work, all his energies were directed toward the construction. In the spring, he did not renew our lease, so we were faced with a fast-approaching deadline of May 1. We all did our part, filling up on bread and potatoes instead of cookies and fruit. Overwhelmed by worries of his own, Father seemed unaware of Mother's struggle to satisfy the increasing appetites of her growing children on a meager allowance; the kitchen was the woman's domain.

Compared to Father, Mother seemed to have time to spare. Except for a flurry of activity in the kitchen before dinner and the daily trip to the grocery store, I wondered how she occupied her time, while we were away at school. Mother didn't much care for housework, which was obvious from the dust that gathered on the bookshelves and the dirty finger marks on the walls. On one of those rare days when a fever kept me home, I discovered that Mother did not sit with her hands idle in her lap; she kept them busy sewing. She balled up the socks she had just mended and took up her needlework. I curled up in one corner of the chesterfield and watched her first admire her work and then begin to embroider. Her fingers worked the needle in and out of the stiff canvas, leaving a trail of colour. Mother looked peaceful, almost happy, and it suddenly struck me that for her, this was not just a hobby; needlework was as necessary to her as Father's work was to him. When she stopped to consult the diagram in the booklet, there was a faraway look in her eyes, as if she could actually see the landscape she was recreating. I pointed to a particular design and asked her what it meant.

"Oh, many things, but mostly that we're Latvian," she answered, dreamily. I made a face and closed my eyes—I knew what she meant.

With time, Mother's hand worked pieces took over the chairs and the couch in the living room, an almost living presence. They made excellent presents too, on birthdays, name days, and Christmas. One of Mother's handsome, embroidered pillows always figured prominently on the lottery table at the church bazaar.

Whenever Mother completed a canvas, I accompanied her to Woolworth's and together we rummaged through the bin of fabric remnants for a scrap of velvet or corduroy big enough and the right shade to use for backing. After a few minutes, I always started sneezing. I like to think now that it was the lint or sizing and not Mother's heavily accented English that sent me outside to wait while she completed her purchase. Sometimes, Mother bought herself a hairnet—she preferred a fine, delicate, almost-invisible mesh to the heavy, sturdier ones—to contain her shoulder-length hair in a smooth pageboy.

One rainy Saturday morning, I moped around the apartment, restless and unable to settle down with a book. Mother was waiting for the dough to rise and sat on the couch, her legs stretched out. She lowered her legs and patted the seat next to her. "Why don't I help you with your sewing?" she suggested. I hesitated; I did not have the patience for fine needlework. Rain hit the window and ran down the pane in sheets.

"*Nu*, Daughter?" Mother's eyes searched my face for an answer, and she patted the sofa again. I was surprised by how beautiful she looked just then, her dark hair swept back from her gently rounded brow, her features regular, her nose just a fraction too long. In a candid moment, she had confessed to disliking her nose, but I would have gladly traded mine for hers, and told her so. Mother squeezed my hand and assured me that I had a very pretty nose, but I knew it was not slender. I take after my father's side of the family, a fact that filled me with apprehension. Would my nose continue to grow to become as prominent as Opap's?

I dragged my feet all the way to my room and returned with my sewing. It, too, looked nothing like Mother's. I smoothed the wrinkled canvas with my hands, spread it out on my lap, and studied it. What a disappointment. The stitches refused to line up in orderly rows; instead they wobbled across the canvas like a snow fence after a winter storm. Some stitches were too loose, others too tight. And the colours! What had possessed me to choose those colours? At the time, I had thought them bold and modern, but now the orange just seemed garish and the turquoise, pretentious. Mother was only being kind when she compared my orange blobs to a Latvian sunset.

"Why don't I help you with that," offered Mother. "You could work on the handkerchief you're embroidering for Father."

I don't know which I disliked more, needlepoint or embroidery. "I have 'til Christmas." The only thing I liked about sewing was being with Mother and hearing her stories, which I only half-believed.

Mother examined my progress. "It's a good start, Ilzite. I remember how impatient my Omite, your great-grandmother, would get if I tangled the thread, and she had to break it, or worse still, I lost a needle. As you know, we lived in the country and couldn't just run to the five-and-dime and buy another one."

I had heard this all before, but I didn't mind. "Tell me about the mittens," I asked.

"Ah yes, the mittens. Before a girl could even dream about getting married, she had to fill her hope chest, not just with embroidered linens, but also with hundreds of warm, knitted mittens."

"You're exaggerating? Hundreds?"

"Really, hundreds. The finest went to her intended, to seal the engagement, and to her future in-laws, to prove to them what a good wife she'd be. The rest were for the wedding guests, relatives, and friends. Even the animals got to wear mittens."

"On their paws?"

Mother smiled at the idea. "No, the mittens adorned the sleigh or carriage; why, even the pigsty out back and the fir tree in front of the house got mittens."

"How many did you knit?"

"You really are full of questions today. I'm not much of a knitter," she admitted, and then added shyly, "There are other ways to catch a man."

The day Father brought home an RCA Victor television set from Eaton's, my interest in needlework as a pastime grew even dimmer. There was no Latvian word for television, but Father preferred *burvju kaste* (magic box) for the wonders it presented. After reading the instructions, Father placed the antenna on top of the wooden cabinet and extended the rabbit ears, two metal rods that did not in any way resemble velvety pink rabbit ears, but were somehow able to grab an image out of thin air. It took a while for the set to warm up and the picture to appear; like an approaching train nearing the station, the light first appeared small, then slowly grew bigger, until it filled the whole glass front. Then, suddenly, an Indian head, complete with feathered headdress, appeared. Father fiddled with the rabbit ears, turning them this way and that, to smooth out the Indian's features. "There, that's the station signal," Father said, and consulted the booklet. "And now, the focus." Underneath the screen, much like Father's radio, were three knobs—one for horizontal hold, another for vertical hold, and a third to adjust the brightness. Father turned off the television, and my brothers and I moaned.

"When can we watch?" I asked.

"After supper, but remember to keep your hands off. It's not a toy. Television will help Mama to learn English."

At first, we were content to watch anything the CBC sent our way, even the Indian head, but soon we realized that not everything CBFT Montreal broadcasted interested us, especially the French programs and the hockey, neither of which we understood. The moment I saw Barbara Ann Scott skate, however, I had a new passion. I wanted to skate like her, wearing a short skirt that flared out when I spun around. I liked the swishing sound her skates made as she carved figure eights in the ice. All I needed were skates. In the meantime, I practised twirling on the slippery wood of the hall, and lifting my leg high behind me, I balanced on one foot.

Father listened patiently as I described my new passion. He believed in the value of sports, but not in letting oneself get carried away. "It's not as easy as it looks," he warned.

"I know that, but I'll practise every day, like Barbara Ann Scott."

"Forget Barbara Ann Scott and be patient. Money doesn't just grow on trees."

"Please, Daddy." I had never before wanted anything as much as this.

I stopped whining and begging when, one day, Father traced the outline of my foot on a sheet of paper and cut carefully along the pencilled line. A few days later, he arrived home with my skates, wrapped in brown paper. My smile faded, when I saw the skates. They were boys' skates, like Peter's, made of brown and black leather with CCM written across the back. "These are not the skates I need," I said, trying not to cry.

"Skates are skates," Father said. "You wanted skates, did you not?"

"Yes, but I need white ones, figure skates, like Barbara Ann Scott. I need skates with thin blades and pointy tips, so I can do tricks."

"Don't confuse need with want," Father admonished. "When I was a boy in Latvia, I made do with blades that buckled to my boots with leather straps."

"But that was the olden days." A voice in my head told me I should be grateful, but I could not help feeling cheated. If I made do with these, I would never become a figure skater.

My dream became possible again on Christmas Eve, when a brand-new pair of white skates with shiny blades winked at me from under the tree. I couldn't wait to get them on and try them out. Even then, I bore little resemblance to Barbara Ann Scott, either in dress or style. Bundled up in baggy woollen trousers that flapped about my ankles and a bulky ski jacket, I made my way along the boards, my ankles folding like worn out playing cards. The spinning happened only in my head, as I tried to keep my balance and remain upright. Other children whizzed by, playing tag around me. I was determined not to give up; I just needed practise. I did, of course, learn to skate, but it was not until the ice turned to slush and the boards came down, that I gave up my dream. Only Mother showed me any sympathy; luckily, Father didn't seem to notice. He was buoyed by world events—the death of Stalin, Hillary's conquest of Mount Everest, and most importantly, the end of the Korean War. "It's only a stalemate," he admitted, but it's over, at least for now." Overseeing the construction of our house in Rosemount took all his spare time and energy.

In the spring, right after Mother's birthday, Father's sister Milda wrote to say they were coming to Canada. They sailed from Southampton to Montreal on one of my uncle's ships and stayed with us for a few days, until they found a place of their own. In many ways, Aunt Milda, with her softly permed, brown hair, hazel eyes, and somewhat fleshy nose, looked a lot like Father's other sisters, Aunt Edite and Aunt Elly, but she was different, too. She was younger but she looked older and more tired, as if she had rowed all the way across the Atlantic herself. However, Uncle Valentine had energy enough for them both and regaled us with shipboard tales of how the boiler nearly blew or how many men he knew who were now lost at sea. During the meal, he chewed his meat with obvious enjoyment and told Mother what a good cook she was, until she felt compelled to offer him another slice. My cousins and I had never met, and we studied each other as we ate. I was not keen on sharing my bed with a complete stranger.

Uncle Valentine's long face ended in a square jaw that moved up and down as he ate. Satisfied, he put down his fork and leaned back. "My first impression of Canada is a good one," he said. "There's plenty of navigable water, open space, and woods."

Father agreed, then he explained that they would go to the shipyards in the morning, so his brother-in-law could apply for work as a stevedore. "It's a first step, of course, until you find something more suitable," Father added.

The next morning when I went into the kitchen, Mother was at the counter preparing sandwiches and my Father and uncle were sitting at the table drinking coffee and eating toast. My uncle had his sleeves rolled up to reveal the lower end of a large anchor tattooed on his upper arm. I knew it was impolite to stare, but I could not make myself turn away; I had never seen anything like it. "Does it hurt?" I asked.

My uncle laughed, showing large teeth, some with gold fillings. "Not anymore."

"We'd better get going," said Father, and they left.

My cousins were a bit of a mystery to me. They spoke Latvian with difficulty, and their English—the King's English, Aunt Milda explained—sounded affected. I thought that my aunt, who had wanted so desperately to come to Canada, should be looking happier than she was. I wondered if it was because she was a pharmacist and dealt mostly with sick people.

With the men gone, Aunt Milda and Mother enjoyed a second, more leisurely cup of coffee. "Everything's so new here—your flat, the motor cars, and the buildings. In England, everywhere it's dusty and crumbling, nothing but rubble."

"It hasn't been easy…" Mother began.

"For sure not. We still can't believe that King George is gone."

Mother looked puzzled, probably wondering what the monarchy had to with anything that concerned us.

Peter, Roland, and I entertained our cousins that weekend, but I refused to call cousin Irene *Princess* like her Mother did, especially when she didn't even lift a finger to help make the bed.

We all breathed easier when Uncle Valentine was taken on at the Montreal waterfront and the Rutkis family rented their own apartment. Mother looked especially tired after shopping and cooking for so many people. I folded the sheet I had just finished ironing and added it to the pile. "Why does Aunt Milda call her *Princess*? She's no princess."

The question surprised Mother. “I don’t know. Maybe it’s what they do in England, call little girls *Princess*. Don’t worry, you’re *my* little princess.”

“I’m serious.”

“Of course she isn’t a princess, we all know that. I think Milda’s trying to make up for the bad times. Irene was born in Dresden, her first baby cries drowned out by the noise of shells exploding all around.”

“So what?” I did not want to feel pity for her. “Didn’t we get bombed, too?” I couldn’t be certain, since my parents never talked about what we had been through, but I had a pretty good idea. “That should be enough to qualify me for princess status.”

“Yes, daughter, we were, around the time of your christening in Swinemünde. ” Mother’s hands began to tremble, and suddenly, I did not want to hear any more. “That whole port city was set ablaze by Allied incendiary bombs, more than once.”

I wanted to feel special, but I was sorry that in satisfying my need, I was hurting Mother. “Let’s talk about something else,” I offered, but just then Roland came in with a cut finger, and Mother got up to attend to it. I was left to brood over the two pet names Father sometimes used, “Little Fly” and “Little Hen”, meant to be endearing, but not especially flattering.

Seventeen

Winter snows melted away, revealing matted lawns and the ugly debris of winter. A few snowdrops on south facing slopes emerged, to bask in the tepid sunshine. Father worried that spring was on the way and our house was far from completed. "We'll be sleeping in the street if it's not finished soon," he said, tapping the calendar before him with his mechanical pencil. "May 1 is almost here."

It was something we all knew, but were powerless to change. As always, our fate rested in Father's broad, capable hands. Mother busied herself at the stove, serving steaming bowls of pea soup riddled with chunks of ham.

"It'll be a relief when this is all over. It hasn't been easy dealing with those builders; they've needed close watching." Absentmindedly, Father stirred his soup as he added up the figures in a long column.

"It will all turn out fine, I'm certain of it," Mother soothed. "When can we see it?"

Father raised the spoon to his lips, and blew on the soup before sucking it up. "Perhaps we could drive out on Sunday and decide on some colours. And if there's time, we might stop at the botanical gardens—if the children's homework is all done by then."

Peter and I both assured Father that our homework would be done long before, and Roland, not yet in school, promised solemnly, "Me, too," making everyone laugh.

From the outside, our house appeared solid and ready for occupancy, but when we stepped inside, we could see why Father was worried. The inside was mostly hollow, looking more like Father's drawings than a finished house. Exposed pipes and tangled wires waited for drywall to cover their nakedness. Father led us on a tour, starting with the kitchen. "The Frigidaire goes here, the stove next to it, with plenty of cupboards and counter space." Father had thought of everything: a balcony in the front, overlooking the street, so that Mother could keep an eye on the children; a window over the sink so Mother could look out when she did the dishes; a modern bathroom with gleaming faucets that were easy to clean; and a driveway for his car.

Mother looked pleased. She would have a fenced backyard and a clothesline. Father leaned over her shoulder, and she rested her cheek on his. "I'll build a sandbox with the leftover lumber," he promised.

At the botanical gardens, Sunday visitors crowded the main rotunda. The overheated air lay thick with the sugary scent of hyacinths, making it hard to breathe. Clumps of daffodils, narcissus, and tulips about to burst into bloom had been artistically arranged. I longed to pick some for Mother, but had to be satisfied with reading the labels. After a while, tired of the slow pace, I tugged impatiently at Mother's hand, "Let's go see the bananas." I wanted to see real bananas, growing on a real tree.

When my mother was at last done admiring the flowers, we moved on to the tropical greenhouse. Father pushed open the door and parted a thick plastic curtain, heavy with moisture. "Whew, it's like a *pirts* in here." With one hand, he removed his glasses, and with the other, he extracted a clean, white handkerchief from his pocket and wiped them. "Look there, the bananas I promised you."

"Those green things?" I was disappointed. They looked nothing like the long, gently curved yellow boats that Mother sometimes brought home from Dominions as a special treat. A bunch of green bananas, no bigger than my little finger, hung from a thick, curved stem. At the tip dangled a fleshy, purple, torpedo-shaped flower.

Up ahead, Peter had discovered an orange tree, thick with blossoms and small green fruit. "I guess the fruit needs real sunshine to turn orange," he said. Just then it struck me that it might not be so bad to have to change schools and make new friends if the botanical gardens were practically on our doorstep.

Soon after our visit to the new house, Mother started packing. First, she gave the books and knickknacks a much-needed dusting and placed them in cardboard boxes. Then, she wrapped most of the dishes in old newspapers, and they, too, found their way into boxes. On moving day, men came and lifted the sofa and beds as if they weighed nothing and loaded them on a truck. We followed the truck across the city. On the way over, Father explained that we would have to be careful: there had been some problems with the wiring, and some of the paint might still be fresh. We entered and were greeted by a heady mix of fresh paint, glue, and varnish. "Don't bang your suitcase against the walls," Father called after us as we struggled up the short flight of stairs.

He did not carry Mother over the threshold, but surrounded by boxes and bundles, Father folded Mother's hands in his. "Mama, welcome to your new home. I promise you will never again be without a roof of your own to shelter you." It was embarrassing to listen to that mushy stuff, so I didn't stick around, but instead followed my brothers down the stairs to check out the basement, something I was loathe to do on my own.

Father believed it was best to finish the year we had started at Van Horne Elementary. So in the weeks that followed, instead of Father having to cross the city each day, Peter and I woke early to catch the first of three buses, from east to west. It was a relief when the school year ended, and we could sleep in. All through the hot summer, Peter and I explored our new neighbourhood. At first, it was strange to hear French spoken on the street and in the stores, as if we had moved to another country, instead of merely across the city. Peter, who had already studied French at school, tried his hand at translating the signs, causing me to giggle and passers-by to stare. However, my first French words had nothing to do with stores or merchandise, but pastry—more correctly, *patisserie*. Not far from the gates of Canadian Vickers, Father discovered a French *patisserie*. Every other Friday, on payday, he arrived home with a white box tied up with string and filled with *milfeuilles*, *éclairs,* and *meringues*. It was the one extravagance he allowed himself and us.

I was ten that first summer on rue Orléans. Sometimes, if I felt like being helpful and big sisterly at the same time, I offered to take Roland to the park. Other days, Peter and I went off on our own, crossed busy Pie IX Boulevard and entered the far, back gate of the botanical gardens to explore its wilder, unkempt side, where the grass reached our knees, and no one else was around. Other days, we aimlessly kicked at pebbles as we wandered the gravel paths around the manicured beds, stopping to read aloud the funny-sounding words on the nameplates—*Quercus, Pelargonium, Sassafras*. I especially liked sassafras; it sounded impolite, like something I shouldn't be saying. Since Peter and I were now familiar with buses, Mother sometimes allowed us to ride the Masson Street bus to the end of the line, at the eastern edge of Mount Royal. We ran up the grassy slope to the path that led us up and up, around the mountain through stands of maple, poplar, and oak. Once, we ventured as far as Beaver Lake and lost track of time, as we watched the model boats sail about its rippled surface. Our late arrival earned us a stern look and a reprimand from Father, but Mother, looking relieved, hurried to warm our dinner.

Our latest escapade reinforced Father's belief that the city was not a suitable place for children to spend the summer months. He worried about bad influences, by which I think he meant the gum-chewing youngsters on street corners, although he never really said so. "Mama, the children need fresh air and sunshine," he said. Then, on rare occasions, when he was feeling nostalgic, he remembered Jurmala and the house his Father had rented each summer. Swimming, tennis, volleyball, and walks on the beach—all were appropriate pastimes. The mere mention of Jurmala brought a far-away, dreamy look to Mother's eyes.

"We really should look around to see if we can't find a suitable summer place, don't you think?" Father often asked Mother what she thought, but in the end, he made the decision on his own, certain that his opinion carried the most weight.

"What on earth are you talking about? I can't squeeze another bite out of my food allowance. You realize the children are growing so fast…"

"I do realize, and that's exactly why."

Mother looked stricken. Father was quick to say, "Of course, you're doing marvels with what I give you, but why don't we see if there's some way we can manage it? Just something small, a lot someplace not too far from the city, that's easy to get to? Besides, I'm due for a promotion soon, and that means a raise." Father had already made up his mind and began putting every spare dollar aside. One Saturday, he arrived home from the hardware store with stiff leather soles, a sharp blade, and tiny nails and glue, and repaired the shoes I was hoping to discard for a new pair. He bent over appliances and replaced frayed electrical cords, scolding us for our carelessness. No lamp could be left burning in an empty room, not even for a minute. Once a month, Mother trimmed Father's thinning hair and hacked away at Roland and Peter's more bountiful locks; I refused to let her scissors touch mine. I was always relieved to see Father bring home the white, pastry-filled box each payday.

One night soon after, we attended a Latvian play. It was late April and patches of winter snow remained only in north-facing, secluded places. Much of the humour on stage was lost on me, and I thought I recognized some of the actors, but the adults enjoyed themselves and I laughed and clapped when they did. Afterward, we went downstairs, as usual. Father stood in a small knot of men, wondering whether to go and sit down, when one of the men announced that he had just put a down payment on a building lot in a small community called Terrasse Vaudreuil. Father listened intently, and asked numerous questions. A lake, lots of trees, fresh air, and only twenty miles from the city—it sounded ideal. That night, when we arrived home, Father got out his map and found Terrasse Vaudreuil, at the west end of Ile Perrot. "Look at all this water," he told Mother, "swimming, boating, and I bet the lake's full of fish just waiting to be caught."

In the morning, he telephoned Juris Beikmanis, who he knew was also interested, and together, and they drove out to see for themselves. Father liked what he saw, and the next Sunday, he took all of us along on his second inspection.

Terrasse Vaudreuil proved to be a small, sleepy community nestled on the edge of a large, blue lake. Father drove slowly along the main, paved road, pointing out the beach, the tennis court, and the general store, and he stopped at Eighth Avenue where the pavement ended. Further on there was nothing to see but a dusty road slicing through the bush. Father turned the corner and pulled over in front of a corner lot with a "*Terrain à vendre*" sign nailed to a tree. "This is it, Mama," he said, patting the large maple as if it were a large animal, "what do you think?"

Mother didn't reply: she was eyeing the nettles, thistles, brambles, trees, and thick bushes that had a stranglehold on the lot. Was that poison ivy, she wondered? Father pointed to the unfinished construction across the street and then recited the other Latvian families that already owned property nearby. "Five are on this very road, the Paeglis across the street, and the Lapiņš down by the lake. Even our minister, Rev. Gaudiņš, bought a lot." There wasn't much to see, so my brothers and I got permission to go down to the lake. A few upturned rowboats with peeling paint rested on the shore like giant, beached turtles. A cool breeze came off the lake, and I buttoned up my windbreaker. At the same time, I kicked off my rubber boots and waded in. Mud oozed through my toes, and the icy water brought tears to my eyes. I sat on a boat to let my feet dry. Soon, Father and Mother arrived to inspect the shoreline, and Father bent down to scoop a handful of water and put it to his lips.

Mother shaded her eyes and looked out at the expanse of water, dotted here and there with small islands. Terrasse Vaudreuil was no Jurmala, but perhaps, because it was not yet summer, it had the right sleepy feel.

"Five hundred dollars is a lot of money," Father admitted, "but it'll be good for all of us. Just think, Mama, all those Latvians, and you'll be able to have a coffee klatch every day!"

"I don't know how we can manage. And where would we sleep?"

"Don't worry, I've thought of everything." Father winked at me, and I knew that he had. He always did. "Just imagine, Mama, our new summer place will be on the island of Ile Perrot!"

"Yes, Ile Perrot?" Mother repeated, not quite sure what Father meant.

"Il. Pe. Ro," cried Father, "it's meant to be. Ilze, Peter, Roland! For once, luck is smiling on me."

"Why, yes," said Mother, and she repeated the name, Ile Perrot, more slowly.

"This place has potential. More Latvians will come here once the news spreads." Arm-in-arm, Father and Mother walked back up the road, and we followed, Roland dragging a stick that left a furrow in the dirt. "I know that the Canadian friends our children have made seem decent enough, but the devil if I can figure out what their fathers do for a living."

By evening, knowing all too well that she could expect no increase in her grocery allowance for the next while, Mother had assented to the purchase. Only when the cheque was signed, did Father admit to any possible drawback. "I'll be honest with you," he said, "it's a bit on the wild side, even for me. Nasty undergrowth chokes the Canadian woods, making walking difficult, not at all like our Latvian forests, but the roads are fine for cycling and the children can run around and swim all they want. I was told there's even a softball diamond, if Peter wants to give it a try."

"That's all good, but we've got to live somewhere."

"Until I figure something out, this summer we can go for the day. No more *privé* signs and fences keeping us back from the water. "

Mother hesitated.

"I know it's a lot a lot of money, but tell me, where else can you buy good health and safe summer activities for five hundred dollars?"

We spent the occasional Saturday or Sunday at our new property, with Mother sitting in a lawn chair by the roadside, waving a leafy branch in the air to keep the mosquitoes from biting, with one eye on Roland and the other on Father hacking away at the bushes. With Peter's help, Father cleared our half-acre of undergrowth, dead tree limbs and many of the smaller saplings, leaving healthy growth. I followed behind, gathering the branches into a pile at the road, to be burned. Using a crowbar, Father jimmied out boulders to expose damp underbellies that teemed with life: ants and beetles that scurried away, millipedes that rolled themselves into a ball, and blind, pink, worms that waved their heads about not knowing where to hide. At the end of the day, we headed down to the lake and the cool water that soothed our bites and scrapes and washed away the dirt and sweat and stench of bug spray. When the Beikmanis family bought a lot down on the main road, I lost interest in helping and joined Anitra in exploring the island.

One day, on one of his many trips to the hardware store in Dorion, Father noticed that the roadside motel was going out of business, and its cabins were for sale. He pulled over, and for ten dollars, bought one. Father then chose a suitable spot and set out cement blocks as a foundation. It cost another ten dollars to have the cabin lifted onto a flatbed truck, transported to our site, and placed firmly on the foundation. Just like magic, we had a summer cabin. All that was needed now was an outhouse, and we could spend the night. Father and Peter dug a deep hole, prying out stubborn rocks with a crowbar and the rest of us, even Roland, helped carry away the stones. When it was deep enough, Father nailed together boards and sheets of plywood to make an outhouse. It was my job to carry water from the public pump, several blocks away. I hobbled back, the heavy pail splashing water down my legs, wishing for the comforts of the city.

During his summer holiday, Father busied himself making our cabin shipshape. He replaced torn screens and laid new linoleum. He built bunk beds for Peter and Roland and a bench along one wall, behind the table, that doubled as a bed at night. As on a boat, no space was wasted, and we squeezed in together. When I slept, I could extend my legs into a hollow space behind the dish cupboard. Mother sewed curtains for our one window and spread a plastic tablecloth over the plywood table to make our cabin more homelike.

The following June, as soon as the school year ended, we drove to the cabin, taking most of our household with us; sheets, blankets, pots and pans, dishes, cutlery, clothes, boots, board games, books and playing cards filled the car with barely any room left over for us. Mother swept up the dead bugs while we brushed the debris of winter from the path and we moved in. Sunday evening, Father returned to his work in the city, and we were on our own.

With Father gone, we could do as we pleased, and each day brought a new adventure. We became strong swimmers and agile climbers, our skin bronzed and our hair bleached by the sun. Even the occasional garter snake slithering around a rock or giant, hairy spider that lurked in the outhouse, could not spoil my happiness. We picked berries—tiny, sweet-smelling, wild strawberries and later, raspberries—that Mother boiled up for jam. We climbed trees to spy on the neighbour, who walked about wearing shorts and only a white brassiere for a top. At night, Mother tended to our bumps and bruises, dabbing on Mercurochrome or offering a bandage, and on a really bad day, teased out the spruce gum stuck in our hair. And she seemed all too eager to poke about with a needle, digging out splinters. Once, after spending some time in the shallows, I found a leech, big with blood, attached to my ankle. Although it did no good at all, I ran around in circles, screeching, until my cries brought a man with a lit cigarette to the rescue.

One disastrous summer, the tree branches were thick with webs filled with wriggling, black larvae. When the hungry horde of tent caterpillars emerged, they were everywhere, stripping the trees of their leaves, and dropping like ripe fruit on our heads and down our backs. I shivered as Father swept them from the door and windows, leaving greenish-yellow streaks. It was impossible to avoid them, and they squished underfoot at every step. I begged Father to take me back to the city with him, but he merely told me not to be such a silly girl. We all welcomed the next heavy rainstorm that washed the path and stones clean. It was a great relief to hear that a program of spraying the roadside trees and bushes would be initiated. "Nature in Latvia was so much gentler," sighed Mother, as she spooned macaroni onto our plates. "After all, it's been massaged for years by the hands of the peasant. The pine forests harbour no underbrush, and the ground is crisscrossed by well-trodden paths; it's a bit like strolling in the park, really, but with mushrooms and berries!" I threw a glance at Peter, who winked in response. When it came to Latvia, we both knew that Mother tended to exaggerate. We had a secret pact that one day when we were grown, we would visit Latvia to see for ourselves, and challenge Mother and her stories.

Despite our frequent run-ins with nature, each summer at the lake was like a new beginning. With Father in the city and school out for the summer, no one worried about grades or good manners or speaking Latvian. We sat around the table in the evening, elbows on the table, and played cards, or Parcheesi or Snakes and Ladders. Mother relaxed, too, enjoying visits with several Latvian women who were around during the week. I slept soundly at night, woken only by the buzz of a mosquito or an annoying itch.

Next door to us, in a permanent, winterized home, lived a French-Canadian family. Our common bond was their large, grey cat that tended to wander. Whenever I heard them calling the cat, I always offered to help and sometimes ended up chasing it home. "*Merci, ma petite*," cried Madame Laporte as she scooped up the naughty bundle of fur. "*Bonjour Madame*," I called from the road. It pleased me to no end, when later that summer, I learned that the Laportes had dubbed us *les anglais*. Soon after, I began referring to Terrasse Vaudreuil as the Terrace, which to my ears, sounded much more elegant.

During the school year, Anitra Beikmanis and I lived at opposite ends of Montreal and we saw each other only at Christmas, Easter, and the occasional Latvian gathering, but in the summer we were constant companions. She was Mother's godchild, making her almost a sister. We spent entire days together, separating only at night or briefly in the day after a falling out. She was an only child, and as such, marginally more mature. Together, we braided daisies, red clover, buttercups, and Queen Anne's lace into wreaths for our heads; we threaded mountain ash berries onto sturdy string to make long, amber necklaces; and we added matchstick legs to fat acorns to create a herd of placid, green cows. We played hopscotch in the road, or with just the right smooth pebbles, jacks. Few grandparents existed in our world; most had stayed behind in Latvia. But on a rare visit to her daughter in Canada, one still-spunky grandmother who had been a dancer in her youth, taught us a vaudeville routine. To the beat of the old woman's stick, Anitra and I strutted and kicked our legs high and sang. When she could do no more with our raw talent, she declared us ready, and we performed before a small audience of parents and siblings and whomever else we managed to corral.

The summer always ended abruptly, before I was ready to relinquish my freedom for the confines of city and school life. Labour Day saw us heading back to Montreal, loaded down with our belongings once again. I felt like a different person, so it came as a surprise to see that not much had changed in my absence, and I quickly fell into a familiar routine.

Over the years, Father worked to improve our rustic, one-room cabin, adding a lean-to just big enough for a bed, giving him a quiet retreat. However, housekeeping without running water and a proper kitchen proved too onerous for Mother, and Father made plans to build a permanent house. I was sad to see the cabin torn down, but not the outhouse. Toward the mid-1960s, Terrasse Vaudreuil began changing into a suburb, a bedroom community with commuters running for the train. Its proximity to the city had made it an ideal summer retreat, but it had also spoiled its wildness. It grew and consumed the woods, its streets were paved, and its lawns seeded, but the blue lake still beckoned, and until I completed high school and got my first summer job before university, Ile Perrot is where I spent my summers.

SWEDEN

We have disembarked the *Baltic Star* the day before and have already said our good-byes to the others. Now, after a day and a half touring Stockholm, Father and I sit at a small table in the airport, waiting for our flights. He is returning to his bungalow in Florida, and I am on my way to meet my husband and sons in Montreal, where our Peter is a student at McGill. For a while, Father and I sit without talking, even though there is so much to say. It has always been like that with us, a complicated mix of reluctance, obstinacy, and respect for each other's privacy. If anyone in this world still believes that children should be seen and not heard, it must be Father.

A flight is called, but it is not Father's. Nervously, he pats his pocket to feel the reassuring bulge of his documents. The coffee shop is clean and modern and filled with happy young people heading off on a holiday. I wonder if Father now regrets having left Sweden in 1951, but I know better than to ask such a useless question. Father is someone who refuses to tread, even ever so gingerly, the road not taken. Instead, we spend the rest of the hour reminiscing over all we have seen and done in Latvia and the relatives we have met these past ten days. Suddenly, Father sets down his cup, and says in a voice so quiet I have to strain to hear, "You know, I sometimes wondered if I'd done the right thing, back in '44, when I made the decision to flee Latvia. At that time, for me, there was no other possible choice, and I don't regret it. But, for Mama, it was different: her parents were still living and her brother also; she missed them greatly and felt some measure of guilt for having abandoned them."

I am at a loss for words, and I mumble something that I hope is appropriate. Father doesn't seem to hear me. He looks away, and bites off a piece of cookie that he chews slowly. "Funny, isn't it? Mama and me, my three sisters, and my brother, for some years, we believed that we were the lost generation, but I now see that the real lost generation is the one that stayed behind in Latvia, them and their children."

"Such a loss. It's evident how hard it's been and still is, but there are signs of hope," I say. "The world is changing." It can't be soon enough for Latvia, I think, it has a lot of catching up to do. Its people have been isolated, oppressed, intimidated, and much, much worse. For the most part, the west has carried on without them. "It was heartbreaking to hear Baiba admit that if she could relive the past, she would escape, run for her life the way we did."

"Certainly, but now I've seen for myself, with my own eyes, the damage the Soviets have done. The suffering and neglect. Bitterness. It's strange to feel vindicated after so many years." Father shakes his head slowly from side to side, then rubs the back of his neck.

Never before has Father spoken so candidly, and I suddenly feel cheated that in all my growing-up years, he never shared his doubts or fears. "Wow," I say. "I'm surprised, Dad. You always showed such certainty in your decisions, and we were never allowed to question anything you said or did."

"Yes, I had to be the mighty lion. The August Leo "

It was true; every birthday Father reminded us he was born under the sign of Leo. I begin to say something, but Father's next words cut me short.

"What good would it have done to show weakness? Everyone counted on me, on what I could earn, what I could make and calculate with this," Father tapped his head. He leaned forward and lowered his voice. "Death and failure were always by my side, ready and waiting for a slip-up."

"What? You never failed at anything you set your mind to." I want to say a lot more, ask more questions, but realize this is not the time or place to do so. We will see each other again in Florida before the year ends.

Father's hazel eyes, magnified behind thick bifocals, observe me coolly. "I'm glad to know that's what you saw."

A loudspeaker announces Father's flight, and he slowly gets to his feet. He extends a hand, and we say "*Ar dievu*". Good-bye. I lean forward and lightly kiss his cheek. Good-byes with Father are never drawn-out or tearful, always matter-of-fact. We part because it is what we must do. "Safe flight," I call after him, but he does not turn, only raises his hand, and I know he has heard.

I get a refill, knowing I will regret it later, and mull over my experiences. It feels as if I have been on an emotional roller coaster, and only now, in Sweden, has the ride stopped. I have learned a lot about Latvia, but I have also learned so much about my own past, both sad and happy. Mother's stories and songs take on new meaning, and Father's determination a new heroism. I feel as if I have regained a part of me that I thought was gone. I have found my lost childhood. The childish resentment I have carried about for far too long, slips from my shoulders onto the tile floor and disappears under passing feet.

Married to a husband who insists on working in difficult, and at times unsafe, developing countries, I consider myself well travelled, but this trip was like no other. It was a homecoming to a place I had never lived. It stirred up memories I had never experienced. I revisited familiar sights I had never seen, except in pictures. Most of all, it made me realize how lucky I was to have grown up in Canada with all its opportunities, but with my Latvian heritage intact. Except for the loss and suffering of my parents and relatives, I would not trade my experiences.

I gather up my things, and head for my gate, fully realizing that Latvia's transition from totalitarianism to democracy and freedom would not be easy. What is needed now is someone brave and strong, perhaps another bear-slayer, to lead the way.

THE END

ACKNOWLEDGMENTS

Thank you to friends and family who expressed an early interest in this book and who gladly sent me material to fill out the narrative. My bothers, Peter and Roland, and many cousins – Walter Zalite who tended to the Zalite family tree; Mara Foster who sent me audio tapes made by her mother, Aunt Elza; Janis Freimanis in Latvia; Biruta Velutini, Milda Lamb, Rita Goba, Dita Mogensen, -- who offered encouragement.

My father was the inspiration for this book and his meticulous record keeping and excellent memory made my work easier. My mother was the heart and soul of our family and instilled in me a love of all things Latvian. My return trip to Latvia in 1990 gave this book its shape and made it possible.

In doing the research I leaned heavily on "The Latvians: A Short History" by Andrejs Plakans and "Latvian Mittens" by Lizbeth Upitis. I was inspired to write my own story after reading "Walking Since Daybreak" by Modris Eksteins.

Much of what I present in this memoir occurred when I was very young, and some, before I was born. The stories and memories of others flesh out the narrative. I hope that those family members who appear in its pages will be accepting of my version of events, even if it differs somewhat from their own.

I owe a big thank you to my husband, Hubert, and to our sons, Peter and Andre, who always encouraged me to write. I would also like to thank Margaret Hart at the HSW Literary Agency for her support and my writers' group, especially Jennifer Hayman who helped with editing. And finally, it must be noted that any errors are my responsibility alone.

A NOTE ABOUT THE AUTHOR

Ilse Zandstra was born in Latvia and grew up in Montreal. A science graduate from McGill University, she is a biologist and a writer. Her husband's international career took her to Colombia, the Philippines and Peru. She is the author of several scientific works as well as two much-loved Spanish-language children's books about a Peruvian spectacled bear: "Ukuku conoce al sol" and "Ukuku salva el bosque" published by Grupo Editorial Norma. Ilse and her husband now reside in Ottawa. They have two sons and five grandchildren.

www.ingramcontent.com/pod-product-compliance
Lightning Source LLC
Chambersburg PA
CBHW031948090426
42739CB00006B/120

* 9 7 8 0 9 9 5 2 9 1 0 0 3 *